DAVID FELLMAN
Vilas Professor of Political Science
University of Wisconsin
ADVISORY EDITOR TO DODD, MEAD & COMPANY

The Political System
of Communism

The Political System
of Communism

Richard C. Gripp

California State University
San Diego

Dodd, Mead & Company
New York   1973   Toronto

To Rosemary

Preface

This study of communism is intended to highlight the essential features of communist-party states, viewed as constituting a specific type of political system. An attempt has not been made to offer a complete, encyclopedic approach to communism, and as a result many aspects of that broad subject are not treated here. The objective is to sketch out only the main structures and patterns of political rule under communism—not to explore deeply the philosophy, history, attributes, and policies of communism, interesting and important though they are. In a way the book is but an introduction to political rule in communist states. The format used to confine the study within certain defined parameters is elaborated in the first chapter.

. A number of scholars have aided my research and writing, some of whom should now be singled out for special acknowledgment. Over a period of several years Don Estes and Jean Hanchett investigated with me various theoretical approaches to the subject and their early research aided my own efforts. Betty Nesvold's recommendations on technique of presentation were welcomed. Wallace Millson worked with me on questions relating to economic development. Dorothy Migdal contributed overall critical evaluations, especially of a methodological nature. John A. Armstrong, David Fellman, Thomas J. Hegarty, and John S. Reshetar, Jr., offered a number of very helpful suggestions for the book. San Diego State College Foundation contributed early support for the study. The author, however, should receive sole credit for the book's shortcomings.

RICHARD C. GRIPP

Contents

Tables

Maps

DAVID FELLMAN
Vilas Professor of Political Science
University of Wisconsin
ADVISORY EDITOR TO DODD, MEAD & COMPANY

The Political System
of Communism

1

Comparative Study of Communist-Party States

The study of communist-party states on a comparative basis is of quite recent origin. Over the years we have become accustomed to a great deal of writing on such subjects as Marxism, Stalinism, communist economics, the history of communism as an ideological and political movement, and communist foreign policies. Separate communist nation studies—for example, on the USSR and Yugoslavia—abound. What has generally been missing is the comparative analysis of communist regimes as a special type of political system.[1]*

This book investigates communist-party states as variants of a single type. Through comparative analysis it is hoped that one can reach a better understanding of the unique structures and features which distinguish this type of system from noncommunist political systems. Indeed, comparative analysis may even strengthen (or

*Footnotes appear at the end of each chapter.

undermine) the initial assumption that a special type of communist political system exists. Is there any basic difference between a communist system and totalitarian structures like those erected by Hitler and Mussolini? Or does the communist system more closely resemble dictatorships of the traditional style, like Franco's Spain or Chiang Kai-shek's China? Approaching the matter from a different standpoint, does the communist system actually constitute a higher form of the democratic political system, as communists themselves claim?

The communist states to be studied are Albania, Bulgaria, China, Cuba, Czechoslovakia, the German Democratic Republic (GDR), Hungary, Mongolia, North Korea, North Vietnam, Poland, Rumania, the USSR, and Yugoslavia. With the exception of Cuba, the communist nature of all of these states is generally recognized, as well as officially proclaimed. Observers such as Richard Lowenthal have questioned Cuba's position, however, noting that the Cuban Revolution was led neither by the communist party nor by communist leaders; formal adherence to communism came several years after the revolution was won.[2] Evidence increasingly suggests that Cuba is at least *becoming* communist. Although in 1959 Castro stated that he was not a communist, in 1961 he apparently had changed his mind enough to claim that he was a Marxist-Leninist. By 1966 Castro was talking about "our communist revolution" and in 1967 he referred to "our" communist party. As Theodore Draper aptly summarizes, Castroism gave communism total power in Cuba, and communism gave Castro an ideology of total power.[3] It is hoped that this study, by comparing Cuba to states whose communist nature is unquestioned, will shed light on the status of Cuba's "communism."

One reason why comparative examination of communist-party states has been rarer than other uses of the comparative approach in political science is that there are special difficulties in data collection and in finding an adequate framework for analysis.[4] Comparative analysis must rest on the availability of comprehensive and detailed cross-national studies, but these have been hindered by the special difficulties just mentioned.

Data on communist states are very uneven both qualitatively and quantitatively—ranging, for example, from an abundance of information on the government and economy of Yugoslavia, to only slight information available on present-day Albania, to practically

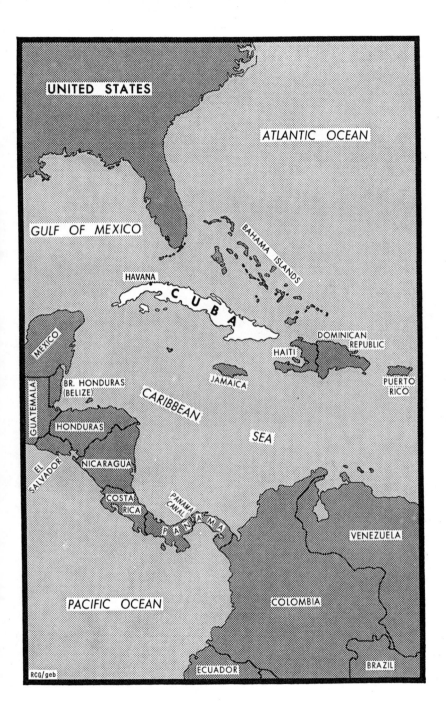

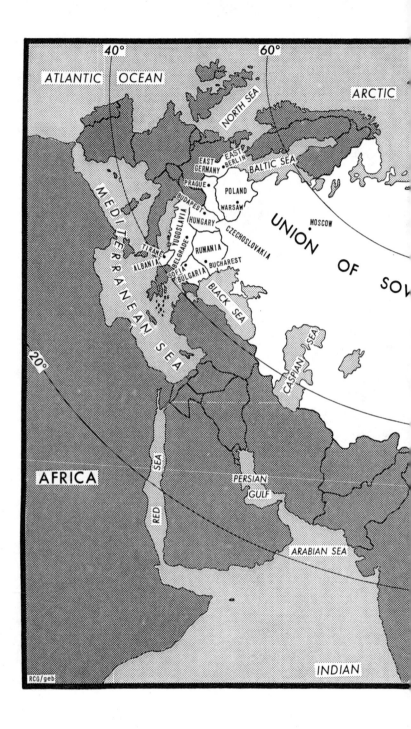

no aggregative data on Communist China for the past few years. In the late 1950's, fairly comprehensive studies of the Eastern European communist states appeared which were informative as broadstroke introductions to those states, but are too dated to be of great value today chiefly because they stressed then-contemporary problems and personalities. The 1960's has seen a renewal of efforts at separate national studies, as well as of general area studies, such as Eastern Europe, and the Soviet Bloc.[5] Present data on communist states vary considerably in quality and coverage depending also on the subject matter. Thus, economic statistics outweigh in volume more sparse social statistics. There is more information on the structures than on the functions of communist states; facts on internal political processes are scanty compared to those relating to foreign policy. Not only is there a need for more comprehensive data on all communist states, then, but we need also to develop criteria for the collecting and ordering of the available data.

An equally forbidding obstacle on the road to comparative study of communist states is the availability of relatively few frameworks for analysis. Methodologically, the main approaches usually relied upon in studies of communism are the historical, the descriptive, and the theoretical. The first two of these approaches are well-known and deserve only brief mention. The third requires elaboration in some detail.

HISTORICAL APPROACH

The historical approach sets forth a series of events, personalities, political crises, and foreign policies normally in chronological order. Historical studies, which exist for all communist states, devote a great deal of attention to each state's history prior to the period of communist rule. The early history of the communist period also is elaborated in similar fashion. These studies tend to stress great detail, at times exhaustively so. They do serve as a useful introduction to and background for understanding the specific cultural, economic, and political determinants of the various national systems. Nevertheless, these studies are not really comparable with each other and at times they treat the more dynamic features of political rule only in a sketchy manner.

DESCRIPTIVE APPROACH

This approach frequently begins with historical information, but in addition describes such aspects of a system as governmental and economic institutions, their structures, numbers, and variations. An example is a description of a national government which includes description of the executive and legislative structures, as well as of the general role which they play within the political system. The descriptive approach, in stressing the details of formal structures, tends to slide into the superficial rather than rise to the analytical; conclusions drawn from such a study usually are unsophisticated. As with the historical, the descriptive approach is not easily fitted into comparability studies.

THEORETICAL APPROACH

The theoretical approach, the most recent approach to be used in comparative analysis, has been tried sparingly in efforts to portray general features of the communist political system.[6] This approach emphasizes the use of models, which might be based on practical experience of communist rule (e.g., a bureaucratic-entrepreneurial model), and the use of ideal types (e.g., elitism, totalitarianism, bureaucracy). A model is a representation, a schematized picture of reality. An ideal type is a perfect, or extreme image of a given class or type.

A frequently used ideal type for the analysis of communist and other dictatorial systems is the totalitarian. This type includes the following features:

1. An official ideology
2. A single mass party
3. A system of terroristic police control
4. A technically conditioned, near-complete monopoly of control of communications and armed combat
5. A central control and direction of the entire economy[7]

Wolfe emphasizes the total in totalitarianism—total power over state and economy. Such extensive control is possible, in Arendt's view, because totalitarian movements are mass organizations of atomized, isolated individuals. In addition, unrestricted, unconditional, and unalterable loyalty is demanded of citizens.[8] As a result of these and related portrayals of totalitarianism, the term carries obvious connotations of total power, total control of material and human resources, and terroristic control over the population of the state.

The totalitarian type may be only slightly useful because it sets forth such a simple, stark, and rare picture. Which communist states, for example, employ extensive and terroristic police controls today, a feature of the totalitarian type? The totalitarian type might be used as a time measure, though. Using it this way, one tries to see when and at what stage of its evolution a communist state most approximates the ideal totalitarian type (e.g., during Stalinism, Maoism?). Fainsod suggests that an extreme case of totalitarian party-state bureaucracy exists in the Soviet Union and China, where political and administrative means both seek to reshape man and society in the collectivized industrial image.[9]

Another ideal type occasionally referred to in discussing communist states is the bureaucratic. Weber's bureaucratic model clearly sets forth certain features of this type, such as fixed jurisdictional areas ordered by rules, laws, and regulations, with the bureaucracy employing only qualified employees who function within assigned boundaries. Weber argues, furthermore, that bureaucracy has destroyed structures of domination which had no rational character.[10] In his types of bureaucracies, Fainsod lists a party-state bureaucracy as a by-product of totalitarian regimes and other one-party dominated political systems.[11]

In some respects communist states match Weber's bureaucratic model. There is in these states, for example, a penchant for hierarchical authority; a strict adherence to rules set down by the regime; qualifications for employees who function within a fixed jurisdiction; and, above all, an accent on rationalism in all societal activities. Bureaucratic rationalism, in fact, forms only a part of a larger, governmental-economic-political rationalism claimed by communists. If the Soviet system were to be evaluated on the single standard of application of rules, Meyer notes, it would achieve a relatively high rating for bureaucratization.[12] In other respects communist states fail to match Weber's model, especially in that higher officials of the bureaucracy—and particularly leaders of the communist party—do not operate within fixed jurisdictional limits nor are they bound by either rules or laws, except as those rules and laws are of the leaders' own choosing and can be changed, or dropped, at the leaders' will. In this respect, the arbitrariness of high communist party officials as they function within communist states is decidedly antibureaucratic.

In addition to these three widely used approaches—historical, descriptive, and theoretical—we will now look into a fourth one which we have labeled the "Marxist-Leninist" approach.

MARXIST-LENINIST APPROACH

This approach is based on Marxist-Leninist ideology. Some of the main elements of this ideology, from Marx on, can now be stated very broadly.

Marx, notably reticent on details of a future communist political system, did refer specifically to a society in which public (or worker) ownership of industry would prevail; in which private ownership of the means of production would be abolished, including property in land; in which credit would be centralized under a state bank; in which communication and transport also would fall under state control.

Lenin inaugurated public ownership and governmental operation of industry, transportation, trade, and centralized banking and finance. He also centralized political rule under a dictatorship of the communist-party elite, with himself at the apex of power; this was his adaptation of Marx's dictatorship of the proletariat.

Stalin's totalitarian model elaborated and built upon the precedents established under the pattern of leadership established by Lenin. In particular, Stalin continued Lenin's style of using the communist party as the instrument through which the dictatorship of the proletariat could be realized. He also completed Lenin's program for nationalizing industry and instituting national economic planning, and collectivized agriculture.

Apart from the writings of these major leaders and founders of communism, certain statements and declarations of later communist leaders and spokesmen have set forth several operational steps and policies which relate to the beginning, the growth, and development of communism in practice. For example, Mikhail Suslov, a modern

Soviet theorist who for a long time has been a member of the ruling elite in the USSR, has set forth several "international" requisites for communism which are applicable, he contends, for all Eastern European communist states. These include:

1. A communist party dictatorship, as the advanced guard (leading element) of the working class
2. Strengthening of the alliance between workers and peasants
3. Liquidation of capitalist ownership of industry, banks, and transport, and their replacement by public ownership and a planned economy
4. Defense of the Socialist Revolution

These requirements appeared in a speech of Suslov's relating to the Hungarian Revolution in 1956 and presumably contain the irreducible minimum below which a communist state cannot fall and still be rated as "communist" by the Soviet leadership.[13]

Thus, the Soviet model, which has served historically as the guide for newer communist states in Eastern Europe and Asia, includes, at a minimum, the following:

1. Dedication to the ideology of Marxism-Leninism
2. Political rule by the communist party, organizing a carefully structured dictatorship
3. Elimination of capitalism and its replacement with socialism
4. Affiliation with and support for other communist nations

All communist states have followed this model in their early years of development, although there have been variations on the model in recent years. The leaders of some of the states, such as Yugoslavia and China, have decided that they, not the Russians, are to interpret the Marxist-Leninist scriptures and determine what constitutes fidelity to them. In addition, the item regarding affiliation with other communist states was followed more in the first years of communist rule than in recent years.

Because several variations on this Soviet model have occurred in practice, its continued utility is questionable, except perhaps for historical comparisons. Thus, it might remain useful for a specific time-period measurement of a given communist state during a specific stage of its development. The first two decades of Soviet rule, for example, might be correlated with the first decade of Chinese communist rule in terms of civil war, nationalizing industry, creating a centralized government, and proceeding through an early period of economic development.[14]

Eastern European communist leaders have on occasion added their voices to those of Soviet leaders in matters relating to communist ideology. The long-time leader of Polish communism, Gomulka, listed four common requirements for building socialism:

1. A Marxist-Leninist party of the working and laboring masses
2. A dictatorship of the proletariat
3. Socialization of production, including central planning and direction
4. Leninist internationalism of socialist countries, including the equality and sovereignty of all states and nations[15]

Perhaps a separate category should be considered for Yugoslavia in view of that state's uniqueness among other communist states. Yugoslavia's dynamic ruling patterns stem partly from its ideological variations on the Soviet model. Yugoslav innovations first appeared after that nation was expelled from the Cominform in 1948 at the insistence of Stalin. Some of the innovations, in fact, were the direct result of that expulsion. Among these, Yugoslavia is most noted for its version of "national communism," or what at times is referred to as an independent road to socialism. In 1956 the Vice President of Yugoslavia, Kardelj, stated: "We do not believe, in a word, that there exist universal political blueprints valid for all countries. . . . Different conditions call for different lines of social development as well as for various forms of economic and political organization."[16] The Yugoslav innovations in the Marxist-Leninist format may be set down as follows:

1. International communism as a system of world revolution is rejected, as is the theory of the inevitability of capitalist hostility and the doctrine of just and unjust wars. Aggression, even communist aggression, is disavowed. Coexistence is mandatory for all nations.
2. The state must begin to wither away, as must also the dictatorship of the proletariat. Only a state which is withering away can be socialist.
3. State control of industry is as bad as capitalist control. What is needed is workers' control.
4. Democracy, although not the Western type, must be introduced. This to include:
   a. Factory management by the workers.
   b. Autonomy in local government.
   c. Greater freedom of individual expression.

  d. Curbing the activities of the political police.
  e. Permitting multiple candidates to run for a given seat in the legislature.
5. A transformation of the communist party from a ruling, controlling dictatorship to an organization which merely leads, guides, and instructs must be effected. The party, then, would begin to wither away.

Marxist-Leninist doctrines have been altered in China, also, to become Marxism-Leninism-Maoism. This sinicization of Marxism-Leninism had its beginnings in Mao Tse-tung's interpretations of that doctrine in the early days of the Chinese communist movement. While Stalin urged the Chinese communists to organize the proletariat, Mao saw the prime necessity for organizing the overwhelmingly important majority class—the peasants. The proletariat, despite Marxian requirements and Stalin's orders, was virtually nonexistent in China at that time. By the mid-1930's Mao had exercised his independence from both Soviet interpretations of Marxism and from political control by Stalin. The origins of the Sino-Soviet split of the 1960's, then, reach back into the period of Mao's early resistance to the Moscow line in the 1920's.

In 1939 Mao pointed out the vacuity of Marxism-Leninism in the abstract, divorced from a given national setting. Thus, if a Chinese communist talks of Marxism-Leninism apart from the peculiarities of China "this Marxism is merely an empty abstraction." Further to this point, Mao called for an end to "writing eight-legged essays on foreign models . . . we must discard our dogmatism and replace it by a new and vital Chinese style and manner. . . ." And, he wrote in 1942, what is needed is a Marxist-Leninist theory *"in accordance with China's real necessities, a theory that is our own and of a specific nature. . . ."* Finally, Mao advised that theory and practice can be combined only if the members of the Chinese Communist party adopt the concepts and methods of Marxism-Leninism and apply them to China, evolving in the process a theory as a result of conscientious study of the realities of Chinese history and of the Chinese revolution.[17]

Despite this early and repeated ideological declaration of independence on the part of Mao Tse-tung, much of Chinese communism is made up of standard Leninist adaptations of Marxism. The purposes of the Chinese Communist party, for example, include the abolition of all class distinctions, the withering away of the state, and the establishment of a communist society stressing mutual assistance and love.[18] Furthermore, after coming to power in 1949, the Chinese communist leaders adopted a version of the Soviet model of a communist system, including rule by the communist party, introduction of public ownership over the economy, and affiliation with other communist states.

Among Maoist innovations in Marxist-Leninist ideology are the doctrines of a protracted revolutionary war from rural guerrilla bases and an emphasis on a peasant foundation for a communist revolution.[19] One of Mao's most famous and original contributions to the ideology is the one on contradictions: socialist society, like capitalist society, develops contradictions between the productive forces and the conditions of production. Thus, even under communism, Mao contended, there will remain contradictions between people; but there is nothing strange about this.[20] This innovation of Mao's is particularly important because, heretofore, communism had been pictured as a perfect society with neither problems nor contradictions.

What Mao has stressed in both his ideology and his political rule is the necessity for a particular, specific national setting for Marxism-Leninism. While this nationalizing of Marxism-Leninism is credited to Mao, and forms a part of "Maoism," it does no more, of course, than follow the history of Soviet communism, which had already adopted Stalin's "socialism in one country" doctrine. However, from the late 1950's Chinese communist ideology has concerned itself with criticizing the "revisionism" of Yugoslavia and the USSR, while at the same time defending Chinese fidelity to a form of pure, orthodox Marxism-Leninism.

All of the foregoing communist leaders have stressed certain features of ideology which we might now summarize in a Marxist-Leninist checklist:

1. A deterministic and materialistic interpretation of history
2. A revolutionary transformation of the old society
3. Rule by a dictatorship of the working class, through the communist party
4. Egalitarianism in all areas of society
5. Anticapitalism and anti-imperialism
6. Public ownership and state-governmental control of the important economic functions of society

7. Building a progressive-humanitarian society which promotes the welfare of all citizens in matters of health, education, employment, and culture

In that by and large they advocate all of the items in the above checklist, all of the communist states appear to be Marxist-Leninist. Their carrying these items into practice, however, is more debatable. While all of the states have a dictatorship, for example (item number 3), it is more a dictatorship of the communist-party elite than of the working class. In the case of Cuba, the dictatorship is comprised more of Castro's personal rule than the rule of the Cuban Communist party. Yugoslavia, moreover, claims its ruling party is "withering away." Egalitarianism (item number 4) has not been realized in all areas in communist states (e.g., in positions of management in society), nor for all citizens (e.g., peasants). If egalitarianism is equated with individual opportunity and fairness in governmental interaction with citizens, then perhaps Yugoslavia has progressed further than other communist states. Where Yugoslavia stresses equal access to opportunity, China emphasizes a maximum level of material abundance above which no one should aspire. Under item number 5, communist states are anticapitalist and anti-imperialist if the latter term rests on Lenin's definition (opposed to the large capitalist-imperialist states). Otherwise, the USSR might be considered imperialistic toward her client states in Eastern Europe, as it occasionally is seen to be by Westerners. Item number 6, public ownership, is carried out to a high degree in all communist states for such activities as industry, transportation, communications, but only in some states (e.g., the USSR) does this include the service and craft industries. A high degree of public ownership in agriculture is rarely obtained if the practical modifications, such as private plots for collective farmers in the USSR, are added to the total.

The question of whether communist states have followed item 7, building a progressive-humanitarian society, is highly debatable. Certainly most of the communist states have striven mightily to improve health care for their citizens, to increase the number of available schools and cultural facilities, and to seek the benefits of industrialization. No doubt the regimes in all of the communist states believe that in fact they are building a progressive-humanitarian society. A noncommunist response to this belief might be that a "progressive-humanitarian society" should include a large degree of personal freedoms—say, to speak, write, and publish at will, or to advocate openly competing political parties—and therefore, of course, communist states have not been progressive. The success of the communist states regarding this item all depends, obviously, on one's definition of "progressive-humanitarian society."

It should now be appropriate to set forth a Marxist-Leninist Model based on the foregoing discussion. The model will rely on the basic ideological foundations of communism as well as on the expressed goals, broadly interpreted, of Marxists-Leninists.[21]

THE MARXIST-LENINIST MODEL

I. *Inaugurate Marxism-Leninism.*
   Replace an old political system with a political system labeled as "Marxist-Leninist."

II. *Establish the communist party as the vanguard of the workers.*
   A. Place the communist party in control of all societal organizations and their related activities, especially in control over the apparatus of government.
   B. Create the communist party to represent the interests of the working class.

III. *Organize a socialist economic structure.*
   A. Abolish capitalistic economic structures and dispossess private owners of economic institutions and facilities.
   B. Establish public ownership of economic institutions and facilities.
   C. Inaugurate national economic planning.
   D. Collectivize/socialize agriculture.

IV. *Establish a structure for popular worker rule.*
   A. Organize a popularly elected legislature.
   B. Establish additional organs of representation, such as trade unions and a public court system.
   C. Set up mass organizations of citizens.

V. *Organize an international association of communist-party states.*
   A. Support a socialist bloc, by treaty and alliance, of communist nations.
   B. Orient individual national foreign policy toward the goals of the socialist bloc.
   C. Oppose capitalist governments and support revolutionary movements.

The treatment of Communist-party states throughout the chapters of this book is oriented around this Marxist-Leninist Model. The chapters cover, in turn, the topics of coming into power (inaugurating Marxism-Leninism), political rule in communist states (establishing the communist party as the vanguard of workers), economic organization and management (organizing a socialist economic structure), popular citizen participation within the state (providing a network for popular worker rule), and communist internationalism (organizing an association of communist-party states). The intent is to compare the various communist states as these states seek to make the Marxist-Leninist Model operational through their political systems. Accordingly, in the next five chapters we shall examine five hypotheses which have been developed from the foregoing model.

Hypothesis 1.   To be communist, a new political system is placed in power which is clearly labeled as "Marxist-Leninist," and which has as its main objective the bringing into full operation of a Marxist-Leninist, or communist, society.

Hypothesis 2.   In a communist political system, the communist party (a) assumes political control over the society; (b) serves as the spokesman for and represents the interests of the working class.

Hypothesis 3.   A communist political system transforms an economy from private ownership to public-socialist ownership and governmental control.

Hypothesis 4.   A communist political system (a) organizes structures for popular participation; (b) achieves viable worker rule through these structures.

Hypothesis 5.   A communist political system (a) supports a bloc of fellow communist states; (b) opposes capitalist governments; (c) supports anticapitalist, anti-imperialist revolutionary movements.

NOTES

1. See the bibliographical essay by Paul Shoup, "Comparing Communist Nations: Prospects for an Empirical Approach," *American Political Science Review,* March, 1968.

2. Richard Lowenthal, "Development versus Utopia in Communist Policy," in *Change in Communist Systems,* Chalmers Johnson, ed. (Stanford: Stanford University Press, 1970), p. 34, n. 1.

3. Theodore Draper, *Castroism: Theory and Practice* (New York: Praeger, 1965), p. 50.

4. See Alfred G. Meyer, "The Comparative Study of Communist Political Systems"; Robert S. Sharlett, "Systematic Political Science and Communist Systems"; John A. Armstrong, "Comparative Politics and Communist Systems," all in the *Slavic Review,* March, 1967; Robert C. Tucker, "On the Comparative Study of Communism," *World Politics,* January, 1967; Richard Cornell, "A Comparative Analysis of Communist Movements," *Journal of Politics,* February, 1968.

5. See Frederic J. Fleron, Jr., "Soviet Area Studies and the Social Sciences: Some Methodological Problems in Communist Studies," *Soviet Studies,* January, 1968.

6. On theories, models, and typologies relating to communist studies, see Frederic J. Fleron, Jr., ed., *Communist Studies and the Social Sciences* (Chicago: Rand-McNally, 1969), p. 19.

7. C. J. Friedrich and Z. K. Brzezinski, *Totalitarian Dictatorship and Autocracy* (Cambridge: Harvard University Press, 1956), pp. 9–10.

8. See Bertram D. Wolfe, *Communist Totalitarianism: Keys to the Soviet System* (Boston: Beacon Press, 1961), p. 275, and Hannah Arendt, *The Origins of Totalitarianism* (New York: Harcourt, Brace and World, 1966), p. 323.

9. Merle Fainsod, "Bureaucracy and Modernization—the Russian and Soviet Case," in *Bureaucracy and Political Development,* Joseph La Palombara, ed., (Princeton: Princeton University Press, 1963), p. 233.

10. *From Max Weber: Essays in Sociology,* H. H. Garth and C. Wright Mills, translators and editors (New York: Oxford University Press, 1946), pp. 196–97, 244.

11. Fainsod, *op. cit.,* p. 235.

12. Alfred G. Meyer, *The Soviet Political System* (New York: Random House, 1965), pp. 3–11, 217.

13. Quoting Mikhail Suslov in the *New York Times,* November 12, 1956. The feared decline of the monopoly of power previously held by the Czechoslovakian Communist party over that nation was a main cause for the Soviet invasion of Czechoslovakia in 1968. See the text of the Warsaw Letter in *Pravda,* July 18, 1968.

14. In this connection see Thomas P. Bernstein, "Leadership and Mass Mobilization in the Soviet and Chinese Collectivization Campaigns of 1929–30 and 1955–56: A Comparison," *China Quarterly,* July-September, 1967.

15. Quoted in Zbigniew K. Brzezinski, *The Soviet Bloc: Unity and Conflict* (Cambridge: Harvard University Press, 1967), p. 294.

16. *Foreign Affairs,* July, 1956, p. 582. This is a paraphrase of Lenin's argument that Marxism is not a system of dogmas; Lenin did not pre-

tend that Marx or Marxists knew the road to socialism in all of its concrete aspects.

17. Stuart R. Schram, *The Political Thought of Mao Tse-tung* (New York: Praeger, 1963), pp. 114–15, 120.

18. Franklin W. Houn, *A Short History of Chinese Communism* (Englewood Cliffs: Prentice-Hall, 1967), p. 78.

19. Mao conceived of the proletariat in China as the entire Chinese people, and so Marxism was wedded to nationalism, thus destroying the tactical as well as theoretical significance of the "class" as a unit of analysis. A. James Gregor, *Contemporary Radical Ideologies* (New York: Random House, 1968), p. 95.

20. Schram, *op. cit.*, p. 236. Yugoslav theory also acknowledges contradictions within a socialist society. See George Zaninovich, in *Contemporary Yugoslavia*, Wayne S. Vucinich, ed. (Berkeley: University of California Press, 1969), p. 303.

21. Paul Shoup writes that communist states should be considered comparable among themselves, or treated as a distinct category for purposes of comparison with other types "if they have adopted the Marxist ideology, if they have experienced a revolution which has destroyed the power structure of the earlier system, and if the Party has acquired a monopoly in the decision-making processes of the societies in question, exercising decisive control over all major political, economic, and cultural organizations." Shoup, *op. cit.* (above n. 1), p. 188.

2

Coming to Power of Communist Parties

A political system includes an organized structure, as well as a particular pattern of behavior which provides political rule. On occasion given political structures die out or are overthrown, and are replaced by others with similar customs, features, and patterns; at other times the differences between the old and the new structures are great enough that the result is a change in political system. Thus, a new political system, in contrast to simply a new ruling group or different political party, is one which markedly differs from the preceding system. The establishment of a military dictatorship in the place of a parliamentary democracy, for example, would result in a change in political system. The Soviet government organized after the October Revolution is one of the most widely cited examples of a new political system replacing an older one; in the process of change there was introduced a new political philosophy as well as a new ruling structure, new practices, and policies.[1]

19

The replacement of one political system with another may be caused by various events and circumstances. Long periods of inefficient rule resulting in a loss of popular confidence in a given political structure, for example, might be aggravated by problems arising from economic underdevelopment, eventually causing a complete change in system. Serious social, economic, and political dislocation —perhaps even chaos—arising as the aftermath of a sizeable war might also be important contributing factors to the supplanting of one political system with another. At any rate, one political system —whether decayed, obsolete, or merely too weak to survive—is replaced by a more viable one.

Ways of establishing new political systems include, among others, revolutionary-independence movements, struggles for power involving civil wars, and *coups-d'état*. Political conventions and mass meetings, as well as elections, might prepare the ground for establishment of new political systems. The American Revolution, for example, cleared away the old political system of English rule over the Colonies and enabled a later constitutional convention and later state legislative action to organize a new political system. The success of General Naguib and Colonel Nasser in replacing the monarchy in Egypt in 1952, or that of General Ayub Khan in coming to power in Pakistan in 1958 illustrate military *coups* replacing monarchical and parliamentary political systems.

Hypothesis 1 states that to be communist a new political system is put into power and is clearly labeled as "Marxist-Leninist," having as its main objective to bring into full operation a Marxist-Leninist society. Older political systems have been replaced with communist ones only in the twentieth century and, in all but two cases, only during the period since World War II. Whatever else might be said about establishing communist systems, then, it is a fairly recent phenomenon. Moreover, the phenomenon has been confined to limited geographical areas, namely Eastern Europe and parts of Asia, plus one nation in the Caribbean Sea.

In discussing ways in which communist parties in these areas have come to power, Seton-Watson sorts the parties into three categories:

1. Those parties which won power principally by their own efforts (Russia, Yugoslavia, Albania, China).
2. Those parties which obtained power by armed intervention from

outside (Azerbaidzhan, Armenia, Georgia, Mongolia, the Baltic states, Poland, Rumania, German Democratic Republic, North Korea).

3. Those parties which combined one and two above (Bulgaria, Hungary, Czechoslovakia).[2]

A somewhat different typology is used by Burks in classifying the build-up of communist movements prior to the change in government:

1. Under enemy occupation, a party built up and carried out a guerrilla action—thus identifying the communist party with the national interest. At the withdrawal of the occupation, the communist guerrillas simply and automatically took over (Albania and Yugoslavia).
2. In states in which the communists enjoyed significant popular support and in which the party had an important history, communists formed an anti-fascist coalition (Czechoslovakia and Hungary).
3. The communist party had a long and dramatic history and had considerable popular support; but the state in question was on the Axis side in World War II, and was therefore attacked and occupied by the Red Army, which then established a puppet government (Bulgaria).
4. In states in which the communist party had little popular support, baggage-train government was brought in as part of the occupying Red Army (German Democratic Republic, Poland, Rumania).[3]

In the typologies of Seton-Watson and Burks, there appear in common several basic types: (1) communist parties installed in power by the occupying Soviet Army; (2) a winning of power by the parties on their own strength and initiative; or (3) a combination of the two. It might be useful, now, to suggest a further breakdown of these and similar typologies.

For the comparative purposes involved here, the ways in which communist parties came into power might be placed into the following two broad groups:

      I. *Independent action by native communists*
        A. Armed *coups*
        B. Nonviolent actions

     II. *Armed intervention by the Soviet Army*
        A. Nationwide occupation
        B. Partial occupation

INDEPENDENT ACTION BY NATIVE COMMUNISTS

Independent action is the most popularly accepted method for setting up communist systems—as practiced for example, by the Bolsheviks in Russia. Although a military struggle may occur with two distinguishable sides (normally the noncommunist government in power opposed by the communist revolutionaries attempting to take power), this category also includes nonviolent actions in coming to power.

Armed coups. Revolutionary-civil wars vary from the slight, several-day sporadic outbreak of the Russian Bolsheviks to the long drawn-out, nation-spanning civil war of the Chinese communists. In the Russian case, however, one should count as part of the broad revolution the Civil War (1918–21) fought between the communists in power and their opposition (in this case the communists were trying to retain and consolidate the power they had recently grasped). In the 1917 revolution, the Bolsheviks had opposed a weak, poorly supported political system, that of the Provisional Government. The Provisional Government was a new (eight months old) political system which had taken over following the collapse of the old, discredited tsarist system in early 1917. Kerensky's leadership of this government was inept and uninspired; its policies were to continue the discredited war against Germany (a war in which Germany effectively, although not technically, had by this time defeated the Russians), to postpone land reform, and to offer no positive solutions to the numerous difficulties facing Russia at the time.

More importantly, by late 1917, Russia was demoralized as a result of its military defeats at the hands of the German armies. Programs of the Provisional Government for internal reforms were many, but its actions in this direction were virtually nonexistent; in effect, its policies called for an indefinite extension of the unenlightened policies of the former tsars. Although it took only a slight push to collapse the Provisional Government, months of intense propaganda on the part of the Bolsheviks had preceded the Revolution—propaganda which revealed their widespread efforts to construct a base of political support among several levels of the population. While not coming to power by way of an election, the Bolsheviks did win some local electoral support in the summer and early fall of 1917 in the form of successful municipal elections. The Bolsheviks enjoyed a tightly organized party which executed a successful overthrow of the Provisional Government. It was advantageous to the Bolsheviks, also, that they constituted the only organized group in Russia in 1917 with a clever leader, a positive program that could win even a minimal level of popular support, and the ability and willingness to employ force. Consequently, their modest military force (some sailors and soldiers, peasants, workers) was adequate to the task of beating the almost defenseless Provisional Government. By late 1917, then, Russia had gone through the creation of two new political systems in but eight months—from an imperial structure, to a semidemocratic one, to a communist one.[4]

The Chinese communists, like the Russian Bolsheviks before them, enjoyed the advantage of having an inept opponent (the Nationalist Government) who rapidly was losing popular support by failing to offer either hope or promise to the nation's citizens. China, too, had gone through a long, debilitating war with Japan which had exhausted what industry there was and caused the citizens to be disenchanted with the Nationalist leaders. In all, there had been a form of civil war between the communists and the Nationalists from the late 1920's until 1949. For more than a decade prior to 1949, the communists under Mao's direction had carefully cultivated the support of citizens of China, mainly the peasants. From the 1930's Chinese communists had taken over certain geographical areas from the Nationalists and then organized Chinese "Soviet republics." The Long March in the mid-1930's and eventual reestablishment in their Yenan retreat, all along being harassed by the Nationalists, measurably added to the communists' experience and confidence. In the process they carried out land reform programs and brought a measure of hope for future improvements to the peasants with whom they came into contact. Between 1945 and 1949 the communists adopted a form of united front by appealing for support from almost all segments of the population (small businessmen, large capitalists, intelligentsia) and by politically organizing each piece of territory which they took over from the Japanese invaders both during and immediately after World War II. Their techniques are summarized by Johnson in outlining the revolutionary strategy of the Chinese communists:

1. Mobilize a sustaining population
2. Organize a mobilized population into mass associations in support of the party
3. Create a large, party-led revolutionary army
4. Adopt guerrilla tactics
5. Carry out a protracted war[5]

The Cuban experience is unique among armed *coups* in that the communists did not begin the Cuban Revolution (the Cuban communists ignored Castro's invasion of Cuba in 1956). By mid-1958, however, the communists contacted Castro at his headquarters in the Sierra Maastra for what resulted in a marriage of convenience between the Cuban communists and Castro's group.

The active period of the revolution which Castro and his companions began in December, 1956, with the invasion from Mexico, extended until January, 1959, when the dictator Batista surrendered. The revolutionary movement led by Castro had romantic aspects stemming from the great odds that confronted Castro's small invasion force of eighty-two men—soon reduced to twelve—who retreated under severe military attacks into the remote mountains of Oriente province, thereby winning, first, the sympathy, then the active support of many Cubans—including students, liberals, workers, and peasants. The revolutionaries built a complete operating base in the mountains from which they fanned out to attack armed forces, bases, depots, cities.

The success of the Cuban revolutionaries stemmed from the popularity of their cause, the choice of battle terrain, and a more competent military leadership (three factors which also were present in the rise to power of the communists in Russia in 1917 and in China in 1949). As Huberman and Sweezy have said, the revolutionary army during the two-year civil war constituted a government, a military force, and a political party all in one.[6]

Thus, in both the Russian and the Chinese cases, a well-coordinated party organization fought a discredited and weak government, opportunely coming to power at a time when near chaos existed in a war-devastated nation. The Chinese communists and the Castro rebels, as well as their Russian predecessors, constituted well-organized and skillfully led groups of revolutionaries who understood the needs and demands of their fellow citizens. In all three cases, the communists seemed effectively to articulate the demands of a great proportion of the nation's citizens. The revolutionaries were also better led militarily than their opponents—exercising more effective strategy, enjoying considerably more discipline over their troops, and profiting from higher morale. Not the least important factor was the more centralized and unified military command which both the Chinese and Russian revolutionaries possessed. In all three instances, finally, a mere change in governments was not what took place, but rather a much deeper, more fundamental replacement of one political system with a quite different one by way of a revolutionary *coup*.

Nonviolent action. In several nations in Europe and one in Asia, communist parties have come to power through nonviolent action. In Albania, a communist-dominated Anti-Fascist National Liberation Committee, an outgrowth of an earlier National Liberation Movement, transformed itself in 1944, into a new, provisional government controlled by native communists. Prior to this time, Yugoslav communists under Tito had been instrumental in organizing, sponsoring, and supporting the National Liberation Movement in Albania. This Yugoslav action was to contribute later on to strained, eventually severed, political relations between Albania and Yugoslavia, as Albania remained fearful of being "swallowed up" (to use a term employed by Stalin's Foreign Minister, Molotov) at some time by Yugoslavia. Following the withdrawal of the German Armies in late 1944, the Albanian communists—through the Provisional Democratic Government of Albania and the Army of National Liberation—established themselves in power in Tirana as the new government of the nation. As an organized, militant political force, the Albanian communists easily eliminated their opposition and succeeded in filling what amounted to a power vacuum. They assumed power by declaring themselves to be the government of Albania with the help of communist or pro-communist army, police, and courts. Their declaration stood without serious challenge.

During the German occupation of Yugoslavia, Tito and his communist partisans in battling the Germans had gained operational control over sizeable areas in 1943; subsequently they formed a provisional (in effect underground) government. This underground government then received military aid from the Western allies to

continue harassing German occupation forces. Following withdrawal from Yugoslavia of units of the Soviet Army (which at war's
end had moved into the Serbian part of Yugoslavia), Tito's government was left in control of large parts of the country. Like the Albanians, the Tito partisans stood up, after the occupying troops of
Germany had left, and simply announced themselves to be the government of the nation. They were to face some opposition, however,
having to fight the Chetniks (a second anti-German guerrilla force
operating against the Nazis during the war in Yugoslavia) under
their leader Mihailovich. Nevertheless, the Chetniks soon were removed by the partisans as an opposition force.

In a situation similar to that of Albania and Yugoslavia, the communists under Ho Chi Minh in what is now Vietnam fought the
Japanese during the latter's occupation of the area. In September,
1945, these nationalist-communists (the Viet Minh) established the
Democratic Republic of Vietnam (DRVN), taking over the north-
ern part of the present Vietnam on the withdrawal of Chinese Nationalist troops. According to Fall, control of Vietnam could have
been taken during this time by anyone with sufficient boldness,
organizational ability, ruthlessness, and armament. Ho Chi Minh and
his Viet Minh forces were able to do so in part of the nation.[7]

In Czechoslovakia, a different political background led to a
unique take-over of power on the part of communists. In prewar
Czechoslovakia the communists were a legal, and an influential,
political force. In the immediate postwar elections for parliament in
1946, the communist party, while not winning a majority of the
total vote, did receive more votes than any other single party (38%
of the vote). This early 1946 success faded in 1947, however, and a
serious defeat in the elections upcoming in 1948 was anticipated as
a distinct possibility by the communists. This motivated them to
carry out a *coup* in February, 1948, thus bypassing the "problem"
of the forthcoming elections. The communists occupied broadcasting
stations, government offices, and various other strategic organizations. At this time the communists held the office of Ministry of the
Interior, making it easier for them to engage in acts of mob violence
without legal repercussions. Also helpful was the fact that Russians
were looked upon by many citizens of Czechoslovakia as their
liberators from Nazism, thus making more acceptable Soviet support
and encouragement to the communists of Czechoslovakia.

ARMED INTERVENTION

In a number of cases, communism has been helped into power by the intervention of the Soviet Army, which occupied certain countries at the end of World War II. The two subcategories under this general heading of armed intervention reflect whether Soviet troops occupied the entire nation, or only part of it.

Nationwide occupation. The Mongolian communist system was established under the hegemony of the Red Army in 1921 when the Provisional, Revolutionary Mongol People's Government was created. Outer Mongolia earlier had been dominated by both Imperial Russia and Imperial China, but when the latter collapsed in a 1911 revolution, the Mongolians won independence for themselves. During the Russian Civil War the White Russians used Mongolia as a base from which to attack the Red Army in Siberia, at the same time that the Whites were fighting the Chinese for control over Mongolia. In the northeastern districts of the country, bordering the Soviet Union, partisan Mongols began forming into a coordinated fighting unit; and, with Soviet backing and support, they proceeded to organize the Provisional Revolutionary Government in March, 1921.[8] With the Red Army and Mongols driving out the Whites from Mongolia in 1921, a communist system was then organized by the Mongolian communists under the tutelage and the leadership of the Soviet Communist party. The new Mongolian government thus became the second communist political system involving a supposedly sovereign nation, to come into existence. Realistically, it was the first of the so-called satellites of the USSR.

In the latter months of World War II the Soviet Army had entered and occupied sizeable areas in Eastern Europe as a direct result of its victories over German troops in these areas. Because of this fortuitous location of Soviet forces, the USSR was in a position to influence both indirectly and directly (occasionally even dictate) the new postwar governments in Eastern Europe. It was thus not accidental that these new governments became communist, fashioned after the Soviet model. In the process, Soviet techniques of takeover included the following:

1. Reliance on agrarian reform to win the support of peasants.

2. Use of the Soviet Army as a pressure force in removing opposition to local communists.
3. Portrayal of the Soviet Army and the USSR as the liberator of the people from Nazism, in the process branding opposition to the communists as "fascist."
4. Use of Moscow-trained communists who were citizens native to each of the countries to infiltrate parties and organizations such as trade unions and justice ministries.
5. Support of (then dominance over) a broad united or popular front of liberal and left forces, and forced mergers of socialist with communist parties. (The united front meant, in effect, that legal opposition was banned; all recognized parties had to participate in the front.)

In Bulgaria a series of events—including a Soviet-backed *coup,* the placing of communists in key governmental posts under the watchful eye of the occupying Soviet Army, and purges of opposition leaders which extended from 1944 until almost the end of 1948 —finally laid the groundwork for the communists to come to power in that country. Through control over the Ministry of the Interior, the communists made key appointments of sympathetic persons to important governmental positions. The communists also applied pressure on leaders of other political parties (e.g., to stop electoral opposition to the communists). Some of these leaders were threatened and imprisoned. In elections held in 1946, accompanied by communist pressure (including arrests), the communist-dominated Fatherland Front won 78 percent of the votes. As a result the new Bulgarian government was headed by a long-time communist and former general-secretary of the Comintern, Georgi Dimitrov.[9]

Again with Soviet assistance—in no small part due to the influence of the occupying Soviet Army—communists were given privileged positions in the post-1944 government of Hungary, including (as in Czechoslovakia and Bulgaria) the position of Minister of the Interior. This privilege was accompanied by Soviet promises to Hungary of territory; and it included purges of dissident, noncommunist political leaders (including arrests and even executions), capped by an enforced unity between socialists and communists. The Soviet Army arrested some leaders of the opposition Smallholder's Party, accusing them, not of opposition to communism as such, but of collaboration with the Nazis. As a result, in 1947 communists won elections (although fraud was involved) to finally establish themselves in power.

The pattern is repeated in Poland where, once more, there was the presence of the Soviet Army, plus successful maneuvers such as a united front; communists in the Interior Ministry as well as in the Polish Army; and arrests of notable anticommunists—all of which aided the Polish communists to seize key governmental posts. These leaders, then, with Soviet help, eventually eliminated the bulk of their opposition. Ostensibly getting rid of Nazis, Soviet forces at the same time eliminated potential opposition from liberal and left political elements in postwar Poland. Furthermore, the Russians were accused of pausing outside of Warsaw just prior to its liberation, to allow the Nazis time to eliminate their underground opposition, an opposition which the Russians believed would be anticommunist.

After taking a part of Eastern Poland in the Nazi-Soviet Pact of 1939, the Russians, following the war, gave a part of Germany to Poland (as promised at the Yalta Conference), thus extending Polish territory westward partially to compensate for the area of Eastern Poland that had been incorporated into the USSR. One effect of this land exchange has been to portray the Russians as a defender of the new Polish-German border, a border initially agreed to by Western nations. This dependency of Poland on the USSR, however, is changing as more nations, including West Germany, recognize the border.

In Rumania, too, there occurred Soviet diplomatic pressures— supported by the painfully obvious presence of their army, which collaborated with local communists (on occasion resorting to mob actions)—as well as Soviet disarming of Rumanian Army units, prohibition of the activity of noncommunist political parties, and restriction of popular suffrage. All of these actions contributed to the establishment of a communist-dominated cabinet in 1945. During this critical period the Soviet representative in Rumania, Vishinsky, forced on King Michael the appointment of Moscow-selected Rumanian communists to such key governmental ministries as interior and defense. Subsequently, elections which were carried out within an atmosphere of severe intimidation (including even murder), enabled the communist-dominated government bloc to win. Finally, the forced abdication of the King was preceded by arrests of opposition political leaders.

In all of the above cases there was at some point in the take-over a seizure of certain key governmental positions by communists who frequently were leaders of a united front, which was, in reality, a communist-dominated coalition of liberal and radical political groups. In several instances communists had already acquired—before the take-over—the very important, even crucial, position of minister of the interior which, among other functions, controls the nation's police. The coalition of liberal and radical political groups was both genuine (in its opposition to fascism) and illusory (in that it was supposed to be—but was not—a broad, democratically-ruled coalition). In all of the cases the Soviet Army contributed the persuasive muscle to threaten dissenters opposed to communist rule. There were purges of political leaders who opposed the communists' coming to power, occasional electoral intimidation (both psychological and physical), and seizure of key governmental and societal offices and facilities. One of the noteworthy factors to be found in these *coups* is that of the high level of organization that existed among communists within the milieu of disorganized societies and enfeebled political systems following World War II.

Partial occupation. The most well-known case of geographical partitioning of a country following World War II was in Germany. The government of East Germany, the German Democratic Republic (GDR), was organized by the Russians within their zone of occupation, the Russians quickly establishing a communist system under the leadership of German communists who were sympathetic to and under the control of Moscow. In early 1946 Soviet authorities backed a united-front merger of East Germany's socialist and communist parties into a single, monolithic party—the Socialist Unity Party (SED)—whose leaders then were placed in key ruling positions in the East Zone of Germany.[10] In the case of East Germany there is a fine line drawn between the coming to power of Moscow-trained German communists and simple occupation by Soviet troops, with actual, albeit indirect, political rule frequently coming from Moscow. In fact, both rule by German communists and Soviet occupation are features of postwar East Germany.

In Korea, at the end of World War II, a similar postwar division of the country occurred at the 38th parallel, for the purpose of completing the surrender of Japanese troops in the area—the Russians militarily occupying the North and the Americans the South. The Russians proceeded quickly to place in authority in the North those Korean communists who were sympathetic to the USSR, some of them even Soviet citizens. The ground was thereby prepared for establishing a communist political system in that part of the country. To a degree, independent North Vietnam too is partially a result of a postwar division of the north and south parts of the nation under separate governments, but, in this case, without the intervention of Soviet troops.

To answer the question now of just how communist parties in general come into power, several techniques and steps might be set down. While not all of these techniques are applicable in any given instance, each of them has played an important role in more than one instance of parties coming to power.

1. Communists work with and through a united, popular front of liberal and left political leaders and parties (in most countries of Eastern Europe, China, and North Vietnam).
2. Communists win support for their leaders and programs by extensive propaganda efforts (most notably, Russian and Chinese), or even by a heroic war record (in North Vietnam and Yugoslavia).
3. On occasion elections strengthen the hand of the communists although not clearly putting them into power (Russian Bolsheviks in the summer and early fall of 1917, and the Czechoslovak Communist party in 1946).
4. Communists gain control by infiltration of key governmental offices, usually the ministry of interior, and by extensive political and military-police pressure (in the countries of Eastern Europe).
5. Communists take physical possession of key installations vital to the stability of the nation, such as government offices and radio stations (in all countries).
6. Communists bring pressure to bear against their political opposition by a number of devices such as discrediting the opposition in the eyes of the nation's citizens; forbidding their enemies to participate in political life; and on occasion even causing the arrest, imprisonment, and execution of opposition leaders. (All communist parties coming to power have used one or more of these tactics.)
7. Communist leaders finding themselves in a political vacuum in which organized political groups are almost nonexistent simply announce their accession to power (in Albania, Yugoslavia, North Vietnam) or are placed in power by a superior military force (in Mongolia, Eastern Europe, North Korea), with acquiescence by the rest of the nation.

A listing of the predominant ways communists have come to power in various states is shown by the categories in Table 1.

One of the fourteen states (Cuba) does not conform to the second part of *hypothesis 1* of the Marxist-Leninist Model: that the new po-

TABLE 1
Categories of Coming to Power by Communists

I. *Independent action*		II. *Armed intervention*	
A. Armed *coup*		A. Nationwide occupation	
USSR	(1917)	Mongolia	(1921)
China	(1949)	Rumania	(1945)
Cuba	(1959)	Bulgaria	(1946)
B. Nonviolent action		Hungary	(1947)
Albania	(1944)	Poland	(1947)
Yugoslavia	(1945)	B. Partial occupation	
North Vietnam	(1945)	North Korea	(1945)
Czechoslovakia	(1948)	GDR	(1949)

litical system comes to power for the specific purpose of bringing
into full operation a Marxist-Leninist society. In the Cuban case
this prime objective was added by Castro at a later time. All of the
other thirteen cases apparently do confirm the hypothesis, as attested
to by the affiliations of their leaders with the communist movement
both at home and abroad, and by their declared Marxist ideology
upon attaining power, if not before.

The communist parties coming to power appear fairly evenly divided between the two main categories of independent action and
armed intervention. Independent actions, at least of the violent type,
appear to be few, with only three of the fourteen states fitting this
category. The importance of the USSR in communist parties' coming
to power is obvious from the table.

PRE-COMMUNIST POLITICAL TRADITIONS

We might now raise the question as to the importance, if any, of
earlier traditions in the communist states. Were there relevant
pre-communist political structures and patterns of rule that had a
bearing or influence on these states as they were transformed into
communist systems? Are there such environments as "pre-communist"
ones? Are there certain preconditions which might have made it
easier for communism to be introduced into a given state? The first
consideration in such a review of possible preconditions should be
that of the nation-states as historical entities.

The breaking up of the Holy Roman Empire—as well as of the Ottoman Turk, the Austro-Hungarian, Prussian, and Russian empires (which started to break up in the early nineteenth century and were finally ended in the early twentieth)—resulted in the creation of a fairly large number of small states in Eastern Europe where the large empires once had existed. Often these new, small states were synthetic fusions of diverse peoples. A main consequence of this synthetic fusion was the rise of a virulent form of nationalism which people associated with their own particular ethnic group.

Czechoslovakia, for example, was created as a new nation in 1918 composed chiefly of the two main groups: Czechs and Slovaks. These two peoples were not close, psychologically, and harbored little love and affection for each other. The problems involved in joining these two peoples into a single nation-state, difficult enough in itself, were aggravated by the number of Germans, Ruthenians, Magyars, and Poles living together. In 1968, incidentally, the Soviet government deliberately widened the Czech-Slovak split by a number of postinvasion actions (such as dealing directly and separately with the Slovak Communist party—by-passing the national Czechoslovak Communist party). The intention, apparently successful, was to play on Slovak independence desires by forcing a virtual separation of Czechs and Slovaks in early 1969, via creation of a new federation, in order to dampen political liberalism within Czechoslovakia and ease Czechoslovakia firmly back into the Soviet bloc. A closely integrated Czechoslovakia is still to be accomplished.

A similar situation is found in another post-World War I creation, Yugoslavia, which was formed of a number of ethnic groups: the two main ones being Serbs (42.1% of the total population in 1961) and Croats (23.7% in 1961). In addition to Slovenes and Macedonians (14.2%), Albanians (4.9%), and Magyars (2.7%), various other ethnic peoples were included in Yugoslavia.[11] Similar problems occurred here because of ethnic differences among the several groups and because some did not want to give up what they considered to be their historic nationality (say, Serbian) for a new, synthetic nationality—Yugoslavian. Some of the other Eastern European nations (Albania, Hungary, Poland) have also attempted to present a national orientation to differing ethnic groups which have been frequently antagonistic to one another.[12] This building of a national, patriotic orientation is, however, a painstakingly slow task (see, for example, North vs. South in the United States of the nineteenth century). In Yugoslavia, for instance, Serbian hero myths were not successfully transformed into Yugoslav ones in the short period between the two world wars.[13] Burks notes, incidentally, that in Eastern Europe numerically weak ethnic groups produce above-average numbers of communists if these groups have had an ethnic or traditional tie to Russia.[14]

The Soviet Union is also a multi-national state composed of numerous ethnic groups (the Russians amounting to slightly more than half of the total Soviet population). Some of these groups (e.g., the Ukrainians) have long harbored separatist tendencies. Ethnic group problems plagued the Russian tsars as they attempted Russification of minority peoples, some of whom (e.g., the Georgians) had earlier lived independently of Russian domination; and national integration of a large number of multi-ethnic groups had not been satisfactorily solved by the old Russian government. In the 1970 Soviet census there were listed, apart from Russian, fifty-nine other ethnic/national peoples in addition to other small groups, some identified and some not.[15]

Even the Chinese, usually considered a fairly homogeneous race, might be considered so only if one means the dominant Han people. Apart from these, there are a number of millions of minority groups in China (Central Asians, Manchus, Mongols, Tibetans, Taiwanese) which have caused integration problems both before and after communism came to power. The officially recognized minority nationalities in China include 54, amounting to some 38 million people occupying some 60 percent of the nation's land area.[16]

Many of these ethnic frictions were aggravated over the years—especially between the world wars—by cultural and even educational policies which catered to various myths of racial superiority and inferiority. Poles were made to believe that they were superior to the Czechs, who in turn considered themselves to be measurably more intelligent than the Slovaks, all of whom were considered by Germans to be of inferior stock. Russians within the old Russian Empire and Han Chinese in old China exhibited similar beliefs in their own racial superiority over minority groups within their respective nations. Extremes of ethnocentrism, in addition to frustrating drives for national integration, made it quite difficult for these people (now spokesmen for nation-states) to cooperate among themselves. It was too easy, both before and after the communists came to power, for historic antagonism to break out once again. Thus Hungarians mistrusted Rumanians, and Poles renewed their centuries-old hate for the Russians. There flare-ups were most apparent following the death of Stalin and the resultant political weakening of his Eastern European empire.

Another noteworthy political tradition in both Eastern Europe and Asia has been the frequency of arbitrary, corrupt, and occasionally harsh bureaucracy. Old Russia is infamous for this feature of its government and in China there has been an almost unbroken succession of such bureaucratic excesses reaching back into the ancient dynasties. Balkan bureaucracy according to Seton-Watson, was centralized, complicated, and above all, corrupt.[17] In a less brutal vein, the tradition of the administrative state in Germany has been of benefit to the postwar regime in the German Democratic Republic. The citizen freely obeys this tradition of old Prussia; in Smith's words, government in the GDR is institutionalized and coercion is bureaucratic.[18] In Bulgaria, Rumania, and Yugoslavia, a bureaucratic, intellectual, and commercial bourgeoisie came into existence in the nineteenth century, developed rapidly after 1918, and formed the ruling class between the wars.[19] Other states in Eastern Europe and Asia have had somewhat similar experiences.

Coexisting with "bureaucratism" in most of these nations is a tradition of authoritarianism, such as that found under the Russian tsars, Albania's King Zog, Bulgaria's King Boris III, Cuba's Batista, Hungary's Admiral Horthy, Rumania's King Carol II, and Yugoslavia's King Alexander—not to mention Germany's Hitler and China's Chiang Kai-shek—all of whom (except for the strong Russian tsars) ruled in the first part of the twentieth century. Authoritarianism was also present in French rule of Indochina, which included the area of present-day Vietnam; and it was present in Japanese rule of Korea between 1910–45. If bureaucratism made government distasteful in the minds of citizens, authoritarianism introduced harsh treatment and a resultant atmosphere of citizen fear toward and mistrust of government officials.

Economic underdevelopment, particularly with respect to industrialization, has typified all of the states of Eastern Europe and Asia which later became communist, as well as Cuba. The only two exceptions are Czechoslovakia and the GDR. The first was industrialized prior to its becoming communist; and, in the case of the GDR, certain attitudes and behavior patterns existed among the people which made them adaptable to industrialization. All of the other states can be classified as agricultural/rural in their precommunist period; the majority of their work force was engaged in agriculture.[20] Land reform, so urgently needed, had been by and large postponed indefinitely in these countries prior to the communist period. Results of economic underdevelopment included a broad range of personal deprivations (e.g., low incomes and inadequate consumer goods) and lost opportunities for the citizens.

Alongside these social, political, and economic disabilities were those of chronic overpopulation, poor health, and low levels of education and literacy. In China, for example, these ills plagued efforts of nation-building and strengthening following the collapse of the imperial dynasties early in the twentieth century. Indeed, in many of these nations life was typified by deprivation in social, educational, economic, and political matters. The term "brutalized poverty" fits life in many of these countries.

Still another phenomenon worth noting under the heading of precommunist patterns of rule is that of the postwar anarchy which immediately preceded the communist period. This was the case during World War I for Russia, the Russian Civil War for Mongolia, and World War II for all of the other communist states of Eastern Europe and Asia. To be found amid this wartime chaos and resulting internal political disruption was a well-organized, native communist-party leadership (Russia, Czechoslovakia, Yugoslavia, China, Vietnam), or in some cases a well-organized political occupation of the territory by the Soviet Army. Nations suffering from dislocations, if not outright devastation, of, say, factories, schools, and railroads were sorely in need of internal reorganization, of firm and wise political leadership. This is when the communists stepped in, offering this reorganization and claiming this wisdom where other voices were weak or nonexistent. Anarchy cries out for order, even if authoritarian.

With but very few exceptions, the conditions in all of the communist states prior to their becoming communist were characterized by extremes of political weakness alternating with authoritarianism; at least some popular alienation from the regime; hypernationalism, at times aggravated by deep ethnic hatreds; and economic underdevelopment and deprivation. In contrast to this weakness was the strength of the communist party, often working in tandem with the Soviet government and its army. Johnson notes that communist parties have come to power in societies that suffered from incoherence resulting from backwardness and the disruptions of initial industrialization (Russia), from colonial rule following on the demise of colonial power (Vietnam and Korea), from semicolonial rule following from abortive nationalist movements (China and Cuba), and from catastrophic defeat and military occupation.[21]

It would be unwise to claim the foregoing factors as preconditions to the initiation of communist political systems. Obviously, too many other nations have suffered from difficulties such as political misrule, economic weakness, and postwar anarchy. Nevertheless, it is easy to see that such political and economic difficulties have opportunely laid the groundwork for well-organized communist movements in coming to power. If too much cannot be made of such preconditions, neither should they be ignored nor discounted in a discussion of how communist political systems originate.

NOTES

1. "A revolution," Huntington notes, "is a rapid, fundamental, and violent domestic change in the dominant values and myths of a society, in its political institutions, social structure, leadership, and government activities and policies." Samuel P. Huntington, *Political Order in Changing Societies* (New Haven: Yale University Press, 1968), p. 264. Lowenthal observes that communist parties seize power in the name of thoroughgoing social changes—in the class structure, the economic system, and societal values. Richard Lowenthal, in *Change in Communist Systems,* Chalmers Johnson, ed. (Stanford: Stanford University Press, 1970), p. 33.

2. Hugh Seton-Watson, *From Lenin to Khrushchev: The History of World Communism* (New York: Praeger, 1960), p. 330. The typology of Dallin and Breslauer also includes three types of cases in which communist parties come to power: (1) through a *coup* and following civil war (Russia); (2) through armed struggle from expanding territorial bases (China, Yugoslavia, Albania, Cuba, Vietnam); and (3) through institution of regimes imposed with help from an external military force (most of Eastern Europe, Mongolia, North Korea). Alexander Dallin and George W. Breslauer, *Political Terror in Communist Systems* (Stanford: Stanford University Press, 1970), p. 14.

3. R. V. Burks, "Eastern Europe," in *Communism and Revolution: The Strategic Uses of Political Violence,* Cyril E. Black and Thomas P. Thornton, eds. (Princeton: Princeton University Press, 1964), pp. 86–89.

4. Black lists these types of communist revolution: (1) violent domestic revolution involving an extended civil war; (2) a revolution from without, with the decisive influence coming from a foreign communist army; (3) a revolution from above, essentially a nonviolent effort with assistance from a foreign communist influence; and (4) an electoral revolution, with little if any political violence. Cyril E. Black, "Anticipation of Communist Revolutions," in Black and Thornton, *ibid.,* pp. 417 ff.

5. Chalmers Johnson, in *The Communist Revolution in Asia: Tactics, Goals, and Achievements,* Robert Scalapino, ed. (Englewood Cliffs: Prentice-Hall, 1965), pp. 50–52.

6. Leo Huberman and Paul M. Sweezy, *Cuba: Anatomy of a Revolution* (New York: Monthly Review Press, 1961), p. 83.

7. Fall summarizes the take-over: "Thus, through the sheer energy and organizational ability of its Communist leadership, Viet-Nam has become a 'people's democracy' in fact as well as in name—even while its territory was still occupied by Chinese Nationalist, British, and French military forces and American observers, and while the nearest Soviet Russian and Chinese Communist troops were still thousands of miles away." Bernard B. Fall, *The Two Viet-Nams* (New York: Praeger, 1963), pp. 61, 66. Another author refers to the Vietnam case as a fine example of a relatively nonviolent seizure of power, a revolutionary *coup* executed with a minimum of violence. See George Modelski, "The Viet Minh Complex," in Black and Thornton, *op. cit.* (above, n. 3), p. 200.

8. M. T. Haggard, "Mongolia, the First Communist State in Asia," in Scalapino, *op. cit.* (above, n. 5), p. 84. Prior to 1921 there had been attempts to set up new communist systems, following the Soviet model, in Persia, by Bela Kun in Hungary, and in Germany. Only the Hungarian attempt succeeded, and that for only a few months.

9. One of the best source books for information concerning communists coming to power in Eastern Europe is that of Hugh Seton-Watson, *The East European Revolution* (London: Methuen and Company, 1952).

10. Smith portrays this merger of Social Democrats with communists as a warm, even festive event. See Jean Edward Smith, *Germany Beyond the Wall: People, Politics and Prosperity* (Boston: Little, Brown, 1967), p. 187.

11. Cited in M. George Zaninovich, *The Development of Socialist Yugoslavia* (Baltimore: Johns Hopkins University Press, 1968), p. 168.

12. Communism coming to power in Albania meant a power transfer from the Gegs to the Tosks (the latter providing most of the leading figures in the Albanian communist movement as well as most of the soldiers for the Army of National Liberation in World War II). Thus the communist Tosks faced the struggle of winning over the northerners —Gegs who had a long tradition of opposition to a central government.

Nicholas C. Pano, *The People's Republic of Albania* (Baltimore: John Hopkins University Press, 1968), p. 62.

13. Zaninovich, *op. cit.*, pp. 19–20.

14. Burks, *op. cit.* (above, n. 3), p. 188.

15. *Izvestiya,* April 17, 1971.

16. June Dreyer, "China's Minority Nationalities: Traditional and Party Elites," *Pacific Affairs,* Winter 1970–71, p. 506.

17. Hugh Seton-Watson, *Eastern Europe Between the Wars, 1918–1941* (Hamden, Connecticut: Archon Books, 1962), p. 147.

18. Smith, *op. cit.* (above, n. 10), p. 80.

19. The political history of Eastern Europe from 1918 to 1941 is the history of these classes. Seton-Watson, *Eastern Europe Between the Wars, op. cit.*, p. 126.

20. Burks, *op. cit.* (above, n. 3), p. 187. There is evidence pointing toward the peasant class as the dominant one among both the communist masses and the communist guerrillas and insurgents in Eastern Europe prior to the communist take-overs.

21. Johnson, *op. cit.* (above, n. 5), p. 5.

3

Political Rule in Communist Systems

Successful political rule in any society rests on a vital link connecting authority with legitimacy. Accordingly, political leaders normally devote considerable time in attempting to legitimate their authority. One might even suggest that when legitimacy of the leaders is questioned seriously, their continued authoritative rule becomes tenuous. Revolution and civil war within a given society, whatever their cause, testify to the complete breakdown of the necessary link between authority and legitimacy.

For communist political systems there is a special problem because they come to power under a cloud of suspicion regarding their legitimacy. Citizens within a specific communist state and many outside of it may challenge the validity of communist rule. As a result, communist leaders must devote a great deal of attention simply to establishing their right to rule.[1]

Hypothesis 2, with which this chapter is concerned, states that the communist party—serving as the spokesman for, and acting in the interest of, the working class—assumes political control over society.

Communists actually begin the long process of validation of their rule long before they get political power. Starting with ideology to justify their power, they proceed through use of party and governmental controls in hopes of winning authoritative recognition. Communist rule by force, occasional purges, sporadic periods of terror have not lessened efforts of these leaders to win voluntary citizen support for their political legitimacy. Toward this purpose, Soviet leaders have relied on the social and humanitarian justice associated with the Marxian ideal, with its simple notions of equity and fairness, as well as on concepts of Russian patriotism. If the acceptance of Marxian ideology can be transferred to the instrumentality of the communist party, then the leaders themselves become legitimated because they own the party. Accordingly, much of Soviet propaganda stresses the philosophical, moral, and practical correctness of the party line for all citizens.

The other communist-party states have followed suit in claiming authoritative legitimacy for their respective communist parties. Pre-communist political traditions of strong, arbitrary rule in Old Russia and in Eastern Europe probably made acceptance of this claim easier; citizens were already accustomed to autocratic governments which left little room for expression of popular democratic attitudes.

In Asia the communist regimes faced greater obstacles in transferring legitimacy to the communist parties. In China, many citizens were not familiar with the idea of granting legitimacy to *any* central or national authority. Because pre-communist China had been family and clan oriented, communist leaders faced unusual problems of building nationalism and patriotism, in addition to seeking wide and deep support for the communist party. Thus, the Constitution of the communist party of China refers to the party as the vanguard of the working class, and to its role as the interpreter of the Marxist-Leninist scriptures. The party is responsible for bringing socialism to China, modernizing the country, fighting off all enemies through leading and, in turn, being led by the masses.[2]

In the other Asian communist states, too, there has been a need to build patriotism and nationalism in areas where they had been submerged under previous colonial regimes (Korea, Mongolia, Vietnam). Korean, as well as Chinese, communists worked to overcome a Confucian bias in their political culture which put the family on a par, authoritatively, with the state. Here again, the unquestioned support of the people for the party was portrayed as the ideological and institutional focus for the society.[3]

Political rule and control involve the making of important decisions which authoritatively govern society. Such rule is the core of a political system and is the main determinant behind the allocation and distribution of much of a nation's resources. In communist systems, too, political rule is at the center of attention for all communists—orthodox conservative leaders as well as liberal reforming ones. Most of the goals of communists—for example, industrialization and an economy of abundance—begin with the key element of Leninism: operational control by the communist party over the main inputs and outputs of the political system. While Marx believed in the primacy of economics over politics—i.e., the structure of the first determines the structure and functions of the second—Lenin acted as if the reverse were true. Subsequent communist political systems, the USSR included, follow Lenin on this point of politics determining economics and thus, in this way, are ideologically more Leninist than Marxist.

Lenin's early leadership of the Bolsheviks (from 1903) and his organization and leadership of the Russian Communist party from 1918 was the successful expression of political domination by an elite party group. From that time on the power center of each and every communist system has centered around its polestar, the communist party. Accordingly, the chief function of any communist party, either in or out of power, is to help shape conditions so that the party can be the instrument for gaining and holding an absolute monopoly of power.[4] The ideological justification for communist-party rule is that it rules in the name of the workers (and under Marxism, of course, workers are to rule society). Because the average worker is ignorant of Marxism and all that it promises him, he must be instructed in Marxism by the communist party. Moreover, he needs help in dispossessing the old capitalist class and taking over political and economic power from them. Setting up a workers' state, a dictatorship of the proletariat, then, requires the services of a skilled, knowledgeable group. Enter the communist party, which promises to lead and guide the worker and to direct the worker toward the Marxian utopia.

After gaining power communist parties consolidate their rule chiefly by eliminating their political opposition and by establishing a governmental structure which carries out their orders. Following this step comes the socialist "revolution," which seeks to replace old structures, institutions, and customs with new ones selected by the communist leadership. In China, one author has seen an evolution of communist-party rule following several successive steps: government by regional party groups (1949–52); the party as a national bureaucracy (1952–58); the party as direct manager of the nation as a total entity (1958–61); and, finally, the party slowly removing itself from the various governmental functions (after 1961).[5] In the USSR, a similar development occurred earlier, as the communist party (CPSU) evolved from an underground revolutionary party into a leadership group which organized the Soviet political system, and eventually into a national ruling bureaucracy. Most recently, the CPSU has been weighing the possibility of relinquishing a bit more of its political rule to some of the formal agencies and offices of the government.

If a simple definition of political rule has reference to significant, authoritative decision-making, the measure of political rule is more difficult to determine. What, for example, is a minimum level or degree of effective political control? At what point in the activities of a given political system does political leadership fail to control? While these and related questions are pertinent for all political systems, including both communist and noncommunist ones, we are concerned here with the questions only as they affect the communist states. The organization to begin with in this investigation is the communist party.

THE COMMUNIST-PARTY APPARATUS

Political rule in a communist state is most visibly expressed through the apparatus of its communist party.[6] Although the party is never the sum total of political power in such a state, it is the essential core and chief motivating force for political rule. The obvious exception is Cuba, where Castro and his close companions —keeping control within their own hands—constitute a barrier to the construction of a communist bureaucracy.[7] Castro himself is Prime

Minister, First Secretary of the Party, Commander-in-Chief of the Armed Forces, President of the Central Planning Board, and Director of the National Institute of Agrarian Reform (INRA).

The main functions of the party with respect to political rule are to interpret the official Marxist-Leninist ideology, establish the political-governmental structures for the society, set forth national policies (both foreign and domestic), and see to their execution. To realize these various functions, the party organizes a structural apparatus approximately as follows:

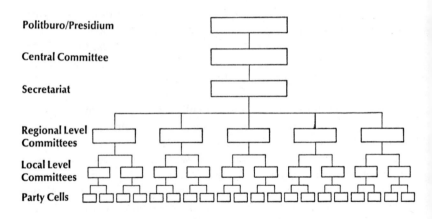

This structure, simplified from the Soviet model, reveals a strict hierarchy with a large number of subordinate (regional and local-level) organizations involved nationwide in the total ruling apparatus. This elaborated organization is necessary, in the view of party leaders, so that effective and efficient direction over policies, programs, and activities of a governmental-political-social nature can be adequately supervised wherever the particular policy or program is carried out. The typical party organization reveals a pyramid-like structure which contains at the bottom a broad base of party cells (basic or primary organizations) in most of the public institutions such as factories, farms, schools, industrial offices. On this base are established local administrative committees, which are responsible for all public functions within their respective areas. Next above these local committees are the regional administrative committees, which coordinate the assignments and functions of a specified number of local committees. The Secretariat, on the national level, is the administrative arm of the central committee. The central committee, which coordinates the work of local and regional committees, is directed by a small inner control organ. This is the Politburo in the USSR, the Standing Committee of the Politburo in China, Politburo or Presidium in most of the Eastern European communist states, and the Executive Committee in Yugoslavia.

Throughout this party hierarchy, administrative and policy discipline is carried out by each subordinate echelon of the apparatus, which, in turn, is strictly accountable in all matters to the next higher echelon of party organization. Control supposedly is carried out from top to bottom in a smooth and expeditious manner; or at least the organizational structure was established with this objective in mind. Following what might be termed the first law of communist control, the hierarchical organization of internal apparatus fans out to establish controls over all nonparty organizations within the particular society. That the party hierarchy does not function all that smoothly in practice, of course, is to be expected. On occasion there is a single national leader—the classical prototypes being Lenin, Stalin, Mao, and Castro—who assumes the power of the party for himself. Other strong leaders have included Tito in Yugoslavia, Ulbricht in the German Democratic Republic, Novotny in Czechoslovakia, Hoxha in Albania, and Kim Il Sung in North Korea. Perhaps because of these numerous strong leaders, some authors suggest that communist systems require, or at least tend toward, a single, strongman dictatorship. Some experience, on the other hand, argues against the single strong-man thesis (e.g., the USSR after Khrushchev, North Vietnam after Ho Chih Minh, post-1956 Hungary, and Rumania).

Communist-party membership, as a percent of a given state's population, varies from an estimated low of .8% in Cuba to a high of 13% in North Korea. Prior to the invasion of Czechoslovakia in 1968, Soviet leaders supposedly informed Czechslovak party officials that their party was too large for that nation's population (12%). The Soviet norm (5%) is adhered to rather closely by other communist states, as shown in the estimates in Table 2. Apart from North Korea and Czechoslovakia, the GDR in 1965 had what the Russians might

TABLE 2
Communist Party Members (estimated)*

State	Party Members & Date		Members as Percentage of Population	Workers in Party (%)	Peasants in Party (%)	Office Workers & Intelligent-sia in Party (%)	Other (%)
Albania	53,659	(1965)	3.0		70.0		30.0
Bulgaria	615,000	(1962)	8.0	38.2	30.0	25.6	6.2
China	18,000,000	(1965)	3.0				
Cuba	70,000	(1969)	0.8				
Czechoslovakia	1,684,416	(1965)	12.0	36.0	6.4		57.6
GDR	1,610,679	(1965)	10.0	47.1	5.8	28.1	19.0
Hungary	520,000	(1965)	5.0	(42.7	)	38.1	19.2
Mongolia	48,570	(1966)	4.0	29.0	21.6		49.4
North Korea	1,700,000	(1969)	13.0	57.0	27.0		16.0
North Vietnam	570,000	(1965)	3.0	11.0	52.0		37.0
Poland	1,614,237	(1965)	5.0	40.2	11.4	42.8	5.6
Rumania	2,000,000	(1970)	10.0	43.6	26.4		7.1
USSR	14,000,000	(1970)	5.0	40.0	15.6	22.9	44.4
Yugoslavia	1,146,084	(1969)	6.0	31.3	7.4		61.3

* Although there is later information on party membership, there is not comparable later information on population.
Area Handbook for Mongolia (Washington, D.C.: Foreign Area, Studies, 1970), p. 233.
Area Handbook for North Korea (Washington, D.C.: Foreign Area, Studies, 1969), pp. 217, 228.
J. F. Brown, *The New Eastern Europe* (New York: Praeger, 1966), p. 290.
Socialist Thought and Practice, July–September, 1969, p. 51.
Supplement to *World Marxist Review,* August, 1970, p. 6.
Hugh Thomas, *Cuba: The Pursuit of Freedom* (New York: Harper and Row, 1971), p. 1456.
World Strength of the Communist Party Organizations (Washington, D.C.: Department of State, January, 1965).

term an excess in party members. Cuba's .8%, on the other hand, appears unusually low for a ruling communist-party state.

COMMUNIST-PARTY FUNCTIONS

One of the first steps taken by a communist party on coming to power is to eliminate both present and potential opposition to its exclusive rule. This is necessary, in view of communists, in order to place the communist party in a clear position of dominance so that it may direct the various functions of society without interference or challenge (much of the opposition, of course, has already been eliminated when the communists first came to power). The party seeks not only to finish off its remaining opponents, but also to set up both machinery and procedures for keeping potential opposition to the party powerless and even preventing its growth. Transformation of a society into communism, then, has been accompanied by the coming to power of a dynamic controlling communist party which is not limited or checked by any other organization.

Here the exception of Stalinist rule in the USSR should be noted. Stalin, during his rise to full power, downgraded the supreme position of the Soviet Communist party to one closer to equality with other organizations (e.g., political police, industrial managers) so that Stalin's own predominant position would remain superior to all other individuals and organizations. As a consequence, the party apparatus instead of dominating these other organizations, was forced to compete with them for Stalin's favor. The party nevertheless retained its ideological legitimacy in national leadership. This was partly because control by Stalin over Soviet society was exercised chiefly through the party's top organ (Politburo). The eclipse of the party apparatus as the ruling force was in any event temporary. Following Stalin's death the party once again was raised to a position of clear and unchallenged supremacy over all other Soviet organizations.

After elimination of its political opposition, the communist party is now in a position to organize its controls over the entire political system—most importantly, over the formal structures of government. The normal governmental apparatus of decision-making within a communist system is the executive arm, including the bureaucracy.

This, of course, does not differ basically from many noncommunist political systems. Structurally, under communism, there is a fair differentiation of government functions among various branches, offices, and organizations. Thus, the Defense Ministry sees to the military protection of the nation, the Foreign Ministry to its diplomacy, and so on. In practice, however, all of these various divisions of the governmental apparatus are but administrative arms of the communist party. As Tomasic portrays it in the case of Rumania, the central apparatus of the Rumanian Communist party (the Politburo members, and central and regional secretaries) is the hard core of the party, while the government and managerial experts are the inner circle of advisors and executives of the party's decisions.[8] Functionally, then, the ruling apparatus is not so differentiated as its formal organization suggests.

The constitutions of China, Czechoslovakia, the German Democratic Republic, Mongolia, North Vietnam, Rumania, and Yugoslavia refer to the leading role played by the communist party within each of these political systems. The Czechoslovak Constitution, for example, establishes the communist party as the guiding force in both the state and society. The Rumanian Constitution places the party organs over those of the state. The Yugoslav Constitution notes the League of Communists (formerly the communist party) as the leading organized force of the working class and the prime mover of political activity. The preamble to the Chinese Constitution of 1954 pays homage to the revolutionary leadership of the Chinese Communist party, while the Mongolian Constitution recognizes the Mongolian People's Revolutionary (Communist) party as the leading core of all governmental apparatus.[9] A Soviet writer describes party control over "state organization" (governmental apparatus) as including (1) provision of leadership, (2) running candidates for public office, and (3) checking up on the work of the state organizations.[10]

Obvious steps on the part of the party toward dominating the governmental apparatus include staffing the executive branch with party leaders and similarly filling key positions in the legislature, as well as other public bodies, with faithful party members. Moreover, all public officials must remain openly in support not only of the goals and policies of the communist party, but also of its rules and, above all, of its leaders. Key positions in the government proper are held by important party leaders; in addition, there are organizations within the communist party which are rough counterparts to governmental offices, such as finance, foreign policy, and the military. One result of these efforts is a close meshing of party and government structures, with the particular organization of the communist party watching over as well as checking on its functionally related governmental organization. In a reorganization of the apparatus of the Polish communist party following Gomulka's downfall, the central party secretariat was listed as follows,[11] testifying to party dominance of specific functions:

Secretary	Functions
Major General Moczar	Army, security organs, administration, and health
Olszowski	Press, culture, youth
Syzdlak	Ideology and propaganda
Barcikowski	Agriculture
Tejchma	Science, parliament, and foreign policy
Babruch	Organizational matters
Starewicz	Politburo matters

Even on the regional and local levels governments are supervised by a regional or local party office.

Party Organizational Structures	correspond to	Governmental Organizational Structures
Politburo		Inner cabinet or committee
Central committee		National Council or cabinet
Regional party organizations		Regional governmental offices
Local party organizations		Local governmental offices

The party also controls the nomination and electoral processes for the legislatures (national and local) to insure the election of adequate numbers of sympathetic supporters of the party leadership. In the Soviet legislature three-fourths of the elected deputies, year in and year out, are members of the communist party. In addition, key officers of the legislature are trusted supporters of the party leadership. Even in Yugoslavia, 184 of the 190 members of the Federal Chamber in 1964 held office in a party organization; and at that time ten out of the fourteen members of the highest body of the Communist League were members of the Federal Chamber. Also, one of the three top leaders of the League (Kardelj) was President of the Federal Assembly.[12] To cite one other example, the Standing Committee (interim executive leadership) of the legislature of North Vietnam has, as its Chairman and Vice-Chairman, two members of the party's Politburo.[13]

Since the apparatus and the activities of government are dominated by organs of the communist party, those organs invariably determine the outputs of communist political systems. Thus, communist policies, as determined by the party leadership, become blueprints for governmental resolutions, decrees, and laws. Eventually, communist-party orders and programs become official rules in the form of instructions and laws issued by governmental bodies, thereby rendering these orders and programs authoritative and legitimate, having legislative, and hence legal, sanctification. The communist Rumanian Workers' party, as an example, officially sets both foreign and domestic policy for the nation, in addition to guiding the work of state organs.[14] Even directions for the economy, including allocations of resources and technological training of workers, are basically party decisions. Rigby portrays the party-state system as one in which a centralized and disciplined voluntary organization (party) wins a monopoly of political power and then superimposes its bureaucracy over the bureaucracy of the state.[15]

Communist-party controls over society include areas such as the economy, the armed forces, education, and a wide range of peripheral activities including art, literature, sports, and the communications media. Of all societal organizations, however, one of the most important is that of the armed forces. If there is a marked loss of support for a regime in the military apparatus of any political system, then that regime, of course, faces serious difficulties. The power of the military apparatus, then, which may at some time be convertible to political power, is neither overlooked nor taken for granted by communist regimes. Indeed, in purpose and goal— support of the leadership and the policies of the communist party— the armed forces in communist states are considered to be political forces. While all armed forces in communist states, of course, are considered to be the first line of defense for the particular nation-state, this defense assignment is not to interfere with the military's political orientation. Furthermore, while the military is to support the party, it is not to challenge it for political rule nor is it to protest against heavy political indoctrination of the members of the armed forces on the part of party spokesmen.

In China, the former Defense Minister Lin Piao, now out of power, had instructed the army to implement the thought of Mao Tse-tung, to resist both revisionist ideology and exploiting-class ideology, to strengthen "revolutionization," to elevate class consciousness, and to raise understanding of policy.[16] Portrayed as a people's army, personally created by Mao, the Chinese Army has been called upon to criticize reactionary bourgeois ideas and to play a major role in the Cultural Revolution of the late 1960's.[17] In 1962, 78.7 percent of the soldiers were either members of the Chinese Communist party or of the Communist Youth League.[18] The Chinese Army has had assigned to it since 1949 many nonmilitary duties, such as flood control, dam building, and agricultural harvesting. These tasks assigned by the party leadership are related to mobilization and modernization of the nation. The tasks may, however, be harmful to the army's potential for defense. Professional army leaders in China have, on occasion, objected to a "weakening" of the readiness and preparation of the armed forces by too frequent a use of them in nonmilitary assignments. For the Maoists, however, all of these nonmilitary uses of the army simply testify to its political role of supporting the party leadership.

The communist party's requirement that a state's armed forces remain loyal to the party has apparently been satisfied, except when the state has suffered a great many war casualties (e.g., five million Soviet prisoners of war taken by the Germans in World War II), or serious internal disorder bordering on civil war (Hungary, 1956; China, 1967–68). At such times the loyalty of the armed forces may be strained, if not seriously questioned.

Within the entire cultural spectrum of music, poetry, literature, and the arts, the various restrictions and prohibitions imposed by ruling communist parties frequently have been severe. Party supervision over culture has as its overriding aim indoctrinating citizens in the advantages, successes, and promises of communism as a social and political system superior to any other. Art, for example, is not permitted solely as a medium of expression for the individual artist. Art for art's sake is insufficient in a mass-mobilizing communist society in which all endeavor (including the artistic) should be devoted to the task of building communism. Thus "socialist realism," wherein art and literature are to be instruments for inspiring citizens to glorify communism, is the party-enforced objective. Literature under Maoism, for example, must be shaped by a clear party spirit and must be designed for the masses—especially for the workers, peasants, and soldiers.[19]

Education, both formal and informal (e.g., extended adult education) under communism is carefully structured and assiduously watched over by the communist-party apparatus. At a minimum, schools include in their curricula many hours of instruction in Marxism-Leninism-Communism. This officially-sponsored philosophy is related in the schools to such subjects as history, economics, law, even on occasion, to the sciences. The schools are also used much more heavily than Western schools are for purposes of regime propaganda, moral and civic training, and what the Russians refer to as "upbringing." All of these various kinds of instruction form a necessary part of political socialization, one of the leading functions of the communist party.

Closely associated with education is a vast array of publishing and broadcasting activities which are included in the communications media. In the media political censorship is brought to bear very heavily—for example, in banning foreign publications—although not always in a manner which is obvious. Thus, instead of nonapproved material simply being sifted through and some of it censored out of publications (which does happen too), the media frequently are reserved and used strictly as a transmitter of information, instructions, and guidelines from the regime down to the citizens. In other words, more often than not, the media form a widespread propaganda apparatus for party policies. Among the communist states there is a wide spectrum from a very light censorship exerted in Yugoslavia, to a very heavy one exerted in the USSR and in China. Ironically, and significantly, just prior to the Soviet invasion of Czechoslovakia in August, 1968, the Czechoslovaks believed they were enjoying measurable progress in what amounted to a lifting of censorship in that country as a part of their general liberalization.

Communist parties, then, function primarily as organs of political control. As this is the norm which has evolved over the several decades of communist-party rule, a communist political system must therefore be considered a party-state system. Whether the party will always retain this dominating, controlling, directing role may be questionable, however.

In the case of Yugoslavia, for example, the party leadership has taken unique steps to de-emphasize the overwhelming dominant position previously exercised by the party within that nation. To signal this change, the party was renamed the Communist League of Yugoslavia in 1958. Henceforth, the League was to play a "conscious" rather than a "leading" role. Its main function was to mobilize the broad masses rather than to continue as the initiator, organizer, and leader of the people's struggles.[20] In 1958, at the League's Seventh Congress, the following policy statement was announced: "The League of the Communists of Yugoslavia considers it untenable dogma to proclaim that absolute monopoly of political power by the Communist Party is a universal and "eternal" principle of the proletariat and of socialist construction."[21]

Tito earlier had said that if the state withers away but the party does not, then the party simply takes the place of the "withered" state and no gain has really been made.[22] One interesting effect these changes have brought about in Yugoslavia has been a sizeable drop in League membership as a number of people evidently have lost enthusiasm for the expectation (now increasingly vague) of advancing their personal position in life through the party apparatus. This development might well be taken as evidence of the decline in both influence and power of the League in Yugoslavia. It may be, as a Yugoslav political scientist states, that the League is still a political party although no longer a mediator between the people and the political system. Thus, the League no longer seeks to take part in all social activities and does not claim to know all the answers to pending questions, but rather strives to be a guiding political force. "It is no longer an instrument of power, but, on the contrary, an expression of conscience. The Communist League has not abdicated its right and its responsibility to seek and eventually to proclaim the truth. But from now on, it publicly declares that truth is not to be enunciated *a priori:* the party has no particular truth of its own. . . ."[23] This development is quite nontypical of communist parties, however; and it should be noted that only Yugoslav leaders have gone to such lengths to downgrade either the theoretical or the practical position of dominance occupied by the communist party within a communist political system.

In 1969 Tito called for establishment of a fifteen-member Executive Bureau of the Communist League's Presidium, the Bureau to be composed in equal numbers of leaders of Yugoslavia's six republics and two autonomous provinces. Tito was to be a member as head of the League.[24] As the Communist League's highest policy-making body, the Bureau supposedly will provide more collective rule than Yugoslavia has had in the past, but its true function may be to pacify the various ethnic nationalities represented by the several Yugoslav republics. This reorganization also reveals that the Communist League is not yet ready to give up dominant political control in Yugoslavia.

Finally, to return to the general discussion of party control in communist states, adequate control over society by the communist party is related to the recruitment of new members into the party and, following this, recruiting some of these new members into the higher ranks of party leadership. Long before the Russian Revolution, at the Second Congress of the Russian Social Democratic Labor party in 1903, Lenin argued the need for a small, devoted, and courageous band of revolutionists as party members. Throughout Soviet history, from 1917 on, membership in the CPSU has been restricted, selective, and frequently quite demanding on the individual party member. Quotas for categories of party members (specified percentages of women, workers, peasants, intelligentsia) have been used by party leaders as they sought both a "representative" and a "workers'" party—but a party that would also be flexible and adaptable enough for a modern and complex society. The obvious dilemma here is how to include in the party large numbers of "workers" (manual workers and peasants) and at the same time to attract intelligent, imaginative, and educated leaders—most of whom are specialists of one sort or another.

LEVELS OF PARTY CONTROL

We might return now to the question of what constitutes minimal levels of effective political (for our purposes, party) control over society within a communist system. The answer to this question depends somewhat on which party is being considered. From Lenin on, the CPSU has been firmly committed to near complete control over Soviet society. Even under the severe periods of Stalinism, the party's control, though restricted, was only temporarily overshadowed—and Stalin himself, it should be remembered, still ruled in the *name* of the party. At the other end of the pole, the Yugoslav Communist League, as discussed above, has been slowly withdrawing from close, direct control over national life.

The position of Soviet leaders as to the minimum level of control which parties in other communist states should exercise has been indicated several times. One Soviet author lists the following as conditions which are essential for establishing a full "dictatorship of the proletariat":

1. The position of the communist party must be fully consolidated and its influence must be greater than that of all other parties combined.
2. Liquidation of the bourgeoisie as an independent political force and removing its members from the state apparatus are necessary.
3. Communists must hold the leading positions in the state apparatus.
4. Key aspects of the economy must be socialized.
5. All workers' parties must be merged into one under the leadership of the Marxist-Leninist party.[25]

Suslov's "international" requisites for communism, mentioned earlier (Chapter 1, p. 10), included the one of a communist party dictatorship as the advanced guard of the working class. The Polish communist leader Gomulka, in listing his four common features for building socialism (Chapter 1, p. 11), also referred to a Marxist-Leninist party of the working masses; at the same time he indicated this party would include as one of its functions the exercise of a dictatorship over the proletariat.

Soviet concern with the minimum level of control exercised by the party in other communist states has by no means been a verbal concern only. In the 1968 Soviet-Czechoslovak controversy, for example, the Russians believed that the Czechoslovak Communist party had lost necessary control over its citizens—so much so that the problem warranted a Soviet invasion of that nation to avoid contamination of the Soviet Bloc with the disease of party enfeeblement. Following this invasion, the Russians demanded that the following be accomplished so that Czechoslovakia could return to the pathway of true communism:

1. The dominant role in the life of Czechoslovakia shall be exercised by the communist party.

2. All other political organs, such as political parties, must be eliminated from public life.
3. The communist party shall control, completely, the press, radio, and television.
4. The party and government shall be reinforced by orthodox (non-liberal) party faithful.[26]

These four points, and particularly the first two, in a way constitute a Soviet definition of communism—at least of its essential political features. Just prior to this demand, the leadership of the Czechoslovak Communist party had pointed out that the unity of party and people formed the only basis on which socialism in that nation was possible, and that destruction of this unity would mean that communists would be written off as the leading political force in both the USSR and Czechoslovakia.[27] Nevertheless, in the Soviet view, unity could be reinstituted only by forcefully returning the Czechoslovak party to a position of dominance and by firm removal of all political opposition within that nation. Through all of these pronouncements, the theme of party control over a nation's political life appears to be the main one. Without such control, the Soviets felt, a communist political system might no longer be communist; for the central core of the system, following Lenin's teaching, would no longer be there to hold it together. The Soviet leaders, in other words, were convinced that the erosion of party control in Czechoslovakia had proceeded to a point at which the continuance of the communist political system in the nation was in serious doubt.

Do the Soviet and Eastern European requirements for a ruling communist party lead to effective political control? The answer apparently is negative for Poland and Hungary in 1956; questionable for Czechoslovakia in 1968; and, by official admission, under reconsideration in Yugoslavia after 1958. Under certain circumstances, moreover, the control of the party may suffer as a result of poor decision-making. Recently, according to one report, the price increases in basic commodities of food, fuel, and clothing which preceded violent riots in Poland in December, 1970, were argued against by the Russians and dumbfounded Ulbricht of the German Democratic Republic. Apparently, the leaders of these latter two communist states believed that political rule would be threatened by such arbitrary governmental action as the price rise. They were correct in their belief.[28] As for the other communist states, the communist party, by dominating the political processes, continued to rule with apparent effectiveness. The only exception other than those listed above is China, where confusion, even chaos, seemed to predominate instead of the party during the latter part of the Great Proletarian Cultural Revolution (1966–69). By the early 1970's the party appeared to be recapturing full political control from the army, which had been called in to restore order.

The effectiveness of communist-party control over society, finally, relates to the effectiveness of its administrative arm, the formal apparatus of government. If that apparatus successfully administers society, and the communist party dominates that apparatus, then overall communist-party rule will have achieved at least a minimum level of operational effectiveness.

GOVERNMENTAL STRUCTURES

Governmental structures and functions in communist systems follow the purpose, goals, and procedures of their guiding communist parties. In a way, this is not entirely different from noncommunist systems. Even the American and British governmental apparatus is expected to respond to the overall policies and directions of the dominant political party as determined by the most recent national election. Communist systems, however, differ from noncommunist ones in that the communist party always remains in power. Moreover, the governmental apparatus under communism is always more responsive to and more directly controlled by the party than is the case with respect to governmental apparatus and the dominant political party in noncommunist systems. As previously described, a communist government attempts to make concrete and operational the abstract and general policies of the party. Thus, such ministries as Culture, Education, and Communications activate in a practical, daily, even routine manner the goals of the party with respect to specifically assigned functions.

Structurally, communist governments follow rather closely the Soviet model. There is an ostensible parliamentary format, including a legislature formed as a result of nationwide elections; and the legislature formally appoints an executive body—usually a council of ministers with a prime minister. There is a Council of Ministers in Albania, Bulgaria, Cuba, Czechoslovakia, the GDR, Hungary, Mongolia, North Vietnam, Poland, and Rumania. China has, instead, a State Council; North Korea, a Cabinet of Ministers.[29] The Soviet legislature (Supreme Council) is a two-house body representing voters by population district, and also by administrative unit (republic, national regions, and districts). Most of the communist states of Eastern Europe refer to their legislatures in a rather similar vein, using a title such as people's assembly, state assembly, or national assembly.

The functions of the legislature in any communist system are both ostensible and real, the main one being to ratify the programs and policies of the regime (as spelled out in detail by the central party and governmental-executive apparatus). The legislature thus performs for the regime a legitimating, supporting function.[30] By means of nationwide elections, the legislature's task is to formally commit the nation's citizens to the goals, policies, and leadership of the regime. If, then, the main function of the legislature is to ratify and legitimate the programs of the communist party, a secondary function (to be discussed in Chapter 5), is to provide a level of popular representation in the political system for the nation's citizens.

The executive organization of communist governments also follows closely on the Soviet model, with a few notable exceptions: in China, there is, additionally, a Chairman of the People's Republic; and in Czechoslovakia, North Vietnam, and Yugoslavia, there is a form of presidency. In the Soviet parliamentary model the prime minister (whose real title is Chairman of the Council of Ministers) technically is selected by the legislature. The Chairman then heads the cabinet (Presidium, or inner group of the Council) in a rather standard parliamentary fashion. This Soviet format differs a bit from Western parliamentary systems, of course, in that the Chairman and members of the Council are actually picked by the communist-party leadership; the selection is merely ratified by the legislature. The Council and its Chairman function as a normal ruling executive, with the proviso that the communist-party leadership organs may at any time assume responsibility for supervising the agencies of government. The function of the Council, somewhat comparable to the Cabinet of the President of the United States, is to administer the daily activities of government, including such areas as defense, internal order, health, education, economic productivity, and foreign relations.

Although the executive structure is similar in China (Premier and State Council), there is an additional post of Chairman of the People's Republic, filled by an election by the legislature (National People's Congress). This special position was created specifically for Mao, who relinquished it, however, after only a few years of occupancy. Thus, initially at least, the Chairman had several important powers, šuch as commanding the armed forces and serving as Chairman of the Council of National Defense. The abbreviated structure of the Chinese government is as follows:

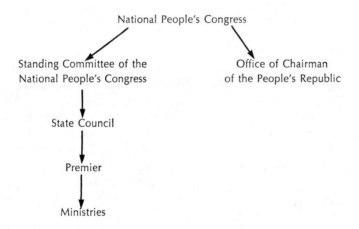

The 1960 Czechoslovak Constitution continues a presidential system on a parliamentary base. For twenty years the number one communist-party leader had also been the President: Gottwald (1948–53), Zapotocky (1953–57), and Novotny (1957–68). Elected for a five-year term, the Czechoslovak President is ultimately responsible to the legislature. The Premier heads the inner cabinet as well as occupying an important position in the hierarchy:

There have been numerous attempts at reorganization of communist governments with the aim of achieving structural simplification as well as organizational and administrative decentralization, all

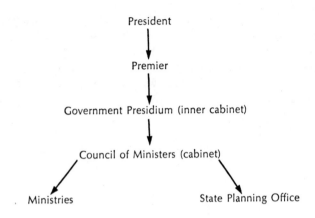

pointing toward heightened functional efficiency. The USSR has undergone the most numerous, although not the most thoroughgoing, structural reorganizations, revealing the great faith held by Soviet leaders, past and present, in the magic of repeated organizational manipulation. Soviet alterations have included a reshuffling of planning bodies; decentralization of management within economic ministries; regionalization of administration; and, most recently, an increase in the independence and authority of lower-level managers, especially on the factory level. Several of the East European communist nations have followed Soviet developments by instituting similar, although not identical, changes. It is to Yugoslavia, however, that other communist nations—perhaps including even the Soviet Union—appear to watch for new alterations and developments in both communist theory and practice.

Yugoslav changes in the Soviet model followed closely on Yugoslavia's ouster from the Soviet Bloc in 1948. Central economic ministries were abolished and a Council of Producers (a chamber of the national legislature) was established, consisting of deputies elected by factory workers, craftsmen, and people in handicraft industries. Counterpart councils of producers exist at regional and local levels of government as well. The national legislature of Yugoslavia, the Federal Assembly, is composed of five chambers representing different subject areas in society. Thus, there is a Federal Chamber representing administrative territories, a Political-Administrative Chamber, a Chamber of Economy, a Chamber of Education, and a Chamber of Social Welfare and Health—all representing specialized constituencies. Of the five, the Federal Chamber predominates over the other four.

In a law passed in 1952, implemented further by the Constitution of 1953, a measure of local autonomy has been given to regional and local governments in Yugoslavia by turning over to them additional powers of administration. All powers not specifically delegated to national and republic governments supposedly are left to the local people's committees, as the sole representative of the central government. The people's committees, as administrative organs for towns and districts, are to perform all of the state functions within their particular jurisdiction. In the Yugoslav view, decentralization of some functions (e.g., economic management) to the local people's committees testifies to a beginning of a withering away of the apparatus of the state, at least on the national level.

The structures of communist governments appear well-designed to realize their basic functions as administrative organs of the communist party. The role of the governments is to carry out the managerial assignments given to them by the party. Consequently, the legislature, the executive, even the judicial organs, are expected to perform as policy executors for the communist party. As the controller of the communist political system, the party employs the governmental apparatus as its agent. Or, to carry the analogy even further, the people are the stockholders in the communist political system; the party is an extremely active and all powerful board of directors; and the government is the general manager who has limited powers.

COMMUNIST POWER ELITE

The ruling elite in the communist-party states is composed of the central hierarchy of the respective parties. Normally, the highest party organization, the Politburo, contains the most important leaders of any of these states. Politburo members make the high-level decisions and are the men who chart national policy, foreign and domestic.

Members of the party elite in the various states all have served a number of years in party or governmental positions of influence and have, with some help from important friends, worked their way up in the hierarchy of political power. By 1965, for example, almost 59 percent of the Soviet Politburo had been recruited into party or political offices at a fairly early career age. Another 41 percent had been co-opted into the Politburo after having served some years in a professional or technical vocation.[31] In both cases, the Politburo members previously had spent many years successfully working in significant posts within the political system. Farrell[32] lists the percentages of Politburo members in the USSR and Eastern Europe possessing a technical as well as career specialization (in 1967) as follows:

Albania	31%	Poland	20%
Bulgaria	33%	Rumania	25%
Czechoslovakia	36%	USSR	44%
GDR	32%	Yugoslavia	51%
Hungary	57%		

Table 3 illustrates an overlapping membership of Soviet Politburo members in other high offices. Of the twenty-one members of the Soviet Politburo, fifteen of them (71%) hold another high post in addition to the Politburo. The table also illustrates how the Politburo members penetrate the executive and legislative branches of the national government. The average age of the members of the Politburo is 61.

From an empirical investigation of Eastern European political leadership, Beck concludes that the leadership has been dominated by careerists in the party apparatus who also have had governmental experience.[33] In the four Asian party states of China, Mongolia, North Korea, and North Vietnam, Scalapino points out the strong to very strong representation of the military in the top echelons of the respective communist parties.[34] And following the Soviet pattern, there has occurred from time to time in other communist states an overlapping of positions.[35] In Poland and Czechoslovakia, for instance, the key leader at times each held simultaneously the top party and the top government posts, the same situation that has occurred in Albania, Bulgaria, Cuba, Hungary, North Vietnam, and Yugoslavia.

Communist politics popularly are considered to be purge prone and, indeed, each of these states has suffered through purges which

TABLE 3
Soviet Elite: Overlapping Politburo Membership

Politburo Member and Age in 1972	Secretariat Central Committee	Council of Ministers	Presidium of Supreme Soviet
Brezhnev (66)	Brezhnev		Brezhnev
Grishin (58)			Grishin
Kirilenko (66)	Kirilenko		
Kosygin (68)		Kosygin, Chairman	
Kulakov (54)	Kulakov		
Kunaev (60)			Kunaev
Mazurov (58)		Mazurov, 1st Dep. Chairman	
Pelshe (72)			
Podgorny (69)			Podgorny, Chairman
Polyanskiy (55)		Polyanskiy, 1st Dep. Chairman	
Shelepin (54)			
Shelest (64)			Shelest
Shcherbitskiy (54)			
Suslov (70)	Suslov		
Voronov (62)			
Candidate Members			
Andropov (58)			
Demichev (54)	Demichev		
Masherov (54)			Masherov
Mzhavanadze (70)			
Rashidov (55)			Rashidov
Ustinov (64)	Ustinov		

Source: *Izvestiya,* July 16, 1970; April 10, 1971.

reflect power struggles among its leaders. The most infamous of these struggles is that of Stalin's Great Purge in the middle 1930's, during which large numbers of citizens were arrested and imprisoned, and a number executed.[36] Concerning the arbitrariness and viciousness of Stalin's direction of the Purge, the former Soviet leader Khrushchev testified: "Mass arrests and deportations of many thousands of people [occurred], execution without trial and without normal investigation . . . of the 139 members and candidates of the party's Central Committee who were elected at the Seventeenth Congress, 98 persons, i.e., 70 percent, were arrested and shot (mostly in 1937–38). . . ."[37]

Lewis compares Stalin's Purge with Mao's in the 1966–69 Cultural Revolution, noting that in each case extraneous forces (NKVD, army, and the Red Guard) were relied upon by the leader to discipline the party, both leaders having bypassed the party as the supreme monopolistic instrument of power—all of the efforts directed toward limiting the independence and autonomy of the party *vis-à-vis* the leader.[38]

In Eastern Europe between 1945–51 there were 3,000 publicly reported political trials, with an estimated 25,000 executions.[39] In Cuba the government under Castro has purged a number of citizens as well as communist-party members. The Cuban purges included house searches without warrant, thefts of property of suspected persons, lengthy interrogations in secret police buildings, and infliction of indignities on prisoners.[40] Following the crackdown on the Czechoslovak liberalizers after 1968, over 1,500,000 party members were interviewed in Czechoslovakia, with 326,817 (21.7%) failing the test and consequently not receiving new party cards.[41]

In all of these cases, the purge, as Brzezinski portrays it,[42] constitutes for some communist leaders a mechanism for cleansing the party of what they believe to be incompetent, bureaucratized, obstructionist, and disloyal colleagues. Despite this history of purges, communist political systems have a mixed record as far as political durability goes. This mixed record is illustrated, in part, by the problem of succession to office. Political succession, in which new leaders replace older ones, appears more peaceful and orderly in democracies than seems to be the case with authoritarian and dictatorial societies. Succession involving communist leaders, popularly, is believed to result from vigorous and bloody struggles for power with the outcome more accidental than planned. Rarely is there machinery which definitely provides for the replacement of the main leader of the communist party.[43]

Upon the death of a prominent communist leader, a succession crisis normally occurs in which a struggle takes place among the contenders for the throne. Following the death of Lenin in 1924, a several-year fight for dominance saw Stalin eventually defeat his opponents to become the single most influential person within the Soviet Communist party. Another struggle among contenders occurred following Stalin's death in 1953. One of the most recent such conflicts was the one between the two hopefuls in North Vietnam,

Truong Chinh and Le Duan, who battled for control following the death of Ho Chi Minh.

Among the fourteen communist states the picture of leadership in the early years seems a bit confused because in several of the states no single leader appeared clearly dominant. In Rumania, Gheorghiu-Dej was at first overshadowed by Pauker and Luca; in Hungary, Gero and Revai shared power with Rakosi; in Czechoslovakia, Gottwald shared top influence with Slansky and Zapatocky; in Mongolia, Choybalsan was one of several early leaders, among whom was Sukhe-Bator; in the GDR, Pieck, Grotewohl, and Ulbricht all were prominent in the early years.[44] In nine of the states, on the other hand, the early leaders were easily identifiable, the most well known being Lenin, Mao, Tito, Ho Chi Minh, and Castro.

The fate of the early communist leaders is suggested by Table 4, which lists the most prominent of the leaders from the time the states became communist, until 1972. The table lists thirty-one leaders, although it does not include all important communists who at some time exercised at least a measure of power and who died in office (GDR's Pieck) or who were thrown out of their positions (such as Rumania's Paulker or China's Liu Shao-chi), or who were even executed (Czechoslovakia's Slansky).

Among the thirty-one leaders, eight died in office, one retired, nine were thrown out of power by their opponents within the communist party, occasionally at the insistence or with the help of the Soviet leaders. Of the remaining thirteen leaders of the communist states, five of the original ones were still in power as of 1972.

Thus, data from Table 4 indicate that, contrary to popular opinion, succession to leadership of the communist-party states is fairly peaceful, although at times involving considerable political struggle. The data also show the durability of the top leadership; less than one-third of the leaders were deposed (nine out of thirty-one), and probably only one or two of the nine actually were executed.[45]

Although a precise calculation of the number of years involved is difficult, the average term of leadership for all thirty-one is approximately twelve years. Sixteen of the leaders served less than ten years each; eight served from ten to twenty years; and seven served more than twenty years. This would appear, without an actual comparison, to equal at least the average length of service of top office holders among the world's noncommunist nations. Apart from relative peace-

TABLE 4
Leadership Succession in Communist States

Nation	Initial Leader	Fate	Successors	Present Leader & Years in Office to 1972
Albania	Hoxha	****		Hoxha (27)
Bulgaria	Dimitrov	*	Chervenkov** Zhivkov****	Zhivkov (17)
China	Mao	****		Mao (22)
Cuba	Castro	****		Castro (13)
Czechoslovakia	Gottwald	*	Novotny** Dubcek** Husak****	Husak (3)
GDR	Ulbricht (with Grotewohl & Pieck)	***	Honecker****	Honecker (1)
Hungary	Rakosi	**	Gero** Nagy** Kadar****	Kadar (15)
Mongolia	Choybalsan (with Sukhe-Bator)	*	Tsedenbal****	Tsedenbal (14)
North Korea	Kim Il Sung	****		Kim Il Sung (26)
North Vietnam	Ho Chih Minh	*	Undetermined	
Poland	Gomulka	**	Bierut* Gomulka** Gierek****	Gierek (2)
Rumania	Gheorghiu-Dej	*	Ceausescu****	Ceausescu (6)
USSR	Lenin	*	Stalin* Malenkov** Khrushchev** Brezhnev****	Brezhnev (7)
Yugoslavia	Tito	****		Tito (26)

* Died in office without losing power.
** Overthrown or eased out by his colleagues.
*** Retired peacefully.
**** Remains in office.

fulness of succession and durability of leaders, history reveals that succession to top political leadership in communist political systems is not predictable. Although we anticipate that the future leader will be one of the key members of the communist party's inner circle, he is not easily identifiable prior to the demise of the top man.

A discussion of communist political elites might well conclude by considering the nature of political stability in communist-party states, and specifically whether such states, as compared with noncommunist ones, enjoy greater or lesser durability in their respective leaders. Rigby notes that not a single change took place in the voting members of the Soviet Politburo in the four years prior to that party's Twenty-third Congress.[46] An interesting comparison is drawn by Szamuely in noting that between 1917 and 1969 the United States had ten Presidents, but the USSR had only seven Heads of State, five of whom were still alive in 1969. To continue the comparison, Britain during the same period had eleven Prime Ministers, nineteen Foreign Ministers, twenty-three Secretaries for War or Defense, while comparative Soviet figures are eight, seven, and ten respectively. Finally, there have been, since 1917, only three occupants in the top USSR post of General or First Secretary.[47] If turnover of top leaders in communist states is taken as a criterion of durability, then, these states appear to be at least as durable as noncommunist ones.

POLITICAL CONTROL IN COMMUNIST SYSTEMS

Political control in communist political systems begins with and is maintained, although not always at a high level of accomplishment, by the communist party. The primary goal, in every case, is party dominance over rule-making and over policy determination for the entire society. In seeking fulfillment of this goal, the party has developed over the years a carefully elaborated organizational hierarchy. Complementing the party organization—centrally, regionally, and locally—is a vast governmental bureaucracy whose function, as handmaiden of the party, is to execute the rules and policies dictated by the party leaders. If the party organization can maintain effective control over the governmental bureaucracy, then the party is well on the way to maintaining its rule over society.

This neat and orderly pattern is not completely successful in all cases, however. The Yugoslav communist leaders, in particular, have altered and modified the simplistic, highly centralized, and dictatorial model as originally fashioned by the CPSU. The focus of these Yugoslav modifications has been gradually to de-emphasize this very dominating and controlling role of the communist party over all aspects of the society. The Yugoslav objective—although not fully achieved in the first decade since 1958, and although carried out in theory more than in practice—has been to change the primary role of the party from that of ruler to that of teacher, from political controller of society to guide of the masses.

The Yugoslav heresy has contributed to political discontent within the communist bloc of states by suggesting a way out of the logical dilemma that stems from trying to organize and direct a workers' society (or "people's democracy") by and through a dictatorship of a small, inner group of communist-party members. While only the Yugoslavs admit the logical and practical inconsistency of trying to achieve democratic self-rule by means of self-selected dictators, the dilemma has resulted in occasional frustrations and resentments among, for example, Poles, Hungarians, Czechoslovaks, even Russians, as they attempt to mesh democratic myth with dictatorial practice. (The Czechoslovaks, indeed, had approached the Yugoslav solution—de-emphasis of the dictatorial role of the party—by the summer of 1968, prior to the Soviet invasion.)

One question raised by these slight alterations in the traditional domineering role of the communist party has been how, given the alterations, a minimum level of political control will be maintained. The Russians have insisted on firm party control both inside and outside the USSR; they used troops to restore such control in Poland and Hungary after the revolts of 1956, and in Czechoslovakia in 1968. Moreover, the Yugoslav de-emphasis on the party has been limited in practice and has not matched Yugoslav theory in this respect. Although the Yugoslav Communist party was renamed the League of Communists to illustrate the changed role of the party, in fact the former party leaders, headed by Tito, have continued to rule the nation under the newly formed League.

Thus—with the possible exceptions of Cuba, Yugoslavia, and very briefly Czechoslovakia—one of the seemingly unchanging features of communist political systems is the continuing overwhelming dominance of the communist-party leadership over society: government, military, culture, education. Other aspects of communist systems change—such as details of economic management, the legislative process, and communist internationalism, as will be noted in succeeding chapters—but control by the party remains a constant. This does not imply total, absolute control, however. In practice the party delegates various aspects of its control to a number of agencies: military, police, managerial bureaucracy, various governmental offices, trade unions—even the legislature on occasion.[48] Central to the concern of party leaders, though, is that the party reserves for itself crucial decision-making authority over the most key elements of society. Beyond this, trends in party control emphasize decentralization of lesser decisions; delegating responsibility for implementing decisions; and, to an extent, allowing lower-level officials a certain degree of reviewing authority, if such does not challenge national supremacy. Cuba appears to lack the network of an elaborated party apparatus extending down into all societal organizations and, on the higher levels, coordinating the functions and articulating the interests of citizens. The low percentage of the communist-party membership compared with the Cuban population further testifies to this assumption. However Marxist-Leninist the Cuban political system is, one hesitates to brand it clearly as a communist-*party* state.

One of the five items of the Marxist-Leninist Model set forth in the first chapter is that of establishing the communist party as the vanguard of the workers, placing it in control of all societal organizations. Thus, the preceding chapter discussed how ruling communist parties came into power and this chapter took up their ruling procedures. What has been absent in the discussion of communist political systems, up to this point, is any evidence that the workers initially sought out the leadership of the communist party to rule and to be the vanguard in the name of the workers. So far we have seen how communist-party leaders are self-selected, or were at first placed in power by the leaders of the Soviet Union. In any event, once in power the communist party in a given state does not permit any open and organized opposition to its rule either from workers or anyone else. At this point it seems the communist party is the ruling vanguard of the workers only because it says it is.

Consequently, this chapter's hypothesis—that communist parties assume political control over society—is only half verified, with a question remaining regarding Cuba. The other half of the hypothesis

—that the party is the spokesman for and represents the interests of the working class—has not been verified. Thus, we are back to the question of authority and legitimacy in communist systems. The gap between workers' rule (Marxism-Leninism) and party rule (communism) is bridged in the written and spoken words of communist leaders. Accordingly, they place heavy reliance on the political socialization of official ideology. If the regime receives support because it is the interpreter of the official ideology, then it proceeds to the next step. This is an attempt to demonstrate, by trying to show extensive and elaborated participation in the communist political system, that workers really do rule themselves.

NOTES

1. Meyer states that authority in communist systems is fluid and insecure chiefly because of their relatively recent revolutions, their very ambitious goals, and the drastic methods used to reach these goals. A. G. Meyer, "Authority in Communist Political Systems," in *Political Leadership in Industrialized Societies*, Lewis J. Edinger, ed., (New York: John Wiley, 1967), p. 84.

2. See Theodore H. E. Chen, *The Chinese Communist Regime* (New York: Praeger, 1967), pp. 127 ff.

3. See *Area Handbook for North Korea* (Washington, D. C.: Foreign Area Studies, 1969), pp. 233 ff.

4. Huntington argues, however, that every major twentieth-century revolution has institutionalized the centralization and expansion of power in a one-party system. Samuel P. Huntington, *Political Order in Changing Societies* (New Haven: Yale University Press, 1968), p. 315.

5. J. M. Lindbeck, in *Soviet and Chinese Communism: Similarities and Differences*, Donald Treadgold, ed. (Seattle: University of Washington Press, 1967), pp. 99–100.

6. The communist party occasionally uses other names, such as the Socialist Unity Party (SED) in the German Democratic Republic, the Polish United Workers' Party, or the League of Communists in Yugoslavia.

7. See the discussion by Carmelo Mesa-Lago in *Cuban Communism*, Irving Louis Horowitz, ed. (Chicago: Aldine Publishing Company, 1970), p. 85.

8. D. A. Tomasic, "The Rumanian Communist Leadership," *Slavic Review*, October, 1961, p. 492. This description well portrays the other communist-party states too.

9. See Jan F. Triska, ed., *Constitutions of the Communist Party States* (Stanford: Hoover Institutions, 1968).

10. V. F. Kotok, ed., *Gosudarstvennoe Pravo Stran Narodnoy Demokratii* (Moscow, 1961), pp. 90–91.

11. *New York Times,* February 9, 1971.

12. See James C. Lowenstein, "Yugoslavia: Parliamentary Model," *Problems of Communism,* March-April, 1965, p. 134.

13. P. J. Honey, ed., *North Vietnam Today* (New York: Praeger, 1962), p. 54.

14. I. Cheterki, *Rumynskaya Narodnaya Respublica—Sotsialisticheskoe Gosudarstvo* (Moscow, 1965), pp. 133, 136.

15. T. H. Rigby, *Communist Party Membership in the USSR, 1917–1967* (Princeton: Princeton University Press, 1968), p. 2.

16. *Peking Review,* no. 42 (1966), p. 7. In 1971, a Soviet report counts ten of the twenty-one member Politburo in China as representing the army. *Izvestiya,* February 3, 1971.

17. From *Chieh-fang-chiiu Pao* (June 6, 1966) in *The Great Cultural Revolution in China* (Rutland, Vermont: Charles Tuttle, 1968), p. 356.

18. See Juergen Domes, in *Aspects of Modern Communism,* Richard F. Staar, ed. (Columbia: University of South Carolina Press, 1968), pp. 275–76. Nevertheless, alienation among peasants in their village because of programs from the Chinese Communist party has been reflected in some soldier disaffection, since most of the soldiers were originally peasant villagers. *Loc. cit.*

19. Howard L. Boorman, "The Literary World of Mao Tse-tung," *China Quarterly,* January-March, 1963, p. 23.

20. Fred Warner Neal, *Titoism in Action* (Berkeley: University of California Press, 1958), p. 43.

21. *Yugoslavia's Way: The Program of the League of Communists of Yugoslavia* (New York: All Nations Press, 1958), p. 165.

22. Neal, *op. cit.,* p. 49. Such thinking by Tito represents an acceptance of the views of the critic Djilas, views which Tito earlier had branded heretical, and for which Djilas had been imprisoned.

23. Jovan Djordjevic, "Political Power in Yugoslavia," *Government and Opposition,* February, 1967, p. 216. The Yugoslav newspaper *Borba* refers to a massive drift away from party membership. See *ABSEES,* July, 1971, p. 269.

24. *New York Times,* March 13, 1969.

25. From A. I. Sovolev, *People's Democracy* (Moscow, 1954), as quoted in Francis J. Kase, *People's Democracy* (Leyden: A. W. Sythoff, 1968), pp. 55–56.

26. *New York Times,* October 5, 1968.

27. Central Committee, Czechoslovak Communist Party, Radio Prague, September 1, 1968.

28. *New York Times,* December 24, 1970.

29. I. P. Ilinskiy and B. Shchetinin, *Gosudarstvennoe Pravo Stran Narodnoi Demokratii* (Moscow, 1964), p. 290.

30. The tendency of legislatures in modern political systems, even the British Parliament and the American Congress, is to act "predominantly

as modifiers and legitimators" of rules that have been initiated by the executive. Gabriel A. Almond and G. Brigham Powell, *Comparative Politics: A Developmental Approach* (Boston: Little, Brown, 1966), p. 138.

31. Frederick Fleron, "Representation of Career Types in the Soviet Political Leadership," in *Political Leadership in Eastern Europe and the Soviet Union*, R. Barry Farrell, ed. (Chicago: Aldine, 1970), p. 127.

32. *Ibid.*, p. 99.

33. Carl Beck, "Career Characteristics of East European Leadership," in Farrell, *op. cit.* (above, n. 31), p. 192.

34. Robert A. Scalapino, ed., *The Communist Revolution in Asia* (Englewood Cliffs: Prentice-Hall, 1965), p. 10.

35. See H. Gordon Skilling, *The Governments of Communist East Europe* (New York: Crowell, 1966), pp. 78–79.

36. See Zbigniew K. Brzezinski, *The Permanent Purge* (Cambridge, Massachusetts: Harvard University Press, 1956).

37. Report of Khrushchev's secret speech in Bertram D. Wolfe, *Khrushchev and Stalin's Ghost* (New York: Praeger, 1957), pp. 110, 124.

38. John Wilson Lewis, ed., *Party Leadership and Revolutionary Power in China* (Cambridge: Cambridge University Press, 1970), p. 142.

39. Joseph Rothschild, *Communist Eastern Europe* (New York: Walker and Company, 1964), p. 126.

40. Hugh Thomas, *Cuba: The Pursuit of Freedom* (New York: Harper and Row, 1971), p. 1461.

41. *Rudé Pravo,* December 15, 1970, quoted in *ABSEES*, April, 1971, pp. 164–65.

42. *Op. cit.* (above, n. 36).

43. The new Chinese Constitution authorized Lin Piao to succeed Mao on the latter's death. No doubt Lin Piao's fall from power negates this provision.

44. See J. F. Brown, *The New Eastern Europe* (New York: Praeger, 1966), p. 7 and H. Gordon Skilling, *op. cit.* (above, no. 35), pp. 74–77.

45. Imre Nagy was killed after the 1956 Hungarian Revolt. The whereabouts of Georgi Malenkov are unknown beyond the Soviet leadership.

46. T. H. Rigby, "The Soviet Leadership: Towards a Self-Stabilizing Oligarchy?" *Soviet Studies,* October, 1970, p. 188.

47. Tibor Szamuely in *Survey,* Summer, 1969, p. 60. He apparently is not counting the very brief tenure of Malenkov as party leader in March, 1953.

48. Ghita Ionescu, *The Politics of the European Communist States* (New York: Praeger, 1967), Part Two.

4

Economic Organization and Management

Much of communist politics, both theoretically and practically, is concerned with economics; and economic organization and management constitute a major function of the party and of governmental structures. Marxian economics, of course, forms the basis for communist ideology, while the two most fundamental goals of communist ideology—economic equality and material abundance for all—are economic ones.

In the first of these goals the hope and expectation exist for an equal sharing of the economic fruits of a society by all of its members. Although some differences are allowed (e.g., in rates of pay for greater output or for higher positions of responsibility), in practice, the differences are not to be excessive. Everyone who contributes something positive to society, in brief, is to be guaranteed a "fair" economic reward from society. There will be, consequently, an end to both rich and poor alike, with all people occupying a broad middle ground in terms of economic rewards. The intention of communist regimes then—and for some states there is a fair degree of accomplishment toward this end—is to provide a minimum level of material benefits for everyone in such matters as food, clothing, housing, and medical care.

The second of the broad economic goals of communism is the achievement of an economy of abundance. This goal, which seeks more and better quality goods for the nation's citizens, is an outgrowth of the underlying humanitarian motivations of Marxism. On the troublesome pathway toward this lofty objective, there usually are shortages (e.g., in consumer goods, which temporarily must await the creation of a heavy producers' goods industry). Thus, although the communist leaders anticipate the eventual triumph of an economy of abundance, they give early priority to building the industrial base for the economy. As evidence of good faith toward reaching the goal of abundance, however, the leaders in at least some of the communist states point to such accomplishments as rapid rates of industrial growth and a steadily increasing abundance and quality of consumer goods. Communist economics, then, points to a future equality of individuals, sharing more or less equally from the total, common wealth of the society, and promising material abundance, eventually. As a consequence of these ambitious objectives, a great deal of organizational energy and managerial concentration in communist political systems are spent on economic problems.[1]

The first economic task for communists in power is to begin a transitional period of socialism called for by Marxism—the first step in converting society from capitalism to communism. Socialism, basically, includes public ownership of, and state control and management over, the means of production. It may also involve considerably more—for example, public ownership of transportation, utilities, communications, and banking.[2] In Marxist-Leninist ideology, socialism is a necessary halfway house toward the eventual millennium of an abundant society—that is, of communism.[3] The task of setting up a socialist system, for communists, starts out as a structural-institutional problem. Moreover, the change in the relationships of production from private ownership and control to public ownership and governmental control is considered by communists to constitute the primary avenue for changing human attitudes from private and individualistic, to public, collectivist, and hence "communist."

The hypothesis we will investigate here, developed from the Marxist-Leninist Model, is *hypothesis 3*, stating that a communist political system transforms an economy from private ownership to public-socialist ownership and governmental control.

Because Marxists have believed that socialist economics can be organized and operated scientifically, they have assumed that efficient supply, production, and distribution of commodities is a simple matter of technological relationships—one organization properly arranged alongside another. Many of the daily functions of communist government, therefore, are concerned with planning for, supervising, and administering the economy. This is reflected in the large number of ministries, agencies, directorates, and boards which are included in the central governmental apparatus of every communist state. In addition, the central committee apparatus of a ruling communist party includes a number of sections whose responsibility and assignment is to watch over various sectors of the economy. Regional and local governmental bodies also are concerned with similar functions.

All aspects of the economy are regulated and directed by one or more governmental agencies. The ideal format which communist systems try to achieve is that of a command economy, one in which the central governmental apparatus allocates resources and gives the orders for the production and distribution of all economic goods. This includes—in addition to planning—governmental financing of both construction and production; seeing to the exploitation of natural resources; setting of prices, fees, and wages; and supervision over production decisions, as well as the transportation and distribution of finished commodities. The organization of the economy, as indicated in the following chart, illustrates both the hierarchical command nature as well as the influence of the apparatus of the communist party.

The financial system of communist-party states is an integral part of the machinery of government. In capitalist countries money is both a means of exchange and an instrument enabling individuals to purchase resources for economic production. Under communism money continues as a means of exchange, of course, but it is not available for individuals to use in ownership of productive wealth. Instead, money is used by governments to develop and manage resources in accordance with national plans.

Organization of Economic Management

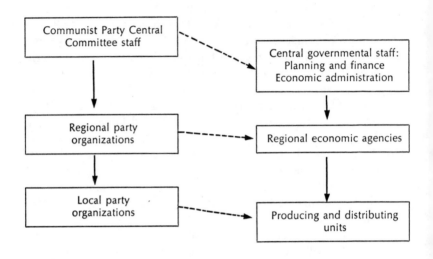

In the USSR the Ministry of Finance is the general manager of subordinate financial organs, including insurance and savings banks. The union republics have their own ministries of finance, acting as regional offices of the central ministry. The Soviet State Bank, with numerous branch offices, is the commercial bank for the nation's economy, issuing bank notes and coordinating the flow of currency and deposits. The State Bank maintains a basic account for each enterprise, makes short-term loans, collects taxes, and controls expenditures. There is an Investment Bank in the Ministry of Finance which extends grants to state enterprises and long-term credits to collective farms, cooperatives, local industry, and to individuals for building houses. There are some 5,000 savings institutions and, finally, a Construction Bank for financing capital investments.

The state budget in the USSR, as the main financial plan for the nation, provides a consolidated account of the national, regional, and local budgets. The budget finances most of the economic expansion, provides administrative audits, helps to formulate and implement national economic plans, and is the central link in the financial and credit system.[4] Taxes in communist states are in the main indirect, the most important one in the USSR being the turnover tax—a tax paid by enterprises on transactions.

The Soviet model is followed in general by most of the communist states.[5] Exceptions to the Soviet model have included charging a five percent interest rate on gross fixed and working capital in Hungary; and abandoning central investment planning, permitting enterprises to lend money, establishing profit-making banks paying dividends to shareholders, and enabling enterprises to sell bonds to the public in Yugoslavia.[6]

NATIONALIZATION

An early step taken by communist parties toward achieving their economic goals after coming to power is to nationalize much of the economic wealth of the nation. This might be limited at first to the critical areas, or what communists have referred to as the "commanding heights" of the economy—such as natural resources, communications and transport, financial institutions and, most particularly, industry. The conscious aim of nationalization is to end private ownership and control of the economy and thereby eliminate economic inequality, exploitation, greed, and avariciousness—replacing the "evils" of capitalism with the "advantages" of collectivity. Areas normally excluded from these early nationalization drives are small-scale handicraft industry, some farming, and various service functions such as shoe repairing.

The pace of nationalization in communist systems has varied from quick, simple take-over of existing industry (as in Albania, Poland, and Yugoslavia) to a slower pace in countries in which a vigorous private sector resisted such quick take-over (Czechoslovakia, Hungary, Rumania). In a few countries specific problems delayed full nationalization, such as having to win sympathy for the communists from several classes of the population (China), and slowness of economic recovery following World War I and the Civil War (USSR). In China and North Vietnam nationalization proceeded by stages, from private to semipublic, and finally to state ownership of the vast majority of industry and commerce. Eventually, though, full nationalization of most of the economy has been carried out in all of the communist states. The notable exceptions are the low levels of nationalized/socialized agriculture in both Poland and Yugoslavia. Table 5 shows the level of nationalization claimed by the communist states by the mid-1960's.[7]

TABLE 5

**Share of the "Socialist Sector" by Branch of Economy,
1958–1965** (in % of total)

State	Gross Industrial Production	Gross Agricultural Production	Retail Trade Turnover	National Income
Albania	99.5	89.7	92.9	91.3
Bulgaria	99.5	99.6	99.9	99.7
China	100.0	99.0	98.0	99.0
Czechoslovakia	100.0	90.9	100.0	99.2
GDR	85.7	90.7	78.1	85.8
Hungary	95.5	96.0	99.0	97.0
Mongolia	100.0	100.0	100.0	100.0
North Korea	100.0	100.0	100.0	100.0
North Vietnam	91.9	78.3	85.0	75.8
Poland	99.6	12.2	98.7	77.8
Rumania	99.7	90.9	100.0	96.2
USSR	100.0	99.9	100.0	99.9
Yugoslavia	100.0	15.0	99.5	

The figures in Table 5, all from Soviet sources, can be misleading. Although gross agricultural production in the USSR, for example, is listed at 99.9% falling within the socialist sector (including state and collective farms), in fact much of agricultural production comes from the private plots of collective farmers and is sold in the collective, "free" markets. Thus, a collective farmer spends so many days working in the "socialist" sector (i.e., on the collective), and a certain amount of time on his private plot. The latter really amounts to private farming, but is counted in Soviet statistics as collectivized, or socialized farming. In one Soviet province for the period 1960–64, 66% of the output of meat, 55% of the milk, and 90% of the eggs were produced on private plots.[8]

ECONOMIC PLANNING

To achieve the dramatically innovative results for which they hope, communist leaders organize an elaborate structure to plan for the reorganization of the economy (from private to public ownership) and then to plan its future development. The rationale for planning is balanced and progressive economic growth, fair reward for all citizens, and organized efficiency. To conserve all of the nation's resources (natural, material, and human) and to develop and expend them most effectively, their planned allocation for production, distribution, and utilization is to be carefully worked out beforehand according to designated proportions. For this purpose, both short-range (annual) and long-range plans are drawn up. Long-range planning is informational; it relates to extended priorities for broad economic development. Short-range plans fill in the detail for the long-range plans, in an operational sense, in the form of specific production targets. It is hoped that duplication, waste, misuse, and mistakes will be avoided through such careful and elaborated planning. Moreover, through such planning the economy can be directed toward fulfilling national goals. For these purposes, a special planning office is established on the national level, which works through regional and local planning offices. These planning bodies set the framework, or outlines, for plans which then are completed in greater detail by the governmental-economic organization whose output is expected to fulfill the plans (e.g., the producing factories).[9]

In addition to the specific planning agencies, many other governmental offices, as well as organs of the communist party, are involved in the formulation, development, supervision, and verification of the planning process—on national, regional, and local levels. Economic planning thus consumes much of the total working time of government and party officials in communist systems.

The process of planning begins with broad goals as established by the nation's leaders. The central planning body then transforms these goals into control figures, which take the form of specific, operational targets for a given period (one, two, or perhaps five years) and for a given segment of the economy. After the specific plans have been detailed, with figures and estimates supplied by intermediate planning bodies and the producing units, the central planning body coordinates the several parts, numerous recommendations, and modifications into one, internally consistent draft plan which then is submitted to the political leaders for final approval.[10]

The Soviet government has experimented with economic planning since the late 1920's, following Lenin's embryonic plan for electrification. Following this came perspective plans (ten to fifteen years), long-range (five years) and annual plans. After suffering through many inefficiencies, partial failures in fulfillment, and general confusion arising out of maladministration, Soviet planning eventually settled down into a routine and fairly consistent procedure in which the plans, as finally decided upon, become obligatory for all individuals and organizations responsible for carrying them out. One result of this massive national planning has been the creation (with periodic re-creations and reorganizations) of a sizeable planning bureaucracy with numerous regional and local planning bodies employing thousands of people.

In the Eastern European nations, early governmental planning (1947–48) was directed at reconstructing war-damaged industries, with long-range plans (usually five years) directed at duplicating in miniature the Soviet model for rapid industrialization. The results were that the combined industrial production of six of these countries rose 114% between 1949 and the early 1950's, Rumania and Hungary having increased their annual output of capital goods 40% in the years 1950 and 1951.[11] A later measurable drop in these early growth rates was aggravated by disproportions in the earlier industrial buildup within these countries. This drop motivated a reform of planning in the late 1950's and early 1960's. In addition to decentralization of the planning operation, long-range (perspective) plans of up to twenty years were formulated, hopefully thereby achieving increased flexibility in short-range plans. These perspective plans were considered by the Soviet leaders as aiding their attempts to integrate the Eastern European nations into a single, coordinated economic entity.

The announced objectives of such integration were the creation of an international socialist division of labor, leading to autarky; a balanced economy in the Soviet Bloc as a whole; heightened economic efficiency; and the opportunity for each of the nations to specialize in a given area of its particular economic strength, thus adding to the overall strength of the Bloc. Moreover, there was anticipated an increased standard of living, with a more-or-less simultaneous transition to communism of these nations within the same period of time.[12]

To bring about this integration, and to come up with a "socialist" equivalent to the Marshall Plan, the USSR in 1949 organized a Council for Mutual Economic Assistance (CMEA, or Comecon). Membership in the new organization included the USSR and the Eastern European communist nations, with the exception of Yugoslavia. Mongolia joined at a later date. A main objective for CMEA has been, at Soviet insistence, to elaborate a division of labor in which each member nation produces its specialty for export to other member nations. There appear to be other Soviet objectives also—for example, supplying raw materials for Soviet industry. As a result of specialty assignments, the German Democratic Republic, Czechoslovakia, and Poland have been assigned, among others, production of machine tools and telecommunications; Hungary—buses and bauxite; Rumania—oil, and oil-drilling and refinery equipment; Poland—shipbuilding, paper-making machines, and coal; Bulgaria—certain chemical products, and fruits and vegetables. Although the Soviet Union has been the motivating force behind CMEA, it has never restricted itself to any given specialty. In the view of a Soviet economist, Bulgaria, Hungary, the GDR, Poland, Rumania, Czechoslovakia, and the USSR supply each other with coal and coke, while the USSR and Rumania provide oil and oil products for the Bloc. The USSR, Bulgaria, Hungary, and the GDR supply iron ore to the metallurgical industry of Hungary, Poland, Rumania, Czechoslovakia, and Bulgaria, while Rumania imports quantities of cast iron and rolled metal. The USSR, Czechoslovakia, the GDR, Hungary, Bulgaria, and Rumania also are cooperating in the use of power plants.[13]

The most obvious limitation on developing an integrated Bloc economy has been the desire on the part of each nation to build an all-round, proficient industry for itself instead of specializing in the production of only a few, selected commodities for the benefit of the other nations. The desire for individual, national autarky has struggled with Soviet plans for a broader international division of labor set into a gigantic cooperative arrangement. Economic nationalism, in other words, is at least as powerful as communist internationalism. Other weaknesses in building such a cooperative scheme arise from differences in cost-price figures, and the absence of common standardization among the several nations. Perhaps one of the leading difficulties has been the lack of clear-cut goals for CMEA, as between the USSR and the Eastern European nations. Soviet goals, in addition to building an economically self-sufficient Bloc, have included servicing and strengthening internal Soviet industry. Obviously, other communist nations cannot be expected to be very sympathetic toward this objective. Moreover the absence of criteria by which the Soviet leadership can measure the goals and performance of its own economy might be a crucial issue, in Kaser's view, on which CMEA has foundered.[14]

INDUSTRIALIZATION

If communism, as Meyer has suggested, is the practice of entrepreneurship—that is, industrialization[15]—the ideological justification for building an industry comes directly from Marxism. Many of the writings of Marx, as well as his political orientation and his overall outlook on society, reflect both an attraction to and a revulsion from industrialization. His fascination and admiration for the accomplishments of industrialization struggled with personal disgust arising from the flagrant injustices of industrial capitalism of the mid-nineteenth century. Marx's objective was to point out to workers that they could take advantage of industrialization without being victimized by it. Marxism-Leninism, most broadly, is a format for organizing society to realize this objective.

Partly because Marx argued for the practical necessity as well as for the historical inevitability of modern industrialization, communist leaders have advanced the ideal of industrialization as their foremost economic goal. For Lenin and Stalin, industrialization meant promoting the growth of heavy industry, creating the necessary stock of producers' goods: machinery, metallurgy, fuel. Once industrialization had been accomplished, then all other economic goals supposedly would follow. This emphasis established not only the Soviet pattern for industrialization, but that of Eastern Europe and China as well. As a result, communist parties and their governments have been structured to function in no small degree as agencies of industrialization—often to the virtual neglect of agricultural output. Five decades of communist rule, from 1917 on, reveal this bias and one-sided development in communist economics. In justification, Marxists have argued that communism is the best and only modern path for any nation to follow if it seeks rapid industrialization.

Successful industrialization, though, relates in no small measure to organization, according to Soviet leaders. The central government apparatus in the USSR, the Soviet Council of Ministers, includes a number of ministries and state committees (approximately fifty in 1970) which are directly concerned with the administration of industry (out of a total of seventy-two such ministries and committees for the entire central government). Moreover, the State Planning Committee devotes the great majority of its time to planning for the growth and the utilization of industry. In addition, the apparatus of the Communist Party's Central Committee (Secretariat) contains a number of subsections which are responsible for supervising the government's management of industry. Functions of the Soviet government and of the communist party on all levels—central, regional, and local—include much effort directed toward organizing, staffing, training for, financing, and in general administering industry. Thus, the Soviet government, to a very considerable degree, has through its history been a government of and for industrialization.

The Soviet model for industrialization has provided a structural and functional design for the communist systems which followed it. This model has included the following:

Industry treated as the leading sector for development.
Growth pattern favors heavy industry.
Stress on advanced technology, economizing on capital, and skilled labor as choices among alternative productive techniques.
Maintenance of a very high rate of investment.
Vocational and technical training emphasized during the period of industrialization.
Adoption of import-substitution policy in international trade.[16]

As mentioned previously, following the Soviet model and under Russian guidance, China and Eastern Europe stressed early development of heavy industry; this was true even of economically backward Albania and Bulgaria. Not surprisingly, economic dislocations developed as a result of each nation trying to de-emphasize its traditional economic production—say, truck garden produce in Bulgaria—and to emphasize instead building of a steel industry.[17] All of the first economic plans of Czechoslovakia, Bulgaria, Hungary, Rumania, and Yugoslavia emphasized the metal working industries first, then the broad sector of all heavy industry. These plans stressed rapid development of electricity, coal, iron, and steel in addition to capital formation. Each stressed a similar "all-round" development.[18] In China, the scale and direction of industrialization, and the choice of techniques—even the size of the industrial establishments (following the advice of Soviet technicians)—were patterned after the Stalinist experience. Table 6 illustrates the similarity in early economic development between the Soviet Union and China.[19]

TABLE 6

Distribution of Public Capital Investment by Economic Sectors: USSR, 1928/29–32, and Communist China, 1953–57 (in % of total)

	USSR 1928/29–32	Communist China 1953–57
Industry	40.9	47.9
Agriculture	19.2	14.9
Transportation and Communications	18.4	15.1
Other	21.5	22.1
Total	100.0	100.0

Despite the almost uniform attention given to the structure and form of industrialization in almost all communist states, then, their achievements vary widely. Neither Mongolia, under communist rule since 1921, nor Albania, since 1944, has become industrialized. Mongolia's main economic activity is animal raising. In all of the industry recorded in 1965, only one-fourth of total workers and employees were occupied in heavy industry.[20] In the case of Albania, when East European communist states and the USSR increased their electrical power output in the period 1950–62 from a low range of 0.8 to 6.0 billion kwh (Bulgaria), to a high range of 91.2 to 369.0

(USSR), Albania's increase was only from 0.02 to 0.24.[21] To cite one more case, North Vietnam into the 1960's remained mainly a rural, peasant society, almost four-fifths of the population living in villages.[22]

On the other hand, serious and concentrated national efforts directed toward industrialization have paid off in rapid progress toward that goal in other countries. The example of the USSR is probably the classical case in this respect. Beyond that nation, industrialization has been, in the view of Ernst, the dominant form of economic growth in Eastern Europe. Thus, the contribution to economic growth of industry and construction was smaller in six out of nine states in Western Europe than in any of the Eastern European states.[23] Table 7 reflects features of industrialization within the several communist states, as these are compared with one another.

TABLE 7
Structure of the National Income by Branch (in % of total income)

Nation	Year	Industry	Construction	Agric. & Forestry	Trans. & Commun.	Trade	Other
Albania	1959	37.1	9.4	42.8	2.8	6.8	1.1
Bulgaria	1964	45.0	7.0	34.0	4.0	8.0	2.0
China	1956	26.4	5.6	48.1	4.4	15.3	—
Czechoslovakia	1964	64.3	8.5	13.8	3.2	9.3	0.9
GDR	1965	64.4	5.2	11.4	4.5	13.2	1.2
Hungary	1965	58.0	10.4	20.5	4.8	5.3	1.0
Mongolia	1958	13.3	8.7	36.6	9.7	31.1	0.6
North Korea	1959	50.9	6.1	28.6	—	—	—
North Vietnam	1962	20.9	3.8	51.8	3.3	20.2	—
Poland	1964	50.9	8.9	22.4	6.2	9.8	1.8
Rumania	1964	48.5	8.5	28.2	4.2	8.0	2.6
USSR	1964	53.6	8.9	21.4	5.4	10.7	—
Yugoslavia	1964	40.1	8.2	27.7	6.5	11.8	5.7

Source: Ekonomika Sotsialisticheskikh Stran v Tsifrakh, p. 7.

Using data presented in this table under the column of *Industry,* the states may be rank ordered and placed in broad groupings separated by approximately ten-point spreads as follows:[24]

Group 1:	GDR	64.4		Group 3:	Yugoslavia	40.1
	Czechoslovakia	64.3			Albania	37.1
	Hungary	58.0		Group 4:	China	26.4
Group 2:	USSR	53.6		Group 5:	North Vietnam	20.9
	Poland	50.9			Mongolia	13.3
	North Korea	50.9				
	Rumania	48.5				
	Bulgaria	45.0				

The limitations of the data presented notwithstanding (disparity among the years showing quite dated information from several of the states; reliance on only the one breakdown, percentage of national income derived from industry), it might not be inappropriate to let the groupings suggest relative rankings of industrialization among the communist states. Thus, the states in Group 1, it might be argued, are fully industrialized and compare with a number of industrialized nations in the world in levels of economic development and industrial capacity. Group 2 states can be thought of as modernizing and industrializing, with a number of accomplishments already recorded—for example, in light and medium industry and in certain areas of heavy industry, such as shipbuilding in Poland and the oil equipment industry in Rumania. Within this grouping there are obvious differences in levels of industrial achievement among the states, for example, between the USSR and Bulgaria. Group 3 states appear to be at an early stage of industrialization and have realized measurable development in selected industries only, such as electro-energy in Yugoslavia and mining of metals and drilling of oil in Albania. Group 4, containing only China, so far reveals some industrial capacity and expansion since World War II—for example, in steel-making and, of course, in nuclear energy. In Group 5 the states of North Vietnam and Mongolia are still in the traditional, pre-industrial state of economic development.

On balance, and based at least on Soviet figures, it appears that communism itself does not ensure rapid industrialization of a nation. Indeed, it appears doubtful that it measurably speeds up the process. Czechoslovakia and the GDR were industrialized prior to their communist period, while Mongolia and North Vietnam remain nonindustrialized after years of communist rule. Although one might point out that North Vietnam has been at war too long to have permitted her to industrialize, whatever her political and economic structure, such is not the case for Mongolia. As for those states in the middle (Groups 2, 3, and 4), the effects of communism *vis-à-vis* rapid industrialization seem unimpressive. One might assume that the command economy helped Hungary and the USSR toward this goal, but why, then, are not Bulgaria, Albania, and China farther along the road toward achieving a modern industry?

COLLECTIVIZATION

The goal of collectivizing agriculture is, for a communist party, the rural equivalent of nationalizing industry. The objectives are similar: to replace private economic structures with public-governmental ones in the interest of greater equity for the peasant farmers than they have enjoyed in the past, in the interest of heightened managerial and productive efficiency, and also of more effective political control by the communist party. Still another goal, although not an admitted one, has been to facilitate confiscation of agricultural produce to help pay the costs of quick industrialization. In addition to the collectivization of agriculture (peasants owning and operating the farms collectively in collective farms) there occurs a common form of simple governmental ownership and management, referred to in the Soviet Union as "state" farms. (Both categories, "collective" and "state," are included together here under the *socialist* or *collectivized* designations given to agriculture under communism.) The organizational format collectivization has taken in Eastern Europe ranges from the loosely structured collectives in the GDR (retaining much private ownership) and the Unified Agricultural Cooperatives of Czechoslovakia, to the more typical Soviet type of joint ownership of both land and livestock.

Collectivization, including establishment of both state and collective farms, had been largely completed in the USSR by the early 1930's. After varied efforts to collectivize agriculture in Eastern Europe in the late 1940's and early 1950's, there occurred a temporary slowdown in the drive following a period of political uncertainty throughout the Soviet Bloc after Stalin's death. A subsequent economic and social "new course" of liberalization in the USSR and in Eastern Europe, as well as efforts to grant more concessions to farmers, resulted from the brief Malenkov period in the USSR and a similar one under Imre Nagy in Hungary. One result of this new course was a temporary halt in the collectivization drive in Eastern Europe, with some collectives being dissolved in Czechoslovakia and Hungary. After Malenkov's fall, the new-course liberalizations faded and collectivization was resumed in the communist states.

Following the 1956 revolutions in Eastern Europe, collectivization drives once again were interrupted in Czechoslovakia and Bulgaria, slowed down considerably in the German Democratic Republic and Hungary, and permanently stopped expanding in Poland and Yugoslavia.[25] Table 8 gives Soviet figures on collectivization for twelve of the communist-party states for the years 1950 and 1965.

TABLE 8

Levels of Collectivization (in % of agricultural area)

Nation	1950	1965
Albania	7.9	89.7
Bulgaria	12.0	99.5
Cuba	—	70.0
Czechoslovakia	22.1	89.3
GDR	5.7	93.9
Hungary	32.2	96.9
Mongolia	39.6	100.0
North Korea	1.9	100.0
Poland	10.3	14.4
Rumania	23.6	91.4
USSR	98.7	99.5
Yugoslavia	10.0	15.0

Source: *Ekonomika Sotsialisticheskikh Stran v Tsifrakh*, pp. 39, 147. Soviet figures differ from estimates by western analysts.

In China, by the early 1950's, the leadership was moving the peasants from private ownership of land (long promised to the peasants by the Chinese communists) to "mutual aid teams," then to "agricultural producers' cooperatives"—each cooperative being composed of forty to fifty households. This pooling of land into common cooperatives was similar to the earlier pattern of collectivization in the USSR. By mid-1956, supposedly 91 percent of peasant households were joined in producers' cooperatives.[26] In 1958 communes were introduced into China as a higher form of socialist organization of agriculture. Each commune included 20,000 or more households and they were so organized as to eliminate private farming once and for all. In addition to land in common, there were added common children's nurseries, even common mess halls. Finally, the Chinese adopted a version of the Soviet collective farmers' private plots as a measure to help solve certain dilemmas arising from the overburdened communes. In Mongolia, contrary to official Soviet figures, collectivization proceeded slowly so that by 1948 the vast majority of stock raisers still had their own herds (with rights of inheritance), and could hire labor and pay wages in kind. Stock raising continues as Mongolia's chief economic activity.[27] The regime in North Vietnam, like that of China, pushed collectivization so that by 1960 some 85 percent of the peasants in North Vietnam were members of some 30,000 collective farms. The other 15 percent of noncollectivized farms consisted of minority peoples living deep in the highlands.[28]

Peasant farmers frequently have resisted efforts to collectivize their farms, beginning with the burning of crops and slaughtering of livestock by Soviet farmers in the late 1920's and early 1930's. These efforts ultimately were overcome by the government's use of troops. As Volin puts it, Soviet policy towards peasants has always consisted of a combination of force, indoctrination, and economic incentives, with only the proportions varying from time to time.[29] In China peasant resistance was milder, although the peasants were not enthusiastic about venturing into such radical schemes as the communes. Some peasant resistance to collectivization also occurred in Eastern Europe in the 1950's. In Yugoslavia peasant resistance, coupled with more astute official reevaluations as to the limited advantages of collectivization, encouraged the regime to end the collectivization drives and allowed the collectives to be dissolved in the early 1950's. A similar development followed shortly thereafter in Poland in the late 1950's and early 1960's. From 1958 to 1961 there were 733 new collective farms established in Poland while 465 were being closed down. In 1961 and 1962 there were 76 new collective farms while 659 were being closed.[30] In these two nations the bulk of farming now is privately owned and operated.

The notable failures of collectivized farming in the USSR and

Eastern Europe to increase agricultural output and to bring to farming the advantages of organized efficiency are well known. The history of collectivization reveals that this form of "public" farming is less efficient than private farming. This is shown by the successful experience of Soviet "collective" farmers in working their small, private plots (see p. 78), as well as the experience nationwide in Poland and Yugoslavia. In the post-1950 reforms in Yugoslav agricultural policy, there were not only calls for an end to further collectivization, but also tax discrimination against the private, non-collectivized peasants was eased, and these peasants were granted certain credit and tax concessions as well as governmental price supports. The one exception to the general limitations and failures of collectivization may be that of the German Democratic Republic. The farmers in that nation believe in the success of collectivization, according to Smith. Productive efficiency has been markedly increased and both the farmers and the state have been rewarded.[31] In structure and organization, however, GDR farms resemble more closely the more private American cooperatives than the public Soviet-type collectives. The farmer in the GDR, for example, can own his land, buy and sell it, although he pools it while in the cooperative.[32] It is questionable, then, whether the GDR type can be classified as truly collective or socialized.

The area of private farming in communist states frequently has been expanded when agricultural reforms have been attempted, for example, permitting an increase in the number and size of private plots (extending even to state farmers in the USSR), or permitting a form of sharecropping (in Hungary in the mid-1960's). Farmers have been allowed to reacquire agricultural land in Yugoslavia, with an upper limit of 25 acres.[33] Evidently Hungarian party leaders also planned, in the latter 1960's, to place more emphasis on private farming than they had earlier, probably because of the importance of the contribution to Hungarian agriculture of the private sector. As of 1965 some 16.1% of the arable land (which included private plots), 55.2% of the orchards and vegetable gardens, and 64.9% of the vineyards were still privately owned.[34] The obvious question raised is why do communist leaders persist in continuing agricultural policies which repeatedly and demonstrably have proven unsuccessful for increasing agricultural output?

From Marxist-Leninism comes a prejudice against capitalism so deep-seated that it frequently inhibits a broad flexibility of choice on the part of the leadership group. Thus, there appears to be an inability on the part of these leaders to accept the suggestion that socialistic/communistic organization and management cannot solve any problem arising in society. Understandably, too, communist leaders are reluctant to return to private ownership in agriculture or industry with all that is implied in a confession that private, capitalistic structures may in some way be equal or superior to public-socialistic forms. In addition, communist leaders, in part because of their ideological commitment to the theory of Marxism-Leninism as well as to their own political goals, have always emphasized the development of industry over agriculture. Consequently, the economic investments in resources, management, planning, and manpower have all been concentrated on industry rather than agriculture. Agriculture has been the stepchild of the economy. It should be noted, on the other hand, that limited investments in agriculture have allowed far greater investments of labor and capital for industrial development. One might argue, as a result, that collectivization has been successful as a contribution toward industrialization.[35]

ECONOMIC REFORMS

From the mid-1950's communist leaders in some countries have planned for and attempted economic reforms to correct deficiencies arising from a number of causes, especially overly rapid industrialization and too heavy concentration of investments in certain narrow sectors of the economy. In attempting to dismantle the older command economy, as Gamarnikow points out, economic planners in Eastern Europe faced the problem of their inheritance from Stalinism—a system which for years was operated in disregard for standards of efficiency and rationality, a system plagued with excess manpower, an artificial price structure, and arbitrary wage scales, with agriculture both neglected and undercapitalized.[36] Problems had arisen also because of poor coordination of demand and supply, accumulation of unwanted goods, low quality of goods, and wasteful use of resources.[37] According to a Hungarian economist, damaging consequences of the planning system involved inefficient investment, waste and low efficiency, a poor product mix, and low incentive.[38]

Eventually Eastern European Communist leaders realized the deficiencies inherent in their particular structures which had resulted in the slowdown in economic growth in most of these nations after the mid-1950's. Analyzing the reaction of Eastern European states to this realization, Montias suggests a scale of reforming states beginning with Albania, which has undergone almost no change, followed by Rumania, with slight changes in allowing enterprises to contact foreign firms. Bulgaria is next, followed by Poland. Then comes the Soviet Union. The three states which have adopted the most significant changes, finally, are Hungary, Czechoslovakia, and the GDR.[39]

To a certain degree, Soviet reforms efforts have set the pace for similar developments in the Eastern European communist states.[40] Soviet economic reforms in management began in 1952 with efforts to reduce the percentage of administrative staffs in proportion to workers, although wide-scale improvements did not begin until after Stalin's death. In a limited managerial decentralization which saw the creation of more than one hundred regional economic offices in 1957, the Soviet leadership launched a decade-long economic reform aimed at ending overcentralization of administration, bureaucratic red tape, duplication of functions, and errors in planning. Great successes have been claimed by the Soviet government in savings from the elimination of superfluous positions and organizations, the achievement of more simplified and rational planning, and the assigning of managerial authority to more appropriate levels of decision-making.

The most recent economic reforms in the USSR (in the 1960's) have involved attempts to free local-enterprise administrators from some of the restrictive controls over their managerial flexibility and independence of decision-making. These reforms, popularly referred to as the Liberman Proposals, authorize some individual producing enterprises to exercise greater leeway in use of their resources, such as in leasing and selling equipment, and more freedom in negotiating contracts with other enterprises, in setting prices and in drafting plans. The success of all of these changes was to be measured in terms of enterprise profit-making. Some marked successes, after several years, have been claimed for this reorganization.[41] Other communist states have picked up this particular type of reform—for example, Bulgaria, which put fifty-two enterprises under the new scheme of greater managerial independence. This was expanded eventually to include most of the industrial enterprises; and it included granting more powers to managers in both production and sales, use of the profit motive instead of quantitative planning indexes to measure efficiency, bank credits instead of budgetary subsidies, and a wage structure tied more closely to production results, rather than arbitrarily set at the central governmental level.[42]

In the late 1950's, in another development, deconcentration of planning in Eastern Europe reduced the role of the central planning authorities *vis-à-vis* those on the regional level, leaving to the latter more of the details of plan formation and at the same time allowing for more flexibility in periodic adjustments of the economic plans. In Bulgaria a new system of both planning and management was announced in 1964 which, among other changes, was to reduce centralism in part by cutting down on the number of compulsory indicators for the national plan.[43] In Czechoslovakia, targets for the national plan were considerably reduced in number and general economic development was shifted in the mid-1960's from the broadly extensive to a more narrowly intensive development.[44]

Poland had been anticipating economic reforms in the late 1950's, but implementation of them was delayed until the late 1960's, with such reforms as stressing more continuity and increased flexibility in planning scheduled to go into effect during the period of 1966–70.[45] By 1970, Poland had launched a broad reform program which included the by-now-typical range of planning simplification, decentralized management, and greater reliance on the market mechanism to guide production.[46] Rumania in the early 1960's also sought greater realism in its economic planning and, like Czechoslovakia, stressed the development of fewer industrial projects—but with the intention to develop those projects already decided upon more carefully.[47] Similar developments took place in China following the economic crisis of 1960–62, when planning was made more realistic and the earlier claims for grandiose economic successes were scaled down.[48] In China, decentralization of control over industry, trade, and taxation dates from 1957. Following the economic folly created by the Great Leap Forward campaign in 1958—an overly ambitious scheme by the Chinese to will themselves to greater production—and the serious decrease in Soviet aid and trade during 1961–62, the economy was ripe for reform by 1963. The reforms have included a slight de-emphasis on capital investment for heavy industry and an increase in trade with noncommunist states.[49] The Yugoslav national plan, finally, was simplified in the 1950's so that the national government now confines itself solely to long-term planning. In lieu of detailed central planning, only the basic proportions necessary to the plan as a whole are to be set by the central government.

The focus of economic reform in Eastern Europe in the 1960's was on decentralization of managerial decision-making.[50] Reforms in Czechoslovakia in the 1960's followed the Soviet format in matters of incentive and guaranteed payments for workers; greater administrative freedom given to enterprises; and, differing from the Soviet example, a general moving away from a command economy to what might be termed a socialist-market one.[51] If the reforms in Czechoslovakia were hailed as the most far-ranging ones in the Bloc by mid-1968, it should be noted that the German Democratic Republic may have initiated some of the same reforms earlier, such as adopting features of the Liberman Proposals. Managerial independence on the factory level also may have gone further in the GDR than in any other East European nation, with the exception of Yugoslavia. Accordingly, the wage and premium system was reorganized, and factories more and more were assigned profit as a measure of success.[52] These reforms were carried out fairly rapidly by the regime and, incidentally, they seem to have been readily accepted by the population.[53]

In Hungary immediate postrevolutionary reforms took place in late 1956 and early 1957, and included decentralizing some of the central governmental ministries while at the same time allowing the growth of a number of new private businesses. For a short time (approximately a year) workers' councils were permitted to help govern factories. Emphasis on profit-making for individual enterprises was stressed in Hungary as early as 1958. In 1964 Hungary, in a further move toward economic rationality, introduced use of an interest rate placed on fixed gross and working capital.[54] Hungary has turned over to a number of factories responsibility for plan preparation, establishment of wages, and setting their own production schedule. Factory output supposedly is now to be based on market demand.[55] The Hungarian economic manager may, since mid-1970, negotiate his own contracts with customers and with suppliers of raw materials in foreign countries.[56]

Similar plans were laid in Poland and Rumania for managerial reforms along lines sketched above. Polish leaders early had argued for the idea that firms should produce on orders of trade agencies rather than on orders of central planners. Indeed, Poland's innovating plans predated even those of the USSR, but in Poland's case many of them were not immediately put into practice.

Until this period of reform, pricing policy in the communist states had been inflexible, being characterized as prices centrally fixed, constant for long periods, formed into two sets (wholesale and retail), and having a special category for agriculture prices.[57] Now, while both Poland and the USSR decided to retain price fixing by central authority, Bulgaria, Czechoslovakia, Hungary, and to a lesser degree the German Democratic Republic, began experimenting with prices set by the market. The GDR scheduled a reform of supply prices in 1967; Poland did so in a third round of reforms in 1967–68; and Czechoslovakia and Hungary were to achieve a complete reform of wholesale and supply prices by 1968.[58] In Rumania, price reform was carefully laid out in advance and then introduced into industries.

Partly as a result of the break between the USSR and Yugoslavia in 1948, Yugoslav leaders in a new era of independence opened the way for extensive reforms in economic management which covered the range from simple improvements in planning to direct worker influences in factory administration. Thus, Yugoslav reforms have both predated and been more extensive than those of any other communist nation, including the USSR. As early as 1950, laws were passed establishing workers' councils and authorizing them to participate in joint governmental-worker factory management. Decentralization of both industrial and agricultural administration also dates from this early period. The abolition of central economic ministries, another in the series of reforms, was an attempt to develop local initiative in industrial management and to decrease the overburdened central bureaucracy. The abolished ministries were replaced by associations called Chambers of Industry, Agriculture, and Trade; and they were governed by representatives elected from workers' councils as well as governmental representatives. Central price controls on producers' goods were abandoned in the 1950's, followed by the near abolition of all wage controls in the early 1960's.[59] Even so, there reportedly were 504 strikes involving some 20,000 workers in Yugoslavia during 1964 and 1965. Causes of the strikes included low earnings, arbitrary increases in piecework rates, inflexible managerial attitudes, and generally poor working conditions.[60] With respect to these reforms, it is important to note that in many instances Yugoslavia has been the bellwether for various communist nations (in part, even the USSR)—in such matters as planning reforms, administrative decentralization, workers' influence on management, and the abandonment of collectivization in favor of private farming.

The main thrust of the Yugoslav reforms signals an effort to create a free market economy within an overall socialist system, with an attempt being made to combine the socialist principles of public ownership and carefully limited inequality in the distribution of income with the use of markets and prices to allocate natural resources and the goods of production. Market socialism is thus contrasted with authoritarian socialism, or as it is usually called, a command economy.[61] As Yugoslavia continued to lead the other communist nations in economic reforms in the late 1960's, the other Eastern European communist countries divided themselves into what Gamarnikow refers to as "pacesetters" (Czechoslovakia, Hungary), which pushed for integral and all-embracing economic reforms, and "footdraggers" (Bulgaria, Poland, and the USSR), which introduced only piecemeal changes in the old model. The German Democratic Republic and Rumania, he argues, are on a third level, that of introducing cautiously pragmatic reforms.[62]

One type of reform so far shunned in the largest communist nations (China and the USSR) is that of extending the private sector of the economy. In Yugoslavia, on the other hand, these extensions have included restaurants, taxis, repair shops, beauty shops, building contractors (for private houses), even travel and advertising agencies. In Poland, since the mid-1960's, the government has encouraged the growth of privately-owned restaurants and cafés, as well as privately-operated restaurants and gas stations which are leased from the state—all of this, by official admission, because of a great need for additional service facilities. By 1965 there were 135,000 private craft workshops in Poland, an increase of 2,400 since the end of 1963.[63] Relative to this encouragement of private ownership, Poland introduced the "agency" system into Eastern Europe, in which a state bureaucracy looks for a private entrepreneur (agent), who then leases the state-owned facility to develop into a profit-making business. There have even been—in addition to private enterprises among doctors, hairdressers, dressmakers, and lawyers—some truck gardeners in Poland who were accused of becoming "zloty millionaires" because of their great profits.[64] The Czechoslovak government too, by the 1960's, endorsed small-scale private enterprise for artisans, small restaurants and shops, laundries, tailor shops, and taxis—in a desire to get the state out of running small and uneconomical enterprises. Hungary, which has the largest number of private businesses among the communist nations, in 1962 counted 68,821 private craftsmen working on their own, of whom 16,423 employed other people.[65] In mid-1965 there were more than 8,800 private traders in such lines as grocery, tobacco, secondhand, florist, and other such service shops.[66]

In the German Democratic Republic in 1966 there were almost ten thousand private and semiprivate factories. Although these were relatively small firms, the state revealed no plans to convert them to the public sector. Interestingly, the government recognizes the advantage of leaving these out of the public sector for reasons of greater efficiency; providing a yardstick for company production costs in state-owned industry; and, finally, insuring a reservoir of technical and managerial expertise.[67] The government also has begun leasing restaurants, cafés, taverns, and beer gardens to private owners on a commission basis.[68]

Economic reforms in the Soviet Union and most of the Eastern European communist states have resulted from official reaction to past weaknesses, in part caused by the peculiarities of communist economic organization and management. Moreover, a too slavish following of Soviet economic structures and policies has given rise to problems in most of the communist states. Part of the reforming impetus comes from a reaction to outmoded methods, methods which may have been useful in the early years of intensive industrialization, but which have become obstacles to economic growth when continued beyond their period of historical justification. Thus, when a socialist system begins overcoming these old methods, it indicates a maturing process.[69] One Polish author lists three models of reform: in the first, the communist party determines long- and short-term "equilibrium" of the economy, with the market playing a broad, but supplementary role (the USSR and most East European states follow this model); in the second, the communist party determines the long-run, but the market the short-run equilibrium (Czechoslovakia and Hungary follow this model); in the third, the market determines both short and long-run equilibrium (only Yugoslavia follows this model.[70]

Sincere, albeit piecemeal, efforts to correct managerial deficiencies have included a simplification and rationalization of economic planning, and in the process there has taken place a de-emphasis in the role of central planning *vis-à-vis* that of regional and local planning. Greater independence for administrators of enterprises carries the intention of giving these administrators needed flexibility in operational decision-making. Most recently, communist-party leaders have been looking toward profit as the most reliable guideline for measuring the efficiency of industrial enterprises. Leaders also are always weighing additional means for stimulating productivity by way of incentives, both collective and individual. Questions not yet answered by these partial reforms relate to whether they are adequate to correct, or at least compensate for, problems found in communist economic organization and management and whether they can keep pace with changing and increasing pressures on these developing economies as they expand and become more complex.

COMMUNIST ECONOMICS

All of the communist states have by and large organized a socialist economic structure, as called for in the third item of the Marxist-Leninist Model. Capitalistic economic structures have been replaced by public ones for at least the important and critical nonagricultural areas of the economy. Economic planning has been inaugurated and a considerable measure of agricultural collectivization has been achieved. It is difficult, however, to arrive at definite conclusions regarding the economic accomplishment *per se* of communist states. In that factories are built, goods are produced, people fed, and improvements recorded, they are, of course, successful. More difficult questions relate to the efficiency of communist economic organizations and to whether communist management is moving these states toward their economic goals in a steady and satisfactory pace. Is the economic organization and management under communism a viable form which facilitates economic development? Clear answers are not easy to find, but certain questions can be discussed and some tentative conclusions set forth.

Has communism, for example, enabled the communist states rapidly to industrialize? Data presented earlier in the chapter suggests that several communist states are industrialized (the GDR, Czechoslovakia, Hungary); a number are definitely on the road to industrialization; some are just beginning industrialization; and at least two are rather completely unindustrialized. Even in these groupings, however, Czechoslovakia and the GDR were industrialized prior to their communist periods and old Russia had begun industrialization by the turn of the century, although to be sure not moving toward completion of this process until some years after the communist period began. Pre-communist Albania, Bulgaria, and Rumania were largely agricultural; and not much has changed in Albania since the communist period. Of the Asian communist states, China and North Korea appear to be industrializing, but North Vietnam and Mongolia do not. On balance, the record of the communist states has not borne out the claims of Marxist leaders that communism leads to early industrialization. The arguments for such claims (command economy, planned allocations, selective investments) are logical, but the experience in these states is not impressive.

On the question of collectivization, we can be more conclusive. By the mid-1960's agricultural production had been collectivized (including cooperatives, collectives, state farms, and communes), officially at least, in all of the thirteen communist states except for Poland and Yugoslavia, states whose leadership apparently has given up on collectivization. Even in the collectivized nations, however, private agriculture persists in various forms. For example, following collapse of the commune system in China in the mid-1960's, occasional reports hinted at renewal of private farming in some areas despite the refusal of the regime to disown the commune system. Even in the USSR, which is almost 100 percent "collectivized," the small private plots (within the collectives) on which farmers produce agricultural commodities and sell them for personal profit in the collective farm markets, account for sizeable amounts of total USSR food production. In addition, the government has promised private plots to the farmers employed on the state farms. One must conclude that much of the agriculture which the government lists as collectivized, in fact is private. The question might honestly be asked, how "collective" is collectivized agriculture, even in the USSR?

Available evidence from the communist states strongly points toward two conclusions concerning collectivization. First, it has had to be forced on the farmers and even then it has on occasion been strongly resisted. Second, it seems inferior to private farming in efficiency of output. Moreover, trends toward more private farming (in Poland, Yugoslavia, perhaps even China and the USSR) point to the possible atrophy of collectivization within the communist states in the future.

Economic administrative reforms in the USSR, the Eastern European communist states, and China have attacked inappropriate organization as well as excesses in bureaucratic administration of the economy. Attempted solutions have included decentralizing managerial decision-making by granting more authority to local administrators, say, on the factory level (most publicized in this respect are the so-called Liberman Proposals, introduced in the USSR, which call for greater responsibility and power for lower-level managers, whose effectiveness will be measured more and more by the level of profit a given enterprise can earn). While these changes are being introduced into several of the Eastern European states as well as the USSR, one trend in all of Eastern Europe is to evaluate more critically the Soviet experience and concentrate on evolving more suitable national patterns for economic development in each country rather than following too closely the Soviet format. The other main thrust of economic reforms in the USSR and Eastern Europe is in the area of simplification and rationalization of the national economic plan. Increasingly, economists in communist states point to the need for greater realism, logic, and flexibility in preparation of and in executing the plan.

In a few of the states (the GDR, Yugoslavia, Poland, Hungary), the private sector has been expanding in the crafts and the service industries. Here, too, a trend seems observable (particularly if one adds the growth of private farming in these countries) toward a long-range increase in the private sector *vis-à-vis* the public, "socialistic" sector. Expectations should be for more moves in this direction in the future as the communist regimes realize the limitations of too severe restrictions against private economic structures and the advantages to be gained from at least piecemeal private ownership.

In Yugoslavia, additional reforms of bureaucracy have included abolition of central economic ministries, resulting in the most extensive decentralization in management of any communist state. To this reform has been added that of establishing workers' councils in factories to enable employees actually to participate in some features of factory management. As Yugoslavia has been a leader in other areas of economic reform (decentralization, plan simplification, private enterprise), one might anticipate that other communist states will adopt the Yugoslav reforms of abolishing central ministries and establishing workers' councils.

This chapter's hypothesis, calling for the transformation of an economy under communism into a socialist economy, is fairly well verified by communist practice. Only in some light and service industries in a few of these states, and in agriculture in Poland and Yugoslavia, are there notable exceptions to the rule of nationalizing economic institutions.

NOTES

1. In Bornstein's view, in practice the CPSU has not relied heavily on ideology with respect to Soviet economics. It has used ideology to "authenticate" and "mask" its actions rather than to guide them. "The more the Soviet economy changes under the pressure of new conditions and new ideas, the more the party needs ideological explanations of continuity, consistency, and legitimacy." See Morris Bornstein, "Ideology and the Soviet Economy," *Soviet Studies,* July, 1966, p. 80.

2. Ward lists the two key elements of social ownership of production in industry and trade, and state control of the rates and directions of economic change. Benjamin N. Ward, *The Socialist Economy: A Study of Organizational Alternatives* (New York: Random House, 1967), p. 7. For Sherman, "pure communism" is any economy with public ownership, central planning, and central commands to producers, but no wages and no prices. Howard J. Sherman, "The Economics of Pure Communism," *Soviet Studies,* July, 1970, p. 25.

3. Some confusion can be avoided by referring to these communist states of the USSR, Eastern Europe, and Asia simply as communist rather than socialist.

4. See Nicolas Spulber, *The Soviet Economy* (New York: W. W. Norton, 1962), pp. 160 ff., and *Soviet Financial System* (Moscow: Progress Publishers, 1966), pp. 62–69, 306–10.

5. See, for example, A. Doak Barnett, *Cadres, Bureaucracy, and Political Power in Communist China* (New York: Columbia University Press, 1967), pp. 293–94; Nicolas Spulber, *The Economics of Communist Eastern Europe* (New York: John Wiley, 1957), pp. 99 ff; Stanislaw Wellisz, *The Economics of the Soviet Bloc* (New York: McGraw-Hill, 1964), p. 2.

6. J. F. Brown, *The New Eastern Europe: Khrushchev and After* (New York: Praeger, 1966), p. 105; Deborah D. Milenkovitch, in *East Europe*, July, 1969, p. 13.

7. Yu. N. Belyaev, *Sblizhenie Urovney Ekonomicheskogo Razvitiya Sotsialisticheskikh Stran* (Moscow, 1967), p. 61; *Ekonomika Sotsialisticheskikh Stran v. Tsifrakh, 1965* (Moscow, 1966), pp. 39, 75, 109, 132, 152, 226; *Soviet Handbook* (London, 1959), p. 18.

8. *Planovoe Khozyaystvo*, no. 1 (January, 1966), p. 79.

9. A primary function of plan-making is to increase the knowledge that the various parts of an organization possess about their environment. Ward, *op. cit.* (above, n. 2), p. 73, 74.

10. See Wellisz, *op. cit.* (above, n. 5), p. 99.

11. Stanley Zyzniewski, in *Eastern Europe in the Sixties*, Stephen Fischer-Galati, ed. (New York: Praeger, 1963), p. 86.

12. Michael Kaser, *Comecon: Integration Problems of the Planned Economics* (London: Oxford University Press, 1965), p. 250.

13. Cited in M. C. Kaser, ed., *Economic Development for Eastern Europe* (New York: Macmillan, 1968), p. 12.

14. Kaser, *Comecon* (above, n. 12), p. 26.

15. Entrepreneurship is the "overriding motive force of Communist rule: that means that the chief aim (or, perhaps, the chief effect) of communism is perhaps the promotion of industrialization." Alfred G. Meyer, "The Comparative Study of Communist Political Systems," *Slavic Review*, March, 1967, p. 6.

16. Charles K. Wilbur, *The Soviet Model and Underdeveloped Countries* (Chapel Hill: University of North Carolina Press, 1969), pp. 76–77.

17. Even the highly industrialized GDR and Czechoslovakia, blindly mimicking the Soviet model, acted on the assumption that they were as underdeveloped as Bulgaria or Rumania. J. F. Brown, *op. cit.* (above, n. 6), p. 77.

18. Spulber, *The Economics of Communist Eastern Europe* (above, n. 5), p. 303.

19. Donald W. Treadgold, ed., *Soviet and Chinese Communism: Similarities and Differences* (Seattle: University of Washington Press, 1967), pp. 334, 340.

20. *Ekonomika Sotsialisticheskikh Stran v Tsifrakh*, p. 156.

21. Cited in Kaser, *Economic Development for Eastern Europe* (above, n. 13), p. 8.

22. See William Kaye, "The Economy of North Vietnam," in *North Vietnam Today*, P. J. Honey, ed. (New York: Praeger, 1962), p. 106.

23. Maurice Ernst, "Postwar Economic Growth in Eastern Europe," in *New Currents in Soviet-type Economics*, George R. Feiwel, ed. (Scranton: International Textbook Company, 1968), p. 84.

24. Other information on per capita income and per capita industrial output from Western sources shows a fairly strong correlation with the rank order set forth in these five groups. See David Simpson in *Scientific American*, November, 1968, pp. 30–31; and Harry G. Shaffer in *East Europe*, November, 1970, p. 24.

25. Brown, *op. cit.* (above, n. 6), pp. 134–36.

26. Theodore H. E. Chen, *The Chinese Communist Regime: Documents and Commentary* (New York: Praeger, 1967), p. 189.

27. George G. S. Murphy, *Soviet Mongolia: A Study of the Oldest Satellite* (Berkeley: University of California Press, 1966), pp. 157–58.

28. Hoang Van Chi in *Aspects of Modern Communism*, Richard F. Staar, ed. (Columbia: University of South Carolina Press, 1968), pp. 350–52. By the end of 1961, allegedly 99% of total value of agriculture production came from cooperatives. Bernard B. Fall, *The Two Viet-Nams* (New York: Praeger, 1963), p. 161.

29. Lazar Volin, in *Comparative Economic Systems: Models and Cases*, Morris Bornstein, ed. (Homewood: Richard D. Irwin, 1965), pp. 341–42.

30. Hansjakob Stehle, *The Independent Satellite, Society and Politics in Poland Since 1945* (New York: Praeger, 1965), p. 134.

31. Jean Edward Smith, *Germany Beyond the Wall, People, Politics, and Prosperity* (Boston: Little, Brown, 1967), p. 79.

32. *Ibid.*, p. 118.

33. *New York Times*, September 30, 1970.

34. Michael Gamarnikow, *Economic Reforms in Eastern Europe* (Detroit: Wayne State University Press, 1968), p. 171. The 16.1% figure differs from the Soviet source in n. 23, above.

35. See Wilbur, *op. cit.* (above, n. 16), pp. 30, 39.

36. Gamarnikow, *op. cit.*, p. 127. In Lowenthal's words, planned revolution from above leads to recurrent conflict with unplanned, spontaneous evolution from below. Richard Lowenthal, "Development vs. Utopia in Communist Policy," in *Change in Communist Systems*, Chalmers Johnson, ed. (Stanford: Stanford University Press, 1970), p. 109.

37. Cf. Gregory Grossman, "Economic Reform: The Interplay of Economics and Politics," in *The Future of Communism in Europe*, R. V. Burks, ed. (Detroit: Wayne State University Press, 1968), p. 110.

38. See Ivan T. Berend of the Hungarian Academy of Sciences, in *East European Quarterly*, March, 1968, pp. 83–84.

39. John M. Montias, in Feiwel, *op. cit.* (above, n. 23), pp. 590–91.

40. This is not entirely true in either Hungary, with respect to Nagy's

New Course in 1953, or in Yugoslavia, with respect to workers' councils and managerial decentralization. Hungary's New Course, inaugurated by Premier Imre Nagy in mid-1953, de-emphasized the crash program of building heavy industry, increased allocations for the light and food industry, made collectivization of agriculture voluntary, and liberalized the labor code.

41. *Kommunist*, no. 8 (May, 1966), pp. 95–96; *Izvestiya*, October 30, 1966. More properly, these reforms might be termed the "Kharkov system," as emanating from Kharkov University economists, one of whom is Liberman. See the discussion in Jere L. Felker, *Soviet Economic Controversies* (Cambridge: The M.I.T. Press, 1966), pp. 58–59.

42. Paul Lendvai, *Eagles in Cobwebs: Nationalism and Communism in the Balkans* (Garden City: Doubleday, 1969), pp. 254–55. Brown cites Bulgarian reforms of decentralization; use of profit motive; wages tied to production; a full use of such economic levers as prices, credit, interest, and taxes—indicating that Bulgarian economic reforms are among the most advanced in Eastern Europe, ranking with those of Czechoslovakia and Hungary. See J. F. Brown, "Reforms in Bulgaria," *Problems of Communism,* May-June, 1966, pp. 20–21.

43. See Brown, *The New Eastern Europe, ibid.* (above, n. 6), pp. 83, 88–89; and *Eastern European Economics,* Spring, 1967, pp. 4–7.

44. George J. Staller, "Czechoslovakia: The New Model of Planning and Management," *American Economic Review,* May, 1968, p. 560.

45. *Eastern European Economics,* Winter, 1967–68, pp. 19–20.

46. Michael Gamarnikow, "The Polish Economy in Transition," *Problems of Communism,* January-February, 1970.

47. Brown, *op. cit.* (above, n. 6), p. 116.

48. Chen, *op. cit.* (above, n. 26), p. 195.

49. Chu-yuan Cheng, in Staar, *op. cit.* (above, n. 28), p. 228.

50. Ward argues that an organization has become centralized with respect to authority if there is an increase in the range of alternatives the authorities can impose on subordinates. Ward, *op. cit.* (above, n. 2), p. 7. A great deal of economic reform focuses on decentralization of the outmoded overcentralized model of an earlier stage of communist economic management. There is only one difficulty with the old model, in the view of Gamarnikow: it worked poorly once the economy got beyond the state of absolute scarcities. Gamarnikow, *op. cit.* (above, n. 34), p. 97. As an economy becomes more complex, it is more difficult to make rational decisions centrally.

51. Staller, *op. cit.* (above, n. 44), p. 560.

52. Brown, *op. cit.* (above, n. 6), pp. 100–102.

53. See Smith, *op. cit.* (above, n. 31), p. 81; and Dorothy Miller and Harry G. Trent, "Economic Reforms in East Germany," in Feiwel, *op. cit.* (above, n. 23), p. 550.

54. Brown, *op. cit.* (above, n. 6), pp. 105–106.

55. From Staar, *op. cit.* (above, n. 28), p. 145.

56. *New York Times,* July 20, 1970.

57. O. Kyn (of Charles University, Prague), in Kaser, *Economic Development for Eastern Europe* (above, n. 13), p. 198. Reforms in Rumania generally have centered on independence from the USSR, development of a diversified modern industry, and heavy reliance on Western technology and trade. George Gross in Feiwel, *op. cit.*, p. 566.

58. Gamarnikow, *op. cit.* (above, n. 34), pp. 63, 91–92.

59. B. Ward, "Political Power and Economic Change in Yugoslavia," *American Economic Review*, May, 1968, p. 572.

60. Gamarnikow, *op. cit.* (above, n. 34), p. 157.

61. Morris Bornstein, ed., *Comparative Economic Systems* (above, n. 29), p. 78. By opting for a commodity economy, in Tito's words, we have not renounced planning, but accept it as a necessity at the present level of development. See *Socialist Thought and Practice*, January-March, 1969, p. 32.

62. Gamarnikow, *op. cit.* (above, n. 34), pp. 175–76.

63. Brown, *op. cit.* (above, n. 6), pp. 118–122.

64. *New York Times*, April 30, 1968.

65. *Hungary-State Pocketbook* (Budapest, 1963), p. 54.

66. *Statistical Pocketbook of Hungary* (Budapest, 1966), p. 114. Also, in Hungary, almost 50% of all repairs and related services are covered by small private craftsmen. *ABSEES*, July, 1970, p. 202.

67. See Smith, *op. cit.* (above, 31), p. 102.

68. John Dornberg, *The Other Germany* (New York: Doubleday and Company, 1968), p. 149.

69. See the discussion in Oskar Lange, "The Role of Planning in Socialist Economy," in Bornstein, *op. cit.* (above, n. 29), p. 201.

70. See *ABSEES*, October, 1970, p. 213.

5

Popular Participation in Communist Political Systems

A desirable if not essential ingredient of successful modern political systems is a rather deep sense of popular participation by citizens in the authoritative outputs for the society.[1] This participation is called for not only by democratic ideology, but also by the ideologies of modernizing political movements. Indeed, the goal of popular government and democratic rule is one toward which all governments in the twentieth century supposedly are heading. Thus, in addition to Western democracies' claiming widespread popular participation, dictatorships often make similar claims, as do one-party states and developing nations.

Fact and fiction are intertwined, of course, in the realization of popular participation for any type of political system. As a process participation can take many forms: direct, indirect, compulsory, volunteer, physical, psychological, dynamic, symbolic. What may be of key importance in the legitimation of a political system, though, is for a large majority of citizens within a given nation to *believe* that wide-scale participation in political decision-making exists, or at the least is potentially available. This can explain the firm convictions held by citizens of many nations that their political systems are both participatory and democratic, even though to outside observers such may not appear to be the case. Participation, for Almond and Powell, commonly has to do with rapid increases in the volume and intensity of demands for sharing in political decision-making by groups and strata within the society.[2] Political participation itself is defined by Sharlet simply as political behavior relevant to the functional inputs of the policy-making process.[3]

Communist ideology highlights the Marxian goal of workers ruling themselves through mass participation in the daily business of politics and government. The attainment of this objective is, of course, the primary argument used by communists for bringing communism into being as a political system in areas where they believe such mass participation is absent. The fourth point in the Marxist-Leninist Model elaborated in the first chapter is to provide a structure for popular-worker rule of the political system, including a legislature, public courts, and mass organizations. Thus, *hypothesis 4* states that a communist political system organizes structures for popular participation and achieves viable worker rule through these structures.

While the long-run objective of popular participation in communist systems is to fulfill the ideological requirement of Marxism-Leninism, a more immediate short-run purpose is to build a solid base of support among citizens which thereby will legitimize political control for the ruling communist party. If a citizen can be brought into active participation in the tasks of the political system, and if he can agree to his own officially assigned role within that system, then this can be interpreted by both citizen and government as giving approval to the regime; it even means that the citizen assumes a certain responsibility for the regime. By these actions the communist-party leadership fully expects that its self-appointed rule is authenticated and made legitimate.

Complementing this objective is the belief, generally held by Marxists, that human nature as reflected in man's behavior can be manipulated, guided, and transformed to permit molding of ideal participant-citizen subjects. Thus, man is perfectible, and if the economic organization of society is suitable (Marxian), then nothing stands in the way of man being in harmony with his society generally, and with his political rulers specifically.

All of this requires a social transformation, however. This is one meaning of a communist revolution—a turnover of obsolete, restrictive social patterns. To begin with the family, communists seek to end traditional customs of economic motives for marriage, of patriarchal and authoritarian family structures, inequality of women and abuse of children.

Women's rights have improved measurably in the Soviet Union compared with old Russia in the areas of higher education, occupations, and law. The old custom of child brides in the Central Asian republics of the Soviet Union, for example, was declared illegal in the 1920's. Even prior to this, though, new laws on marriage and the family were adopted in 1917 and 1918. By 1960, the percentages of women employed in the Soviet economy included 45% of the work force in industry, 41% in agriculture, 85% in health services, 69% in education and science, and 51% in public administration. Comparable figures for 1929 are 28% in industry, 28% in agriculture, 65% in health services, 54% in education and science, and 19% in administration.[4] Women are a long way from winning equal rights in higher governmental and political circles, however. Women rarely achieve high communist party office in the Soviet Union (one woman served on the Politburo during part of Khrushchev's leadership).[5]

In China, where close family-centered society existed for centuries, the communists after 1949 introduced a number of changes related to equal rights for women. Arranged marriages officially were abolished, as were both prostitution and concubinage. Monogamy became the rule, with women receiving the rights to divorce their husbands. In addition, wages were thereafter paid directly to working women, instead of to their husbands.[6] In Mongolia and North Korea, following the Chinese communist example, women were granted equality after the communists came to power in those states. By 1967, reportedly, one-half of all employed persons in North Korea were women.[7] Increased women's rights illustrate the communist approach to the family and to society generally.

Young people in communist states are being politically socialized early—chiefly through their schools and youth groups—so that they will adopt national, patriotic, and communist attitudes. Education under the communists involves many more citizens, both young and old, formally and informally, than was the case during the pre-communist period. Education is used both to end illiteracy and to train the population in modern communist life.[8] Accordingly it emphasizes, apart from Marxian indoctrination, greater objectivity in science and technology than was present prior to communism.

In this social revolution religion has been attacked, downgraded, and seriously weakened in virtually all of the communist states (the notable exceptions are Hungary and Poland, where the church has continued to survive with some strength). Atheism, of course, is endorsed officially by all communist leaders with the goal, an end to what they view as backward and obsolete mysticism which inhibits a society's progress toward modernity.

The transformation of society under communism, then, includes a change in old family structures, greater emphasis on politically socializing young people, expansion and reform of the educational system, and attempts to curtail religious beliefs. All of this points toward a "new" type of society. Consequently, there is to be, in the view of communist leaders, a mass participation of all citizens in mobilizing and communizing their nation. In the process, of course, many individuals have suffered considerable hardship—such as being denounced as reactionary by one's own relatives, imprisoned, and even, on occasion, executed for old beliefs. Apart from having their religious practices curbed, individuals also have suffered disruption of their nuclear family life. Nevertheless, communist leaders argue that in the long run such social revolutions will improve society. Through it all, the main technique relied upon by these leaders is to emphasize community ("collective") attitudes over individual desires. This is to be achieved through mass citizen participation in building the new communist society.

Citizen participation then is but a part of a larger process of political mobilization; it involves persuading and directing a national community into a planned and coordinated effort toward meeting definite goals of modernization. All of this demands great societal commitment, including a large measure of individual and collective sacrifice. As a result, citizens are organized into groups, movements, associations, and committees. That this citizen participation is directed by the communist party only testifies (for the communist leader) to the inevitable and desirable connection between politics and the society at large.[9]

ROLE OF THE COMMUNIST PARTY

The communist party itself plays several roles toward stimulating popular participation; one of these is by opening up enrollment into its ranks, theoretically at least, to all citizens of the nation. Any member of the society supposedly can become a participant-member in the ruling party. By so doing eventually he may even become involved in policy-making and policy execution at the most important levels of the political hierarchy. No matter that actual entrance into party membership may on occasion be restricted by various barriers (such as quotas or given occupations). What matters, from the standpoint of the party leaders, is the wide-scale popular belief that the ruling party remains open potentially to all of the nation's citizens. In this way the party is portrayed as a popular, participant organization.

Once in the party, the member takes part in elections for party officials and in some decision-making, at least on a local if not a regional level. If the individual member feels that he is participating in party rule, then the regime's objectives are served. In addition, rules of the Soviet Communist party authorize individual members to question high party officials on any party matter. In the early 1960's in Poland lists of candidates for elections to local party committees (as usual, drawn up by higher party officials) were supplemented by local party meetings, which in turn were instructed to include at least 25 percent more candidates than the original list. Secret voting subsequently removed some of the former party officials from office.[10]

An important function of communist-party members in the routine fulfillment of their responsibilities is that of seeing to political socialization for the system as a whole. This building of patriotism among the citizenry is a regularly assigned and continuous responsibility for all party members. If most of the nation's citizens can be persuaded to accept the national goals, policies, myths, and, of course, the leadership group of the communist party, then they are effectively supporting the system. The main focus of popular participation, in fact, centers on political socialization, in which all citizens are expected to become involved in the society in an active, supportive role.[11]

Political socialization via the mechanism of the communist party has included civic education for children, adults, specialized, and mass organizations. In schools, for example, the education includes anticapitalist indoctrination, the theory of Marxism-Leninism, political economy, the advantages of socialism and communism, and the particular virtues and great accomplishments of the nation since it began functioning under a communist party. In two years of "Staatsburgerkunde, Klasse 9 and 10" in the GDR in the early 1960's, eighty-nine hours of class time were devoted to political socialization.[12] During the first four years of university education in the Soviet Union, approximately one-fifth of the student's classroom time is occupied with political socialization.[13]

Citizens in communist systems express their demands most effectively through the officials and the apparatus of the communist party. From the leadership's point of view, the party is the most important as well as the final articulator of "valid" demands. While the party uses numerous agents (government bureaucracy, trade unions, economic administrators, mass organizations) to sort out and articulate these many demands of both citizen and special interest, the party apparatus still is viewed by everyone in the system as the main arbiter of conflicting demands. Moreover, the party seeks out citizen complaints, suggestions, and recommendations, hoping thereby to articulate at least some of the popular desires and wishes. All of the media in the Soviet Union, including editorial boards of broadcasting stations, have letter departments whose staffs are supposed to record the letters received, to which organization the complaint is forwarded, and what action is taken on the complaint—all of this information to be given to the letter writer.[14]

A citizen has but to gain the support of communist-party officials to be able to see his demands given attention. No other organization is as important for this purpose as is the communist party. Nevertheless, the party is not the only channel for expressing citizen desires. The position of supremacy enjoyed by the party, while not being challenged, is being partially eroded to the point where it is being forced to share the articulating function with other organizations, among the more important of these, the national legislature.

FORMAL REPRESENTATIVE STRUCTURES

A form of popular referendum has been used in the USSR, Albania, Czechoslovakia, Poland, Rumania, and Yugoslavia, where public opinion regarding certain proposed laws is solicited prior to the enactment of the laws. Accordingly, suggestions have been forthcoming from various social, industrial, and professional organizations. Prior to the passage of a pensions act in the USSR, for instance, such preliminary discussions gave rise to more than 13,000 suggestions from Soviet citizens. The argument was made, in this situation, that nationwide discussions add a new dimension to popular democracy.[15] A draft law on marriage and the family was also prepared by several commissions of the national legislature and circulated in the USSR for general comment and discussion prior to enactment of the draft into law. According to a press account, many people contributed to preparing the law—including scientists, teachers, doctors, trade union representatives, the Young Communist League, and employees of the courts and prosecutors' offices. Moreover, the draft law was published in a number of enterprises, on state and collective farms, and in educational institutions.[16] To take another example, there were in the GDR in 1956, 1,445 popular suggestions concerning a widely circulated draft law on local organs of government.[17] Table 9 lists some communist states and popular suggestions offered concerning the proposed draft constitutions in those states.[18] What is missing from the table, for one to estimate the impact of the popular referenda, are data on the extent and types of critical comments offered and, especially, those accepted by the authors of the legislation. Therefore, analysis of the efficacy of such participation is necessarily quite restricted.

Communist ideology implies that representation under communism is direct, unlike the indirect representation known in parliamentary systems. Under communism people take possession of state power (in Ionescu's words)—legislating, executing, and judging so that a formal, hence artificial, separation of powers is unnecessary.[19]

TABLE 9
Discussions of Draft Constitutions

State	Period of National Discussions	No. of Meetings	Partici- pants in Meetings	No. Making Suggestions & No. of Suggestions	No. of Amend- ments Accepted
Bulgaria	10/46–5/47	——	——	——	74
Czechoslovakia	4–7/60	47,400	4 mill.+	732,800 individuals 19,000 suggestions	50+
GDR	10/48–5/49	9,000	——	500 suggestions	52
Hungary	8/49	——	——	——	5
Mongolia	6–7/60	1,166	208,000	2,902 individuals	47
Poland	1–4/52	200,000+	11.5 mill.	1,800,000 individuals	91
Rumania	7–9/52	——	10 mill.+	18,836 suggestions	51
Yugoslavia	9/62–2/63	——	6 mill.+	300,000 individuals	—

Political representation is referred to by a Polish writer as a process of mutual interaction between governmental policy and popular attitudes resulting in a similarity, a consensus. This requires the government to open all possible channels of interaction between people and policies in order to achieve a minimum degree of popular consensus on governmental policy.[20] The interaction does not mean identity of views between government and the electorate, however. In the national interest, the government may have to rule against the "mood of popular opinion," that is, against "irrational" popular demands.[21]

Legislatures. Slowly and incrementally legislatures in some communist states are assuming more importance as articulators of popular demands. There are three reasons for this. First, legislatures have for some time been organized and visible—acting as magnets to attract citizen requests, demands, and complaints which from time to time come their way. The formality of legislatures giving their consent to party-executive proposals, thereby legitimizing these proposals, places these legislators increasingly in a strategic position to articulate, and perhaps in the future even aggregate citizen needs and desires. Thus, as legislatures continue to work closely with the ruling groups, they begin to acquire a position from which they may be able to start bargaining with the rulers. Here the legislators may begin to trade continued support for the rulers for political concessions from them. This has, of course, occurred in Western legislatures and it may now be taking place in the Soviet legislature.

A second reason for the increasing importance of communist legislatures is that legislative functions are constitutionally based; as the people's official representatives they also are paid lip service by the party. Communist legislatures are cited as sovereign expressions of legislative and executive functions through which the "working classes are guaranteed participation in the administration of the state."[22] Thus, over the long run legislators are tempted to act more and more as viable representatives of the people, acting both from the legal-constitutional justification and, indirectly, in response to party propaganda. The communist party is hard pressed to justify its actions of bypassing and neglecting the authority of the legislature. It thus becomes ever more embarrassing for party leaders to ignore this branch of government in the actual decision-making processes. Pressure builds on the regime to match ruling practice with ruling myth and to accord the legislature more of a voice in political rule.

A third reason for increasing importance is that communist parties are falling short of satisfying adequately the popular demands made on the political system. The demands are too many and citizens articulate them more effectively than they once did. The effect is to encourage parties to use the legislatures as convenient channels to handle the overload of demands.[23]

Examples of the increased importance of communist legislatures can be found in Poland, Yugoslavia, and Hungary. The Polish legislature (*Sejm*) gained a measure of independence from strict party dominance in the 1950's, at which time the Yugoslav legislature (*Skupcina*) was revealing internal factions made up of various interest groups. However, more and more of the draft laws and plans originated in the Yugoslav Legislative Assembly in the 1960's and those introduced by the government occasionally were subjected to heavy amendments.[24] The draft law of the 1965 economic plan for

Yugoslavia frequently was amended by two of the legislature's five chambers. The outcome, finally, was legislative adoption of the twelfth revised version of the plan.[25] In another example, in the November, 1965, session of the Hungarian Legislature, a reply by the Minister of Heavy Industry to a query from the legislature was rejected by that body.[26]

A most daring posture taken by a communist legislature was to be seen in Czechoslovakia following the Soviet invasion of 1968. In November of that year the Executive Committee of the legislature asked the government to take adequate measures to stop circulation of a Soviet-sponsored propaganda newspaper then being distributed in Czechoslovakia. This same Executive Committee also inquired of the government as to the legality of other Soviet-backed governmental actions. Another committee, along with some of the Assembly deputies, raised points concerning Soviet control in general.[27] This legislative defiance of the Soviet invading force presumably ended shortly thereafter.

Meanwhile, demands for the rehabilitation of the legislatures were being made both in Hungary and in the GDR.[28] Regime spokesmen in Hungary suggested that the legislature become a forum for preparing legislation, for discussing important problems, and even for holding investigations.[29] In 1966 the Hungarian leaders called for the role of the legislature to be measurably upgraded. Deputies to the National Assembly were urged to assert all of their rights and prerogatives in order to permit legislative "control" over the government. One communist party secretary pointed to the necessity for the government to report to the legislature. The deputy's voice, the secretary continued, "is the master's voice—the voice of the electorate, that is, the people."[30] For the 1971 parliamentary elections in Hungary, new laws made it easier to nominate candidates and to provide contests for some of the seats.

In Bulgaria, too, there has been a call for strengthening the role of representative bodies (the People's Assembly and local councils) and for greater control by the People's Assembly over the executive and administrative organs of the government.[31] There have been calls by Soviet academicians as well, urging an increased role in decision-making for the Soviet legislature. These have followed in part from a gradual expansion in this legislature's functions as reviewer of the government's annual budget and economic plan.

In still another example of increasing importance for legislatures, the Rumanian national legislature voted itself additional functions, one of which is to receive reports on a regular basis from the head of the government. Moreover, every government minister was to be responsible directly to the legislature.[32]

With the possible exception of Yugoslavia's *Skupcina*, the most viable of communist legislatures has been the Polish *Sejm*. In 1959 a government bill calling for a passport law was amended by the *Sejm*, rejected three times, and finally approved after including additional rights of citizens to appeal a government refusal to grant a passport.[33] A government proposal for a new criminal code was approved by the *Sejm* only after the code was heavily amended.[34] Of 174 laws passed by the *Sejm* in the period 1957–61, only 34 were adopted without amendments.[35] The *Sejm* also has seen negative voting by some of its members, a rather unusual occurrence in communist parliaments. Some of the voting, however, was by the small, openly independent group of Catholic deputies (called the Znak Circle; see p. 135 in the legislature.

In any dynamic legislature there are active and responsible committees working on a large number of legislative matters. Thus, the *Sejm* committees were increased in number from seven to nineteen in 1957. Apparently in these committee meetings pending legislation at times is vigorously debated; on occasion governmental ministers and their representatives are sharply questioned in the committee sessions, and the committees are active in the interim period between sessions of the *Sejm*. In 1961, for example, there were fifty-three committee meetings on the budget at which time about one hundred amendments were proposed.[36]

By the early 1970's the legislature as an articulator of popular demands in communist states had not yet become significantly important. Traditionally, communist legislatures have been "rubber stamp" bodies which serve as simple instruments by which policies and programs of the party leadership are given quick and automatic ratification. In the process there normally is neither dissension nor opposition to the party leadership. This format, as discussed above, may now be changing. The legislature is becoming visible as an institution through which popular participation in the political system is rising. The experience of heightened legislative vigor in

Poland and Yugoslavia—and to a lesser degree in Hungary and Czechoslovakia—in the period from the late 1950's through the late 1960's, gives testimony to the promise which might be held out for increased popular influence on the communist political system through its legislature. This trend in Eastern Europe is matched in the Soviet Union, which has seen—particularly since 1966, when new, enlarged committees of the legislature were formed—a rise in the level of decision-making authority of its legislature *vis-à-vis* the government and the communist party. Moreover, since the late 1950's, individual legislators had been participating (mainly through the committees) in minor decision-making, such as increasing the national budget and careful examining of the annual economic plan prior to its adoption by the legislature; legislators also had begun submitting recommendations on legislation and administrative performance to the Council of Ministers. More significant still—as a mark of the heightened respect which the party leadership had acquired for a legislature that was progressively adding to its influence within the overall Soviet political system—was the action of the Central Committee of the CPSU in 1966, which increased its representation on the executive Presidium of the legislature from its own membership from six to twenty-two Central Committee members.[37]

Elections.   Elections to communist legislatures are used by ruling communist parties as nationwide plebiscites for the endorsement of the party's programs and policies. The elections are very rarely used as contests for office between candidates, and are never used to oppose the communist party. The widely adopted Soviet format is for the overwhelming majority of voters to elect the officially (communist-party) supported list, containing one candidate per seat to be filled. The usual choice open to the individual voter is to vote either for or against this one list. In certain communist countries some changes in this format have occurred since the mid-1960's, however.

As part of the general reforms in Czechoslovakia in 1967, terms of deputies for the National Assembly were extended from four to six years. Multi-candidate elections were authorized, although all candidates still were to receive endorsement from the party-dominated National Front.[38] In 1966, one writer in Slovakia recommended that the legislature, as the nation's main representative body, must formulate a political line (independent of the communist party); and deputies must be elected on a basis of free choice by the voter.[39]

Apart from these Czechoslovak adaptations and suggestions, which flowered briefly during the liberalization period in the late 1960's, the most apparent exception to the typical communist electoral format is found, again, in Yugoslavia. The trend in that state is for multi-candidate nominations. Furthermore, Yugoslav law forbids the re-election of candidates to successive terms of public office.[40] In the 1967 parliamentary elections in Yugoslavia, for instance, there were electoral contests in eighty-six districts. In these districts twenty-four of the candidates who had been endorsed by the Communist League were defeated. In the Republic of Slovenia, League-endorsed nominees lost nine of the twenty-one contests in which they were running.[41] For the five chambers of the national legislature in these elections there were 656 candidates running for 322 seats. Similar multi-candidacies were reported for seats in the republican assemblies.[42] In Hungary in 1967 voters also faced a choice of alternate candidates in Budapest's sixty-six parliamentary districts and in several other counties. In the 1971 parliamentary elections there were contests in 49 of the 352 seats.[43]

In North Vietnam, elections serve the socializing function of building grassroots support for the political system, as they do in the communist countries of Eastern Europe, but they also carry out an additional function. Regular electoral turnover of office holders encourages training and indoctrination of large numbers of the rural population. This complements an institutionalization of change carried out through semipermanent electioneering in the villages. Peasants thereby become acquainted with dynamic change in local life and with nation-building as well as with national policies. The national leadership anticipates that elections will aid peasants in breaking with the past and as a result the peasants will more readily accept modernizing policies.[44] In the 1971 general election for a new National Assembly, 529 candidates were running for 420 seats; all but seven of the 529 were officially endorsed by the Fatherland Front.[45] In the process, popular participation in the political system of North Vietnam has been enhanced through the modernizing effects of elections.

Local assemblies. Local legislative assemblies are even more important than the national legislature as focal points around which popular demands are made known in communist societies. A Polish scholar contrasts People's Councils in Poland with local government in the West in an attempt to illustrate the advantages of popular participation under communism. While local governments in the West are restricted to a narrow range of functions, he argues, People's Councils suffer no such limitations and have, in fact, had their powers increased by legislation in 1958 and 1963. Moreover, a close working relationship between the national legislature and the local councils provides opportunities to adjust national plans to particular territorial and local needs.[46]

In the Soviet Union, city governments may well be the most important formal agency through which the average citizen participates in his political system. By the 1960's thousands of citizen demands were coming into formal agencies (boroughs) of the city governments of Moscow and Leningrad. These demands dealt with matters of housing space and repair, food services in stores and restaurants, quality of services to consumers, and health as well as transportation facilities. Moreover, the regime apparently encourages and welcomes such popular demands being brought to agencies of the city government.[47]

The practice of representation under communist systems includes (in Poland) village assemblies of all adults who supposedly participate in local decision-making. Inhabitants of apartments in the various communist states are organized into block committees to supervise administration of the apartments, as well as to help in the orderly upkeep of houses, streets, and open spaces. In addition, there are numerous factory-worker organizations through which workers supposedly influence some aspects of plant management. One Yugoslav writer explained the purpose of a particular governmental reorganization in Yugoslavia as: ". . . the attempt to broaden the scope of political participation and to find a more immediate social basis for institutions and political power. . . . But behind all this there lies a very clear political motive: the transfer of leadership and decision-making in government and management to the organs closest to the citizens which are not as liable as the executive organs to turn their activities into a permanent monopoly."[48] In the GDR, where there may be at least 100,000 elected representatives to local legislative organizations, the twofold purpose is to build wide popular support for the regime and to help execute central governmental policy.[49]

Courts. When communist leaders organize a court system, following the Soviet format, they normally include elected judges (people's assessors) serving for a year's time along with professionally trained and permanently appointed judges. In the USSR two such assessors, along with one professional judge, constitutes the normal court. In the GDR, however, the appointed judiciary as such has been abolished, with all judges and lay jurors elected by national and local legislatures for terms of four years. In Hungary, Poland, Czechoslovakia, and Yugoslavia, on the other hand, judicial administration is entrusted only to professional judges. In Yugoslavia, furthermore, constitutional courts have been given the power of judicial review over virtually all acts of government, including legislation.[50]

In the working plants of the USSR there are also lower-level "comrades' courts," made up of amateur citizen members who handle minor law infractions. In small plants the comrades' courts are composed of five to seven members, and in larger plants from eleven to fifteen members. These courts are elected by the workers; and they are allowed to process minor offenses such as unapproved leaves, late arrivals and early departures from work, drunkenness, and, in general, infractions of working rules. Punishments, like the offenses, are minor. This Soviet structure, again, has its counterpart in the GDR, where there are "conflict" and "arbitration" commissions for lesser crimes.[51] In Poland also there are workers' social courts operating in several cities and, since 1960, in the more important enterprises, although these differ in many respects from the Soviet comrades' courts.[52]

The goal in all of these quasi-courts is a form of direct and quick justice for individuals, as meted out by one's fellow citizens. One result may be that professionalism in court procedure is traded, perhaps, for greater equity, as well as for an opportunity on the part of the accused to accept censure from his colleagues on the job and in the community. Citizen representation in the legal court procedures of his nation (even though the appearance may be more convincing than the reality) is a matter occasionally separable from whether the individual receives "justice" as such. Indeed, it is always debatable, in any system, whether justice equates with popular representation in the courts or elsewhere. What is important for this discussion is whether citizens feel that they enjoy representation somewhere in their legal processes.

Trade unions. Trade unions should be one of the natural avenues of popular participation in any industrialized society. In communist systems, however, unions carry out only minor, non-policy-making functions assigned to them by the party and the government, since no organization is permitted to challenge the policies and decisions of the communist party. The consequent subordination of union activity to the control, even manipulation, of communist-party elite should be embarrassing to communist leaders who claim ideological descendancy from Marxism. Since the early 1920's, when the Soviet trade unions capitulated before the overwhelming political dominance of the communist party, trade unions in communist states have been weak and ineffectual representatives of the claims and demands of industrial workers. By the early 1960's, however, this picture had begun to change in some of the states.

Yugoslavia, again, was a leader. Following submission of the economic plan for 1965 to the Yugoslav trade unions for their prior approval, the unions rejected the first draft of the plan.[53] At the Twenty-first Congress of the Hungarian Trade Unions in 1966, the communist-party chief of Hungary, Janos Kadar, told the Congress that henceforth the unions should have a more important role and authority in society. No longer, he continued, were the unions to serve merely as a transmission belt (Lenin's directive) for the orders of the communist party. Also in 1966, the head of the Hungarian Trade Union Council argued for the unions to assume the stance of "true representative" of organized workers, taking an "independent position" in all areas of economic, social, and cultural life.[54] In July of 1968, Hungarian trade unions vetoed two decrees from the Ministry of Transportation and Telecommunications because the unions were not consulted beforehand. The Ministry then agreed to negotiate with the unions. This was the first time that unions took disputes above the level of the local enterprises, where earlier they had been settled behind closed doors.[55] Presumably this action signaled a greater degree of union independence from the party and government apparatus than had been the case before.

Examples of increasing strength of trade unions were found in other communist states as well. Czechoslovak trade union officials called for their unions to be both independent and voluntary; hopefully workers thereby would become more involved in the plans of their enterprises. In Czechoslovakia unions already have forced changes in draft laws on unemployment and have gained improved safety standards in industry.[56] Even in the Soviet Union, the newspaper of the trade unions (*Trud*) frequently has criticized individual factory trade union committees for not making full use of their rights, for example, in allowing management to dismiss workers without first getting the approval of the respective trade union committee.[57] During the last few years in Turkmenistan, 33 percent of employees dismissed by managers were reinstated to their jobs by the courts because the dismissals did not have the approval of the local trade unions.[58]

One form of worker "participation" in society has been the strike. While all of the East European communist states have suffered workers' strikes, this maneuver has occurred in recent years only in Czechoslovakia, Poland, and Yugoslavia. (In the USSR, there have been occasional reports in the past, however, of striking workers, work stoppages, and general expressions of worker dissatisfaction.)[59] In Yugoslavia, for instance, for a few-year period in the late 1960's, there were recorded 513 strikes involving 72,000 workers.[60] In the Polish workers' riots of December, 1970, protesting an increase in prices of food and clothing accompanied by a complex change in incentive pay, the workers not only protested these policies, but they also attacked trade union headquarters, demanding even a resignation of union leaders. As a result, in addition to the ousting of the communist-party leader Gomulka, party newspapers began criticizing the weakness of the unions. The government promised more independence for unions to defend the rights of workers more vigorously. In some instances mixed management-worker committees bargained with government ministers over wages and for the replacement of plant officials.[61] All of these "concessions" won by Polish workers might yet prove transitory, however, as memory of the riots begins to fade.

The farthest steps toward independence for trade unions, as already suggested, seem to have taken place, expectedly, in Yugoslavia. The national head of the trade unions has stated, for example, that when dealing with personal income of union members, the unions "cannot act as ordinary executors of a fixed planned policy, but must strive to have their point of view adopted by the state administration."[62] Nevertheless, if trade unions have been increasing their authority and responsibility only slightly—with the exceptions noted above—more progress toward representing workers in the political system may well lie in less traditional organizations, specifically in workers' councils.

Workers' councils. Perhaps growing pressures from industrial laborers, together with continuing regime embarrassment over the weaknesses of trade unions, have combined to permit greater involvement of workers in some degree of factory self-management. The structure around which this self-management has focused in Eastern Europe has been the workers' council. The idealized version of workers' councils involves worker control over factories, while the more practical version calls for at least some worker influence in the management of factories and similar installations. While particular versions of the workers' councils arose in Yugoslavia in 1950 and spread into Poland and Hungary by 1956, their origins go back at least into pre-revolutionary Russia.

The St. Petersburg Soviet (council), created in 1905, was made up chiefly of workers and soldiers, its formation and subsequent political activity evidencing a rise in citizen demands for more participation in the tsarist autocracy. Other workers' councils were formed in Russian factories before and during the revolution of 1917. There followed a rather brief period of considerable worker influence on management by way of factory committees (the basic units of the councils). Collective agreements between workers and management were encouraged by a decree of the Soviet government in 1918 which covered hiring and firing, working hours, and wage rates. These early factory committees and councils did exert considerable managerial power in representing workers. By the early 1920's, however, the committees were rendered powerless when they were replaced by trade unions which, in turn, were closely controlled by the communist party, thus ending the experiment of worker control in Russian and Soviet factories.

When Yugoslavia introduced workers' councils into Eastern Europe in 1950, a procedure was worked out under which employees were to manage their factories themselves. In addition, the councils were to perform entrepreneurial decision-making functions. Elected by factory workers, the councils were to determine the commodities to be produced, as well as to decide questions of pricing, selling, scheduling, even the disposal of capital funds. As a result of exercising a number of these powers, including the right (shared with trade unions and economic associations) to hire and fire the directors of factories, the councils' influence on management has been measurable.[63] On occasion, the factory director has been caught between the desires of the workers' councils on one side and what may be thought of as the interests of the state in matters of wage levels or budget cutting on the other side. As a result of these cross-pressures, by 1967 one report noted that 66 percent of all directors were abandoning their positions to find new jobs.[64] Besides such cross-pressures, other limitations on the power and autonomy of the councils have been certain restrictions imposed on the national plan; jealous governmental officials on all levels; trade unions; and, not least, the Communist League itself. The party, even though renamed and de-emphasized, has not given up ruling Yugoslavia—and part of such rule involves retaining significant controls over industrial management. One effect of the Yugoslav experience with workers' councils, however, has been to encourage their adoption, or adoption of a version of them, in several other Eastern European states.

By 1956 workers' councils were being introduced into Poland and Hungary even prior to the October revolts in those states. In 1959 a law on very limited workers' self-government was passed in Poland which provided for worker "conferences" to control and supervise through a council all activities in the factories. While this council appears to have been only advisory, it supposedly approved all plans for the factory as well as issues "directives" for the factory's investment policy.[65] Workers' councils in Hungary during the 1956 revolt managed not only factories, but in some cases city government as well. However, after the communist party regained firm control in both of these states following 1956, such control effectively checkmated the worker power and influence which previously had been exercised through the councils. By late 1957, a postrevolutionary malaise had set in, and the influence and autonomy of workers' councils in Hungary and Poland were noticeably on the decline.

In 1957 the GDR initiated a form of workers' councils which were very restricted in their authority; they were limited in practice to questions of social welfare. In 1961, Czechoslovakia, too, expanded the functions and strengthened the position of its workers' factory committees.[66] The workers' councils in that state then increased in numbers in conformity with the general liberalizations in 1967 and 1968. This was the case to such a degree that the Council of the Skoda Manufacturing Works commissioned a three-man group to advertise, in the name of the Skoda Works Council, for a new general manager to be hired by the Council. Following the Soviet invasion, however, and the resultant clamp-down on all of the liberalizing measures in Czechoslovakia, the functions of the councils were again curtailed.

During the Great Proletarian Cultural Revolution in China, workers took control of some factories, according to an account of one such takeover in the Tsingtao Locomotive and Rolling-Stock Plant in East China: "Power was seized at the plant on January 23, 1967. Then in early April, the revolutionary mass organizations of the plant formed a revolutionary great alliance and set up a federation of proletarian revolutionaries. A little later, a revolutionary committee was established as a provisional organ of power. When the revolutionaries first came into power, a number of liaison members were appointed to take over the leadership of the workshops and groups of workers in the different sections."[67] No additional information is available, however, as to why the "revolutionaries" took power (to run the factories? to insure ideological purity?), nor as to their successes or failures in factory administration.

From the standpoint of popular participation in communist political systems, the experience of workers' councils in the states mentioned appears to have made two contributions. First, there is now a record of some experience, albeit slight, of at least limited worker control—experience which has no doubt led to a greater vitality for trade unions than might have existed without the example set by the councils. Second, local government has been encouraged both to cooperate with councils (and with trade unions) and to supervise their activities. This has the double advantage of strengthening local government while lending greater official sanction to the councils. The most solid achievement of the councils, even though short-lived in some instances, has been to add to the general feeling of an increase in popular participation in these states. In Yugoslavia the councils have gone so far as to replace units of local government and certain agencies of the state administration in such functions as social services, health, insurance, education, culture, and science.[68]

Although the influential period of workers' councils in some of the communist states (Hungary, Poland, USSR) was only a brief one, their long-run contributions to a growth in the idea of self-government, or "direct democracy," may yet become significant. In Yugoslavia, for instance, the regime by the late 1960's was more and more referring to the idea of "direct socialist democracy" as a step in the withering away of the state apparatus. As Zaninovich notes, the Yugoslav system of representation has taken on a strongly functional or interest-group aspect.[69] It does not seem illogical to assume a rub-off effect of both desire for and experience in self-government.

SEMIFORMAL REPRESENTATIVE STRUCTURES

Semiformal popular representation includes both mass organizations (such as national fronts and youth associations) and interest groups (such as the bureaucracy, military, intelligentsia, peasants). Increasingly, citizens in communist states have been turning to some of these more informal structures for the articulation and satisfaction of some of their demands, as these demands remain largely unfulfilled by the formal channels. This development, it would seem, follows naturally when the apparatus of the party and the government has restricted itself chiefly to satisfying the demands of the party elite. It is conceivable, furthermore, that in the absence of open and approved opposition groups—for example, an opposition party—that some of these more informal representational groups within a communist system might become the nuclei around which at least some modest opposition views may be given a form of expression.

Mass organizations. National fronts were the earliest form of communist-sponsored mass organization, arising as coalitions of antirightist and antifascist groups seeking power after World War II. The national fronts are outgrowths of popular fronts, which were unions of socialists and communists striving to gain power for the political left in prewar Europe. Following communist victories after the war, the national fronts continued as large coalitions, now closely directed by the communists; their main purpose became that of mobilizing voters behind the official (communist) list of candidates for election to public office.[70]

The national fronts usually contained a sizeable majority of a nation's adult population, as in Albania, where the Democratic Front included all politically acceptable Albanians, excluding the former "bourgeoisie."[71] The significance of these large national fronts dominated by communists is that they gave the communists a bit of historical legitimacy during the period covering the national-front experience. The communists used this experience to claim justification for their political rule. Even in the new (1968) Constitution of the German Democratic Republic, there is the statement: "In the National Front of Democratic Germany the political parties and mass organizations pool all forces of the people for joint action for the development of socialist society."[72] In addition, specialized organizations are created on occasion in all of the countries which relate to current problems of interest to the regime, such as the League of Nazi Victims in the GDR. Mass organizations in the GDR include the following:

Consumer Cooperatives	German Union of Culture
Democratic Women's Union	National Front
Ernst Thalmann Pioneers	People's Solidarity
Free German Youth	Peasants' Mutual Aid Association
German-Soviet Friendship	Society for Dissemination of
Society	Scientific Knowledge[73]

Front organizations in all communist states follow a pattern of including a large number of more specialized organizations—usually including organizations for youth, women, writers, and cultural groups, as well as paramilitary organizations. In North Korea, for instance, the large Democratic People's Coalition Front included such mass organizations as:

General Federation of Korean Literature and Arts	Korean Democratic Women's Union
General Federation of Trade Unions	Korean Journalists' Union
Korean Buddhist Federation	Korean Red Cross Society
Korean Christian Federation	Korean Students' Committee
Korean Democratic Lawyers' Association	Socialist Working Youth League
	Young Friends' Party[74]

In addition to enrolling functional organizations within the national fronts, communist regimes enroll large numbers of volunteers as agents of mobilization. One borough leader in the city of Moscow claimed that five percent of his borough's population was engaged in a variety of volunteer work: people's militia, comrades' courts, housing repair, libraries, internal passport control, sanitary and cultural activities, food inspection, and even babysitting committees.[75] The GDR regime has claimed that over 100,000 volunteers work in organs of the Workers and Farmers Inspection; 154,000 serve on parents' advisory committees; 189,767 serve on dispute commissions (in large enterprises); 55,000 on arbitration commissions (in residential areas, cooperatives, and in private undertakings); and 48,000 serve as lay judges.[76]

In North Vietnam street committees have been formed to communicate government decisions to the people and to maintain public order and safety. In Hanoi itself, in the early 1960's, there were a reported 4,600 block chiefs and deputy chiefs.[77] In Cuba, committees for the Defense of the Revolution (CDR) were created in 1960 and numbered some 100,000 (in every streetblock of the big cities and in towns, villages, and farms) two years later. The CDR's were to be responsible for supervising local internal security, census, rationing, vaccinations, housing, and political indoctrination.[78]

Youth organizations (groups which range in age from young children up into the mid-twenties) obviously are one of the most important types of mass organization in communist states. They are structured to carry out political socialization among young people. Indeed, youth organizations constitute the main recruitment agencies for bringing new members into the communist party. In Czechoslovakia, the Czechoslovak Union of Youth (CSM) officially represents young people and supposedly helps them find a place for themselves "in the life of a socialist society" by preparing them for jobs and for participation in public activities.[79] In North Korea, members of the Democratic Youth League help local officials with a wide range of tasks, including land reform, conscription, adult education, road repair, elections, and tax collection; and they serve on occasion as auxiliaries to the police, even to the army.[80]

While there are numerous mass organizations in the Soviet Union, their success is limited in part because of poor supervision. Although small-scale volunteer groups help out in law enforcement and civic clean-up campaigns, the task of organizing and maintaining these groups constitutes a measurable drain on the time of local officials. Thus, the volunteer organizations may be as likely to increase the work load of local officials as to reduce it.[81]

It should be possible to gain greater insight into the use to which mass organizations are put in communist political systems if we examine one such system in more depth. A clearer picture might be drawn, also, if the political system is in an earlier stage of development and is one in which mass organizations have been heavily relied upon for political socialization.

Perhaps China has accomplished more than most other communist states in mobilizing its masses, in large part through mass organizations and mass movements. It has done so in a nation which was largely rural; mostly illiterate; and not accustomed to officially sponsored, carefully organized mobilizing efforts carried out nationwide. If the communist regime is successful in mobilizing China's masses, it will have been so in defiance of Chinese customs and history, which have been tied to the traditional family structure.

One of the most serious drawbacks of the pre-communist family structure of Chinese society, a structure which had evolved over centuries, was the deleterious effect it had on the nation's politics. Extreme family orientation (including the extended family, or clan) resulted in deep and widespread nepotism, accompanied by corruption in both official and semiofficial governmental functions; a noted absence of nation-building energy; a lack of modern methods of political and governmental organization and management; and, above all, an inadequately developed popular feeling of nationalism.[82] The Chinese were situated within the confines of a given geographical area, but a deep felt belief in China as a unity, as a collective body, as a nation, simply did not exist in the minds of millions upon millions of Chinese citizens—particularly those living in the rural areas. The second task of the Chinese communists (the first being to gain political power), then, was to begin the imposing effort to create national integration, including psychological nation building with given physical ingredients (population, land, and resources). What the communists faced, therefore, was creating in the minds of individual Chinese the idea of China as a nation, and the idea of *being* Chinese—of a "Chineseness." They had, in brief, to cultivate patriotism and nationalism for the first time in this century in many places where it had not previously existed.[83]

To accomplish this task the communists sought to destroy what they felt to be harmful structures and customs, such as a citizen's primary devotion to his family, great reverence for older citizens (a part of so-called ancestor worship), inferiority of women, and other Confucian inspired stratifications within society.[84] In place of these structures the communists tried to revolutionize Chinese society with such radical measures as land reform, mass literacy campaigns, accent on modern practices in science and technology, and above all an attempted transfer of the citizen's primary loyalty and devotion from the family to the state. Only by making such changes, the communists believed, could a modern system be built which would permit China to take her proper place in the competitive world dominated by large and powerful nation-states.

Perhaps because of this unique history, mass mobilization has received more attention in China than it has in other communist states. From the beginning of communist rule in 1949, mass organizations have been a part of "a style of government execution and administration in movements and drives which have followed upon, overlapped, and coincided with one another in fatiguing succession."[85] Mass movements geared to Mao's faith in the mass line have related to practically all aspects of Chinese communist rule: purges, economic policies, battles with nature, conservation, collectivization, even foreign policies.[86]

Mass mobilization in China began with a battle against illiteracy and has included the opening of new schools, especially numerous technical and engineering institutes[87] (although at the same time a number of universities were closed, and others were amalgamated to put an end to private schools and universities); establishing neighborhood groups called residents' committees; setting up water-work brigades, production brigades, and eventually communes in rural areas; and finally organizing a number of mass organizations, including youth groups, students, women's organizations, and labor unions. Mass organizations have numbered in the dozens, then; and they have related to the affairs of small economic and social units that do not form a part of the formal governmental structure. These organizations are firmly controlled by the Chinese Communist party (CCP); all are ruled from the top of their respective structures (democratic centralism); they possess a well-developed basic-level apparatus; and they perform a "transmission belt" function between the CCP and Chinese citizens.[88]

Complementing the organizations has been a series of programs in which great numbers of the population have been enlisted—such as small-scale steel production in backyard furnaces and the several "anti" programs. In 1950, for example, there was the land reform movement, the marriage law, and the Resist America—Aid Korea Movement. In 1951, there was the Suppression of Counterrevolutionaries Movement, the Three-anti Movement (anti-corruption, anti-waste, and anti-bureaucracy), and the Five-anti Movement (anti-bribery, anti-tax-invasion, anti-theft of state property, anti-cheating on government contracts, and anti-stealing of state economic secrets). Probably every citizen in China, Townsend believes, was involved in at least two or three of these mass movements by way of meetings, parades, rallies.[89]

Accompanying the organizations and programs has been an underlying propaganda from the regime—especially the thought-reform campaigns which at times have been all-pervasive in attempting to remodel the thinking and reactive patterns of individual Chinese citizens. Thought reform, occasionally referred to in the west as "brainwashing," has been tried on an extensive basis in Communist China, although its effects and successes are difficult to measure. In Schurmann's view, thought reform is the basic method of ideological indoctrination of the Chinese communists, the method by which ideology is created within the individual.[90]

The actual process of thought reform apparently is reserved for important cadres. It begins with intensive discussion, self-examination and cross-examination in small group meetings. After lengthy, repetitive sessions of the small group, all of an individual's faults are aired, criticized, and carefully analyzed (in Chinese-communist parlance, he is "struggled against"). The individual then is helped to an understanding of himself, of the social revolution taking place in China, and of the proper course of action to take on his part in the future in order that he might find his place in the new society. As to the effects of such thought reform, Schurmann suggests that, through using a range of instruments to produce individual motivation and commitment, in all probability the process is widely successful in achieving identity transformations in individuals.[91] Individuals completing the thought-reform program are expected to have acquired a deep feeling of very active participation in the developing "new" Chinese political system.

Apart from the select cadres and communist-party members who receive special attention by way of thought-reform sessions, the remainder of the population in China is subjected to various types of materials of an information-propaganda nature. These materials are disseminated through schools, factories, and places such as one's work, public parks, streets, and buildings. A large amount of propaganda material is disseminated by means of the several instruments of mass media—such as radios, books, newspapers, journals, posters, and banners—in addition to the ubiquitous discussion sessions.

In 1966 Mao and some of his close supporters, chief among whom was Defense Minister Lin Piao, launched what came to be known as the Great Proletarian Cultural Revolution. It amounted to one of the most thoroughgoing campaigns of mass mobilization undertaken anywhere in recent years. The main cause for this new "revolution" centered on the question of which pathway toward progress was desirable for China. Mao was disappointed over economic failures, setbacks in foreign policy, the rise of "bureaucratism," and the CCP's inability to socialize the population adequately. Above all, there was a waning in selfless devotion to the CCP by a number of its members. The communist revolution in China which had begun decades ago was running down; and Mao and the Maoists looked for a dramatic way to rekindle this lost revolutionary fervor. The Proletarian Cultural Revolution was Mao's answer to the revisionists within the party who had become tired, disillusioned, compromising, and too practical-minded—who preferred routine solutions to tough problems over mystical incantations of Maoist aphorisms. No matter that all other revolutions had run down, Mao was determined that the unique Chinese communist revolution would not meet this fate.

The chief technique of the Cultural Revolution was one of nationwide mass participation in the various campaigns of the revolution. This participation included denouncing old customs and habits, disclaiming any desire for earthly wealth or treasures, purging from positions of leadership all but the most flaming devotees of the Cultural Revolution—i.e., Maoists. The Maoist cult of personality which was a result of these efforts reached its peak during the years of the revolution: 1966–69. For ideological purposes, in the view of one observer, the thought of Mao Tse-tung—following two and a half years of mass struggle, mass criticism, and mass transformation —has become sacred on the Chinese mainland.[92]

One instrument used very heavily by the Maoists to carry out the

Cultural Revolution was that of the Red Guards. Numbering perhaps twenty-two million at peak strength, the Red Guards were youths of proletarian or peasant background, trained and led by military officers. The guards mainly demonstrated by means of huge parades—but also renamed streets on their own, smashed many old art treasures, burned old books, tore down historical monuments and religious symbols. They also denounced a number of Chinese leaders, chief among whom was Liu Shao-chi, then President of China.[93] Various factions of the Red Guards also engaged in bitter fighting until eventually they were sent back to the countryside; some were arrested by troops; and others were persecuted by workers later in 1968 to their apparent demise.[94]

Serious effects of the revolution included the closing of most schools in China for a two-year period while students toured the nation "making revolution." Factories also were disrupted, as was the normal work of government in domestic affairs. Economic losses alone from the revolution, although incalculable, are in all probability very high. If there were any positive accomplishments of the Cultural Revolution, they might lie in further mobilization of the masses in a nationwide effort to "think" revolution and, as a result, to get rid of a number of old, conservative habits and customs which impede modernization. But even here, the seriousness of awakening and unleashing on the populace millions of youth who apparently set their own standards of what should be permitted in Chinese society and what should not can only be surmised. It should be a reasonable assumption that the results could be quite harmful. It may be difficult, for example, to turn this youthful energy of the Red Guards into constructive channels—say, school attendance, after its many destructive actions. Thus, while there is no doubt that wide-scale popular participation has been achieved in the Cultural Revolution, how beneficial will be its effects for the future of China, however, is not at all clear.

What has taken place in China since 1949 is a very elaborated series of campaigns and programs, highly organized and carefully supervised by the communist party, which has sought to mobilize the masses of Chinese and to remake the entire culture—especially the political culture—in the Leninist-Maoist-Communist mold. The long-range goal is to enable, even force, the overwhelming majority of citizens to participate politically in building a new, revolutionizing modern China. The objective has not been to introduce popular formulation or control over policy, but rather popular execution of party policy. A notable result of these many efforts has been to blur the distinction between governmental and nongovernmental activity by using both state and mass organization to win popular acceptance of party goals.[95] The Chinese experience with mass organizations illustrates an extensive and extreme use of a technique relied upon by all communist political systems, to a greater or lesser degree; and their experience may eventually demonstrate the upper limits of the practical effectiveness of mass mobilization.

Interest groups.   Another form of informal popular representation is found in the interest group, which is an organized effort to promote the welfare of a specific element of society—such as manual workers, farmers, or industrial managers. The interest group is neither organized nor encouraged by the communist party, but arises out of its own efforts.[96] Interest groups in communist states are very poorly developed, for they cannot appear to assume the role of an opposition political force. Unable either to challenge party leaders or party doctrine, such groups, unlike their counterparts in the West, must articulate their demands softly, respectfully, even subtly, before high party officials. Barnett, in referring to China, for example, points out that interest groups influence the implementation of policy more by showing passive resistance than by exerting active pressure.[97]

Although communist interest groups are more latent than their Western counterparts, they nevertheless appear visible from time to time depending on the current political climate; their effectiveness seems inversely proportionate to the vitality and strength of the communist party. They have arisen in the past decade as a reflection of growing popular demands—in recent years, for example, in Poland, where everyone made demands on the government. Intellectuals wanted more freedoms and greater cultural variety; workers wanted higher wages, lower norms, and better working conditions; peasants wanted lower compulsory delivery quotas, higher prices for their commodities, and an end to the collectivization drive; most people wanted freer travel, more contacts with the West, an end to persecution of the Catholic Church, and more independence from Soviet control.[98] A Warsaw University professor lists several types of Polish interest groups: (1) economic (trade unions, peasant associations); (2) professional (writers' union); (3) segments of society (Women's League); (4) religious and national organizations (Ukrainian); and (5) regional groups.[99] The Polish interest group formed from the few deputies elected to the Parliament as Catholic representatives is both visible and active. This group, known as the Znak Circle, supposedly acts as something of a parliamentary caucus to articulate Catholic opinion on proposals brought before the parliament. Wiatr states, furthermore, that the Catholic Church is the strongest pressure group in present-day Poland, pointing out that it directly intervened in elections to the parliament in 1957 in support of the political course of the then party leader, Gomulka.[100]

The Polish developments just outlined reflect a long-range trend in Eastern Europe toward a more pluralistic society in which interest groups are beginning to be recognized, and on occasion even granted a measure of autonomy. In some of these states the mass organizations themselves are emerging as embryonic interest groups.[101] In North Vietnam, Fall identifies the intellectuals, the urban labor forces, and the peasantry as interest groups; and the communist party, the army, the administrators and managers as power groups. While the army is a power group perhaps second in size only to the communist party itself, the peasants in North Vietnam have on occasion succeeded in exerting their influence, for example, in forcing the government to ease up on further collectivization in 1961.[102]

Traditional and identifiable interest groups begin with the peasants, the most typical of the groups in the communist states. Before World War II peasants in Eastern Europe even had their own political parties. Today, their actual or potential strength as an interest group results chiefly from their large numbers. Peasants can be a silent interest group whose importance nevertheless is sufficient to cause the regime to act (as in increasing annual incomes in the USSR and in stopping collectivization in Poland and Yugoslavia) as if they were an organized group regularly articulating their demands into the system.

Workers constitute a large class in almost all of the communist states and represent at least potentially a very influential interest group. To date they have functioned, weakly though it has been, through trade unions and workers' councils. On occasion workers have engaged in minor strikes and even major uprisings in a few of the states (Czechoslovakia, the GDR, Hungary, Poland, Yugoslavia, and, perhaps, the USSR). Their influence on the political system, however, like that of the peasants, rests more in its potentiality than in its accomplishment to date. This, despite the claim of Marxists that they have inaugurated the dictatorship of the proletariat.

Western scholars believe that the military constitutes an interest group in communist states, somewhat as it does in noncommunist ones. As military leaders are held responsible for defense of the nation, they can be expected to support heavy investments for armaments, a tough line toward the West, and firm (even forced) alliances with other communist states. Ionescu refers to a military-industrial complex which stands for investment priority in heavy industry, and maintenance of foreign bases as part of defense policy.[103] It is also a popular assumption in the West that the ouster of Khrushchev in 1964 was due in no small part to the influence of the Soviet military hierarchy. According to Kolkowicz, there is in the Soviet Union a military point of view which on occasion has expressed "opposition or self-interest demands." In the post-Stalin period, again according to Kolkowicz, relations between party and military might be portrayed as "a dialogue between two powerful institutional bureaucracies, some of whose vital interests had come into conflict."[104] In China, military commanders supposedly had won influence in high party positions (regional bureaus of the Central Committee and on the Politburo), gained control over the mass media, and taken over civil administration in much of the nation, at least in the latter 1960's.[105] During the Chinese Cultural Revolution (1966–69), the army replaced a number of local party officials and party units as the controlling ruling force. Throughout the Chinese Communist party, in fact, sizeable numbers of military officers occupy influential positions.

In Communist states the intelligentsia forms an interest group which has few of the resources of peasants, workers, or the military. The intelligentsia do not have large numbers, and they usually are not in economically critical occupations, except for the subgroup of managers themselves. It may be, however, that the managerial segment of the intelligentsia class is growing in importance in the Eastern European states.[106] As for the Soviet Union, it has been assumed in the West that its managerial segment is dynamic and long has been influential in policy-making. Here, the managers function not in opposition to the communist party, and not as an organized group, but as key influences on the party leadership.[107] Stewart states that members of interest groups in the Soviet Union, while acknowledging the predominance of the communist party, nevertheless may promote specific policies (or oppose them) while still under consideration, with the intent of influencing the leaders as they are making policy.[108] One study reports a decline in the degree of party control in the Soviet Union during the period 1952–65, with a concomitant rise in the policy-making influence of the nonparty elites: the central economic bureaucrats, the military, the literary intelligentsia, and the legal profession. The author of this study is persuaded enough by this trend to declare the Soviet political system to be a competitive one.[109]

Other segments of the intelligentsia include writers, poets, and artists—intellectuals who, as a group, seek greater individual freedom from governmental controls, chiefly that of censorship. They are considerably less influential and less successful in the satisfaction of their demands than are the managers. In the period 1955–57, however, Polish intellectuals were measurably influential both within and outside of the party. This influence was reflected in nonparty controls over important periodicals and a wider selection of music, art, and literature.[110] In the Soviet Union, novelists and poets have attempted to bring great pressure on the regime to achieve relief from such odious practices as censorship and imprisonment for publishing stories abroad. These efforts have included petitions to party officials, letters to editors, protests to the government, even rare (and very small) demonstrations.[111] All of this effort since the mid-1960's appears to be of very slight, if any, benefit to these petitioners. More successful interest articulation in the USSR has seen jurists and academicians win revisions of some of the more Stalin-like laws and a turn of the regime toward more legal protections for citizens.

Some journalists in Hungary, all party members, have succeeded in reducing party restrictions over their work.[112] In the USSR, the editors of the Young Communist newspaper, *Komsomolskaya Pravda,* have successfully campaigned for a ban on use of some pesticides, and criticized a Soviet novelist who was antiliberal and anti-Semitic.[113]

In a way, even local administrative bureaucracy constitutes an interest group as it pressures central authorities for greater freedoms in decision-making, additional expenditures from the central government, and more favorable allocations from the annual plan. These local administrators are not without some authority, of which they seem increasingly to be aware. In Czechoslovakia, for instance, people's committees have until recently controlled 30 percent of total state expenditures, and were made responsible for agricultural production, local industry, warehouses and shops, construction enterprises, hospitals, and schools.[114]

In Hungary, as well as Poland (see earlier discussion, p. 109), the Catholic Church constitutes an interest group whose influence with the government is small but persistent. In Poland the Church has conducted kindergartens and children's homes, a university, and a printing press. Following the Polish workers' riots of 1970, the Catholic Church there demanded certain "rights" from the government. The rights were to include freedom of expression and conscience, an end to governmental suppressive measures, the right to social justice, and the right to adequate material commodities.[115] Both in Poland and the GDR, Catholic bishops have run up against governmental controls and battled mightily to hold their position within society.

All in all, interest groups in communist states are more embryonic than developed. They are poorly organized and function always within a framework imposed by the communist party. They certainly do not challenge the party for power—not openly nor obviously at least. Communist states continue to be centralist and dictatorial more than they are pluralistic. And yet, some of the interest groups are growing in importance, inceasingly learning how to articulate popular demands, and from time to time even influencing policy.

Communist political systems, in Skilling's view,[116] can be divided roughly into five categories depending upon the vitality of their political interest groups, as follows:

1. *Quasi-totalitarian*
     USSR, 1929–35
     China, before 1965
     Eastern Europe at various periods
2. *Consultative authoritarian*
     GDR after 1961
     Rumania, Bulgaria, and Hungary in the 1960's

Poland after March, 1968
USSR after Khrushchev
3. *Quasi-pluralistic authoritarian*
Hungary and Poland during the thaw of 1953–56
USSR under Khrushchev
Czechoslovakia and Poland in the mid-1960's
4. *Democratizing and pluralistic authoritarian*
Czechoslovakia between January-August, 1968
Yugoslavia after 1966
5. *Anarchic authoritarian*
China, 1965–69

Here, Skilling associates interest-group vitality with pluralistic democracy, and assumes that some communist states at least, move into and out of these stages somewhat in conformity with their current degree of internal democracy. As pluralism increases in the communist states and as life becomes more complex, no doubt there will be a concomitant rise in the vitality and efficacy of the interest groups, which already are beginning to function more effectively within the communist political system.

POPULAR PARTICIPATION

The two basic goals for which communist states strive through popular participation are to fulfill the Marxist-Leninist requirement for worker rule and to build widespread support for the political leadership of the communist party. They seek, in brief, to legitimize the communist political system as it has developed over the years. While these two goals might appear to some to be contradictory, the communist, of course, argues that they are in reality complimentary. Here, the form of political participation may be more important than its substance, as citizens are likely to support a system with which they can easily identify.

As in most other areas of communist political life, the level of popular participation, its depth, seriousness, and success depend in part on the boundaries for such participation which are established and permitted by the communist party.[117] If the party is committed to and actively supports wide-scale popular participation, as in Yugoslavia, then its effects reverberate throughout the system, expanding and seeking new avenues for expression. If, on the other hand, the communist party does not allow popular participation to any great extent, as in Albania, then such participation is limited and tends to be more covert than overt. A deeper question is whether popular participation can be reduced below a certain minimum level without undermining a required minimal support for the system as a whole.

How much participation does every system need? A study of communist political systems reveals that there is some such participation (even under Stalinism) in each communist system; that at times it seems to be viable whether or not the communist party stimulates it; and that, on occasion, it appears to have grown despite party efforts to keep it confined to a few, approved channels. A related question is whether the structures for representation discussed above, both formal and informal, are in fact representative of the citizens as a whole, or even of large parts of the citizenry.

A typical feature of communist political systems is a heavy reliance for popular participation on officially endorsed, but informal organizations. These organizations are numerous, of varied types, often volunteer, and always watched over and guided by the communist party. Their objective is to mobilize popular support for the political system generally and for the communist-party regime particularly. While in the past informal organizations under communism have been more important than formal ones with respect to citizen participation, this situation may be in the process of change as the more formal organizations—legislatures, for example—gain in functional responsibility within the system as a whole. Although signs of vigor have faded somewhat from the Polish *Sejm*, since the mid- and late-1950's, some other legislatures in communist systems appear to have been growing in influence since the early 1960's (USSR, Yugoslavia, Hungary). For several reasons—constitutional authority, the ideological myth structure, growing citizen awareness as translated into greater articulation of demands, and the practical necessities of governing complex societies—we can anticipate increasing legislative vigor and growing independence of legislators within communist political systems in the future.

Some writers in the communist states point up the necessity for developing more democratic procedures than have been in existence earlier. In Czechoslovakia, where more liberalizations came faster and stopped more abruptly than in any other communist state, in the late 1960's there appeared the following statement: "The continued development of the new system of management of the national economy definitely requires a simultaneous development of democratic forms, methods, and institutions within the social system, in accordance with the principle of socialist pluralism, which is obviously a higher form of political development than the old, partly fictitious, partly formal, monolithic forms of the past."[118] In Hungary, a secretary of the communist party's central committee stated that to promote socialist democracy it is necessary to carry out a limited political reform which would increase parliament's role in the system and give additional prerogatives to the deputies.[119] If not the communist leadership, at least the liberal reformers within communist states view popular participation within the system as being necessary, important, perhaps even crucial to the future configuration of communist political systems.

With respect to *hypothesis 4*, stated at the beginning of the chapter, all communist systems do establish organizational structures to achieve worker rule. The problem, for communist as for all political systems, is one of having reality catch up with myth. The practical realities of communist-party dictatorship more often than not fail to match the participatory myth of Marxist-Leninist ideology. Although the structures for popular participation are there, for example, in established trade unions, the dictatorial requisites of communist systems carefully restrict anywhere near a full expression of participation within these structures. Elitist dictatorships do not easily evolve into participatory democracies. There remains a doubt, of course, that the elites desire such an evolution, Marxist ideology notwithstanding. It becomes a question of power versus ideology; those holding power are the interpreters of the ideology. In the confrontation of the two concepts, only the Yugoslav leaders seriously have pledged the supremacy of ideology over power. Apart from the Yugoslav trends, the short-lived Hungarian revolt of 1956, and the Czechoslovak liberalizations in 1968, the hypothesis of workers' rule in communist systems is not verified in practice.

An equally important question, perhaps, is whether communist systems—which include elite rule plus minimum popular participation—effectively carry out the socialization process of winning and holding popular support for the system. Is the structure of participation instrumental to the needs and desires of the regime? A reasonable answer is that the structure only partially fulfills the function of political socialization and renewing support for the system. There are, in fact, a number of instances in which the socialization-supportive function of participation in the communist states reveals a number of shortcomings. In the USSR some of the intellectuals have become increasingly alienated from the regime since 1966, due chiefly to an absence of satisfied demands. In parts of Eastern Europe representatives of various groups (intelligentsia, youth, workers) have expressed the need for improvements and changes in their political system. The workers' riots in 1953 in the GDR, the Hungarian Revolution and the threatened Polish revolt in 1956, workers' strikes in Yugoslavia, the Polish riots in 1970 all suggest that the traditional socialization-supportive function under communism has not been overly successful. In China, one can only guess at whether there might have developed some alienation toward the regime as a result of the Cultural Revolution. Barnett, however, suggests that the Chinese regime seems to have created a strong base of organized support, but at the same time the regime does face widespread dissatisfaction and tension.[120] A case might even be made, as Pye does, that one aftermath of the Cultural Revolution probably will be a decline, at least for a time, in participation of the masses in Chinese politics. Emotions in China became ritualized and mass participation became a new form of public pretense, with Mao being placed in a role isolated at the top, not unlike the Chinese emperors of old. And so, after twenty years under Maoist rule forced mass mobilization appears to have backfired somewhat and to have produced a growing sense of individual citizen privatization. The effect just may be a gradual drift back toward the traditional equilibrium of the Chinese political system.[121]

Trends in political development among some communist societies in the 1960's have seen a de-emphasis of the dictatorship, an increase in the influence of the legislature, a wider articulation of popular demands, and a slight increase in political diversity. All of the communist states have partially de-emphasized their respective dictatorships; a few (Poland, Hungary, Czechoslovakia, Yugoslavia, the USSR) have seen slight increases in the vitality of their legislatures; and several see a widening in the articulation of popular demands, although more in spite of wishes of the elite than because of them.

The results of a recent study on political participation involving six noncommunist nations imply that economic development increases mass political participation because associated with economic development are greater numbers of citizens in the middle and upper social classes, as well as greater numbers involved in organizations.[122] One can see in communist economic development similar factors at work. Moreover, economic reforms in the communist states have increased the number of citizens now involved in lower-level economic decision-making (industrial managers, local administrators, consumers at the marketplace). More political diversity, consequently, might be anticipated in those states which are developing economically at a fairly rapid rate, thus giving rise to more and more popular demands—many of which, however, cannot be satisfied rapidly enough. Thus, more diversity and perhaps more dissension can be expected from Yugoslavia than Albania, more from the USSR than Mongolia, and more from Poland than North Korea. All of these developments, though, do not add up to the Western-conceived image of democratic participation. None of the communist states, for example, has seen the rise of political opposition groups. Overt parties, organizations, or movements which in any way could oppose the policies and leadership of the communist party simply are not permitted to exist.

Trends and prospects on balance seem favorable for increased popular participation in communist systems for several reasons. The shortcomings referred to above with regard to participation must reveal to communist leaders that they are inadequately achieving the political socialization and supportive functions, while yet claiming the existence of popular sovereignty within their states. In addition, youthful alienation where it exists (USSR, Poland, Czechoslovakia, China) testifies to limitations in past and present political socialization. More and more it appears that a complex society which seeks and needs greater popular involvement in the economy (both from the standpoint of managerial initiative and increased consumer sovereignty) has difficulty in preventing a rise in popular participation. Thus, legislative elections, mass organizations, budding interest groups, modern communications and education, greater market socialism—all stimulate increased popular participation within communist political systems, even though the leadership tries to maintain the structure of a one-party, elitist dictatorship and strives mightily with at least short-run success in curbing popular participation.

NOTES

1. Milbrath notes that all citizens participate in their political systems at least passively, for example, through obedience to laws and paying taxes. Lester Milbrath, *Political Participation* (Chicago: Rand-McNally, 1969), p. 9.

2. Gabriel A. Almond and G. Bingham Powell, Jr., *Comparative Politics: A Developmental Approach* (Boston: Little, Brown, 1966), p. 36. Interestingly, Sharlet believes that political scientists have conceptualized political participation as behavior in democratic systems, a view which does not have either an empirical referent or theoretical significance for communist political systems. Robert S. Sharlet, "Concept Formation in Political Science and Communist Studies: Conceptualizing Political Participation," in *Communist Studies and the Social Sciences,* Frederic J. Fleron, Jr., ed. (Chicago: Rand-McNally, 1969), p. 248.

3. Sharlet, *ibid.*, p. 245.

4. A. G. Kharchev, *Communism and the Family* (New York: Crosscurrents Press, 1964), p. 23.

5. The following table shows women elected to some of the national legislatures:

Country	Date	Total Deputies	Women	Percent
Bulgaria	1966	416	70	17
GDR	1967	500	153	30
Hungary	1967	349	69	30
Mongolia	1969	297	65	22
Poland	1969	460	62	13
Rumania	1969	465	67	14
USSR	1970	1517	463	30
Yugoslavia	1969	620	49	8

SOURCE: *World Marxist Review,* Supplement to vol. 13, no. 8 (August, 1970), p. 17. Cf. also the interesting article by Lotta Lemmon, "Women in the USSR," *Problems of Communism,* July–August, 1971.

6. Sripati Chandra-Sekhar, *Red China: An Asian View* (New York: Praeger, 1961), p. 113.

7. *Area Handbook for North Korea* (Washington, D. C.: Foreign Area Studies, 1969), p. 105. As one author depicts the communist transformation, communist ideology has been substituted for the Confucian ethic; a party-affiliated elite for the traditional status group; and the nuclear family system, for the extended one. *Ibid.*, p. 70.

8. Meyer notes that communists seek to create a new political culture with new views, new attitudes, new behavioral and ideological guides.

This involves a restructuring of the entire nation's personality, a far more ambitious task than simply legitimating a new ruling elite. A. G. Meyer, "Authority in Communist Political Systems," in *Political Leadership in Industrialized Societies,* Lewis J. Edinger, ed. (New York: John Wiley, 1967), pp. 93–94.

9. Sharlet, *op. cit.* (above, n. 2), p. 247.

10. Hansjakob Stehle, *The Independent Satellite: Society and Politics in Poland Since 1945* (New York: Praeger, 1965), p. 13.

11. Rigby equates socialization with political mobilization and notes that the party carries out the function of socialization through the mass media, the soviets, the trade unions, and other mass organizations. T. H. Rigby, *Communist Party Membership in the USSR, 1917–1967* (Princeton: Princeton University Press, 1968), p. 36.

12. Arthur M. Hanhardt, Jr., "Political Socialization in the German Democratic Republic," paper delivered at the Sixty-sixth Annual Meeting of the American Political Science Association, September, 1970, pp. 14–15.

13. Darrell P. Hammer, in *Problems of Communism,* July-August, 1964, p. 15.

14. Mark W. Hopkins, *Mass Media in the Soviet Union* (New York: Praeger, 1970), p. 303.

15. *Parliaments* (London: Cassel and Company, 1961), pp. 153–54. One Soviet letter writer puts it that discussions such as these reveal the "profoundly democratic nature of our system," *Moscow News,* June 28, 1968, p. 3.

16. *Moscow News,* June 22, 1968, p. 3. Some draft laws are published in several of the Soviet national journals, such as *Soviet State and Law, Soviet Justice, Soviet Legality, Soviet Trade Unions, Socialist Labor,* and *Economic Problems.* See *Nash Narodnyy Parliament* (Moscow, 1966), p. 145.

17. V. F. Kotok, *Referendum v. Sisteme Sotsialisticheskoy Demokratii* (Moscow, 1964), p. 98.

18. *Ibid.,* p. 102.

19. Ghita Ionescu, *The Politics of the European Communist States* (New York: Praeger, 1967), p. 29. Of course, as Ionescu points out, in practice direct democracy and self-administration have not yet appeared in communist states.

20. Marek Sobolewski, "Electors and Representatives: A Contribution to the Theory of Representation," in *Representation,* J. Roland Pennock, ed. (New York: Atherton Press, 1968), p. 107.

21. *Ibid.,* p. 102. The author does not spell out what he means by "irrational" demands, but perhaps he means those found unacceptable to the government.

22. V. F. Kotok, ed., *Gosudarstvennoe Pravo Stran Narodnoy Demokratii* (Moscow, 1961), pp. 81–82.

23. In a criticism of certain features of the Soviet system, three Soviet

scientists have recently compared their economy to traffic at an inter-section. When the volume of traffic grows, the traffic controller loses his ability to ensure a smooth flow of traffic, and "The only solution is to widen the crossing." Obstacles blocking economic development, accord-ing to these writers, reside in the "socio-political" sphere. *Survey,* Sum-mer, 1970, p. 164.

24. Ionescu, *op. cit.* (above, n. 19), p. 259. As "debating bodies" debate local problems, they become more interested in general problems; and local groups and factions find company among other local groups across the region or country. Thus, a large debate becomes inevitable and parliaments become the natural arena for fractional consultation. *Ibid.,* pp. 253–54.

25. *Ibid.,* p. 262. The power of government, theoretically and struc-turally, is centered in the Yugoslav Legislative Assembly system. See Winston M. Fisk, "The Constitutionalism Movement in Yugoslavia," *Slavic Review,* June, 1971, p. 288.

26. *East Europe,* January, 1967, p. 38.

27. *New York Times,* November 29, November 30, 1968.

28. Ionescu, *op. cit.* (above, n. 19), p. 253.

29. *East Europe,* January, 1967, p. 38.

30. Quoted in Michael Gamarnikow, *Problems of Communism,* March-April, 1969, p. 18.

31. Stanko Todorov in *World Marxist Review,* April, 1967, p. 26. In 1962 a Politburo member pointed to the necessity for the Assembly to control the work of the ministries. *East Europe,* May, 1962, p. 43.

32. *New York Times,* December 23, 1965.

33. Stehle, *op. cit.* (above, fn. 10), p. 194.

34. Ionescu, *op. cit.* (above, n. 19), p. 258.

35. *East Europe,* January, 1965, p. 22.

36. Stehle, *op. cit.* (above, fn. 10), pp. 178–79; *Problems of Commu-nism,* March-April 1965 p. 130.

37. Richard C. Gripp, *Patterns of Soviet Politics* (Homewood, Illinois: The Dorsey Press, 1967), pp. 224–26.

38. *East Europe,* January, 1968, p. 44.

39. *Ibid.,* June, 1966, p. 22.

40. M. George Zaninovich, *The Development of Socialist Yugoslavia* (Baltimore: Johns Hopkins University Press, 1968), p. 118. Tito, how-ever, has been elected President of Yugoslavia for life.

41. *East Europe,* May, 1967, p. 25.

42. "Assembly Elections in 1967," *Yugoslav Survey,* November, 1967, pp. 13–16. In the 969 federal elections there were three candidates for every seat in some of the districts. *Socialist Thought and Practice,* April-June, 1969, p. 61.

43. *East Europe,* April, 1967, p. 46; *New York Times,* April 26, 1971.

44. George Ginsburgs, "Local Government, 1945–54," in *North Viet-nam Today,* P. J. Honey, ed. (New York: Praeger, 1962), p. 139.

45. *New York Times,* April 12, 1971.

46. Witold Zakrzewski, "The Mechanism of Popular Activity in the Exercise of State Authority in People's Poland," in Pennock, *op. cit.* (above, n. 20), p. 261. In elections to the people's councils, however, more than 50% of the elected councilors are members of the communist party. See *Twenty Years of the Polish People's Republic* (Warsaw, 1964), p. 53.

47. See the discussion in James H. Oliver, "Citizen Demands and the Soviet Political System," *American Political Science Review*, June, 1969, pp. 466 ff. Local governments have recently begun to exercise their rights to examine production plans of farms and institutions. *ABSEES*, July, 1971, p. 47.

48. Jovan Djordjevic, "Political Power in Yugoslavia," *Government and Opposition*, February, 1967, p. 213.

49. Arnold J. Heidenheimer, *The Governments of Germany* (New York: Crowell, 1971), p. 281.

50. René David and John E. Brierly, *Major Legal Systems in the World Today* (London: The Free Press [Collier-Macmillan]), 1968, p. 254; Fisk, *op. cit.* (above, n. 25), p. 292.

51. John Dornberg, *The Other Germany* (New York: Doubleday, 1968), pp. 254–55.

52. David and Brierly, *op. cit.*, p. 249.

53. Ionescu, *op. cit.* (above, n. 19), p. 262.

54. *East Europe*, January, 1967, p. 30; April, 1967, p. 20.

55. *Ibid.*, September, 1968, p. 45.

56. *Ibid.*, April, 1967, p. 24.

57. Mary McAuley, *Labour Disputes in Soviet Russia, 1957–1965* (London: Oxford University Press, 1969), p. 123.

58. *Turkmenskaya Iskra*, October 13, 1970, cited in *ABSEES*, April, 1971, p. 38.

59. *New Republic*, March 9, 1963, p. 7.

60. Neva Jovanov in *Review of International Affairs*, November 20, 1969, p. 26.

61. *New York Times*, January 16; February 16, 1971.

62. *East Europe*, April, 1967, p. 25. A Yugoslav source argues that trade unions in that country have extensive rights in the enterprise, including independent decision-making and the right of veto. *Review of International Affairs*, October 20, 1969, p. 16.

63. See the discussion in Zaninovich, *op. cit.* (above, n. 40), pp. 79–81. According to one Yugoslav scholar, workers' self-management in that nation is not yet fully implemented, the economy still being marked by a "dualistic structure of management." Niclos Scmardzija and George Klein, "A Perspective View of Self-Management in a Socialist Context." Paper (mimeographed, unpublished) read at the Annual Meeting of the American Political Science Association, September, 1970, p. 3.

64. Namad D. Popovic, *Yugoslavia: The New Class in Crisis* (Syracuse: Syracuse University Press, 1968), p. 148.

65. Stehle, *op. cit.* (above, n. 10), p. 166.

66. K. Grzybowski and J. L. Alder, "Eastern Europe: Legislative Trends," *Problems of Communism*, March-April, 1965 p. 129.

67. *Peking Review*, March 22, 1968, p. 19.

68. Djordjevic, *op. cit.* (above, n. 48), p. 211.

69. Zaninovich, *op. cit.* (above, n. 40), p. 114.

70. See Joseph Rothschild, *Communist Eastern Europe* (New York: Walker, 1964), p. 130.

71. Stavro Skendi, ed., *Albania* (New York: Praeger, 1956), p. 87.

72. *Democracy in the GDR* (Dresden, 1968), p. 24.

73. See *Yearbook of International Communist Affairs, 1966*, p. 55.

74. *Area Handbook for North Korea*, op. cit. (above, n. 7), p. 229.

75. Henry W. Morton, "The Leningrad District of Moscow—An Inside Look," *Soviet Studies*, October, 1968, pp. 212–13.

76. *Democracy in the GDR, op. cit.* (above, n. 72), p. 13.

77. Bernard B. Fall, *The Two Viet-Nams* (New York: Praeger, 1963), p. 181.

78. Boris Goldenberg, *The Cuban Revolution and Latin America* (New York: Praeger, 1965), pp. 270–71.

79. *Problems of Communism*, March-April, 1969, p. 27.

80. *North Korea: A Case Study in the Techniques of Takeover* (Department of State, Washington, D.C.: U.S. Government Printing Office, 1961), p. 51.

81. Oliver, *op. cit.* (above, n. 47), p. 470.

82. The family life of old China was more than the source of an individual's strength and courage, it was society itself. See Valentin Chu, *Ta Ta Tan Tan* (New York: W. W. Norton, 1963), p. 127.

83. Almond and Powell cite "nation building" as one of the system-development problems constituting challenges to political systems. *Op. cit.* (above, n. 2), p. 35.

84. Earlier Kuomintang efforts had called for an end to a number of these societal inequities, but little progress in this direction occurred prior to the communists.

85. Richard L. Walker, in *Aspects of Modern Communism*, Richard F. Staar, ed. (Columbia: University of South Carolina Press, 1968), pp. 204–05.

86. *Loc. cit.*

87. The school enrollment increased from 117,000 to 441,000 between 1949 and 1958, and to 810,000 by 1960. See Immanual C. Y. Hsu, "Higher Education in Communist China, 1949–61," in *China Quarterly*, July-September, 1964, p. 147.

88. James R. Townsend, *Political Participation in Communist China* (Berkeley: University of California Press, 1967), pp. 151–53, 173.

89. *Ibid.*, pp. 87–88. From the Great Leap Forward (1958) the common people of China, for the first time, were made aware of a relationship between what they did as individuals and the overall purposes of the state. Ping-ti Ho and Tang Tsou, eds., *China in Crisis* (Chicago:

University of Chicago Press, 1968), vol. 1, p. 605. North Vietnam has had three "anti" (corruption, waste, and red tape) and three "pro" administrative reform campaigns (responsibility, financial management, improving technical knowledge). See John C. Donnell in *The Communist Revolution in Asia,* Robert A. Scalapino, ed. (Englewood Cliffs: Prentice-Hall, 1965), p. 163.

90. Franz Schurmann, *Ideology and Organization in Communist China* (Berkeley: University of California Press, 1966), p. 48.

91. *Ibid.,* p. 50. Thought reform in North Vietnam was adopted from the Chinese format. Although implemented in a wider circle, it otherwise appears rather similar. See Hoang Van Chi, *From Colonialism to Communism* (New York: Praeger, 1964), p. 118.

92. Chung Hua-min, *Communist China, 1968* (Hong Kong: Union Research Institute, 1969), p. 493.

93. See the discussion in the *New York Times,* March 5, 1967.

94. Chang Man, in *Communist China, 1968, op. cit.* p. 53.

95. Townsend, *op. cit.* (above, n. 88), p. 74. As Vogel argues, the major economic, cultural, educational, and rural activities were brought under governmental management. Ezra F. Vogel, *Canton Under Communism* (Cambridge, Massachusetts: Harvard University Press, 1969), p. 351.

96. In a totalitarian system, as in all other political systems, structures and subsystems exist; but they are not autonomous and their interactions are hierarchically controlled. See Almond and Powell, *op. cit.* (above, n. 2), p. 312.

97. A. Doak Barnett, *Cadres, Bureaucracy, and Political Power in Communist China* (New York: Columbia University Press, 1967), p. 441.

98. James F. Morrison, *Polish People's Republic* (Baltimore: Johns Hopkins University Press, 1968), pp. 85–86.

99. Jerzy J. Wiatr, "Political Parties, Interest Representation and Economic Development in Poland," *American Political Science Review,* December, 1970, p. 1242.

100. Jerzy J. Wiatr, "The Hegemonic Party System in Poland," in *Mass Politics,* Erik Allardt and Stein Rokkan, eds. (New York: Free Press, 1970), p. 382, n. 11.

101. See J. F. Brown, "Rumania Today," *Problems of Communism,* January-February, 1969, p. 13. Brown refers to the "liberal reform" states (Yugoslavia, Hungary, Czechoslovakia), not to Rumania.

102. Bernard B. Fall, "Power and Pressure Groups in North Vietnam," *China Quarterly,* January-March, 1962, pp. 42, 45.

103. Ionescu, *op. cit.* (above, n. 19), pp. 99–100.

104. Roman Kolkowicz, *The Soviet Military and the Communist Party* (Princeton: Princeton University Press, 1967), pp. 12–15.

105. See Ralph L. Powell, "The Increasing Power of Lin Piao and the Party-Soldier, 1959–1966," *The China Quarterly,* April-June, 1968, pp. 38, ff. In Bulgaria, too, an unusually large number of military officials

have appeared on the party Politburo. See J. F. Brown, *Bulgaria Under Communist Rule* (New York: Praeger, 1970), p. 35.

106. See Carl Beck, "Bureaucracy and Political Development in Eastern Europe," in *Bureaucracy and Political Development,* Joseph La Palombara, ed. (Princeton: Princeton University Press, 1963), p. 296.

107. Jeremy R. Azrael, *Managerial Power and Soviet Politics* (Cambridge: Harvard University Press, 1966), p. 173.

108. Philip D. Stewart, "Soviet Interest Groups and the Policy Process," *World Politics,* October, 1969, p. 47.

109. Milton Lodge, "Soviet Elite Participatory Attitudes in the Post-Stalin Period," *American Political Science Review,* September, 1968, p. 839.

110. Morrison, *op. cit.* (above, n. 98), pp. 90–91.

111. See the extensive documentation in *Problems of Communism* for July-August and for September-October, 1968.

112. *New York Times,* April 15, 1970.

113. *Ibid.,* May 4, 1970.

114. Beck, *op. cit.* (above, n. 107), p. 280.

115. *New York Times,* January 2, 1971.

116. H. Gordon Skilling, "Group Conflict and Political Change," in *Change in Communist Systems,* Chalmers Johnson, ed. (Stanford: Stanford University Press, 1970), pp. 222–228.

117. According to one view, popular participation in the United States is indirect, segmented, and pluralist; in the USSR it is direct, hierarchial, and centralized. Zbigniew Brzezinski and Samuel P. Huntington, *Political Power: USA/USSR* (New York: Viking Press, 1964), pp. 90–91. And yet, Gitelman notes that in the context of Eastern European politics, participation in social and economic spheres may be as significant as direct political participation in the Western sense. Eric Gitelman, "Power and Authority in Eastern Europe," in Johnson, *op. cit.* (above, n. 117), p. 253.

118. From *Literarni Noviny* (Prague), quoted in Gamarnikow, *op. cit.* (above, n. 103), p. 14. Of course, the 1968 invasion cancelled moves in this direction.

119. From *Nepszabadsag* (Budapest), quoted in Gamarnikow, *op. cit.* (above, n. 103), p. 18.

120. Barnett, *op. cit.* (above, n. 97), p. 444.

121. Lucien W. Pye, "Mass Participation in Communist China: Its Limitations and the Continuity of Culture" in *China, Management of a Revolutionary Society,* John M. H. Lindbeck, ed. (Seattle: University of Washington Press, 1971), pp. 30–33.

122. Norman H. Nie, G. Bingham Powell, Kenneth Prewitt, "Social Structure and Political Participation: Developmental Relationships, Part I," *American Political Science Review,* June, 1969, p. 368. Or, as Ionescu argues, the more a society develops, the more pluralistic it needs to become—economically, socially, and politically. Ionescu, *op. cit.* (above, n. 19), p. 273.

6

Communist Internationalism

The international relations of nation-states have their origins in the particular circumstances within which these states operate. Several of the determinants which shape the various foreign policies of communist states—and indirectly shape communist internationalism—include such variables as the special history, geography, and political experience of these states. Each communist-party state therefore has certain givens which often take the form of limitations and restrictions on its flexibility, all of which have an inevitable bearing on the role which that state can play in any international communist movement.[1]

HISTORICAL-POLITICAL EXPERIENCES

It is not surprising that the historical-political experiences of the communist-party states have measurably influenced international communism in a great variety of ways. Old Russia's relations with Europe in the latter part of the nineteenth and early part of the twentieth centuries, and Soviet attempts to promote a sphere of influence in the area, culminated in Germany's invasion of Russia in World Wars I and II. This motivated the Russians to erect a post-World War II defensive barrier, consisting of the Eastern Europe communist states, between the USSR and Western Europe. Consequently, the use of Eastern Europe for Soviet national interest planted seeds of nationalistic dissension (which bore fruit in the late 1950's and in the 1960's) between the USSR and these communist states.

Throughout Eastern Europe, long-standing elements such as "Balkanization" and a resultant growth of extreme chauvinism and nationalism have inhibited the development of a trusting, cooperative internationalism among the Eastern European states. The continuing hostility between Albania and Yugoslavia, for example, testifies to this traditional attitude. In addition, the merger of differing ethnic/national groups into synthetic nations after World War I (Yugoslavia and Czechoslovakia) made it difficult to integrate these states and give them a single national orientation.

Relations between the USSR and communist China have been aggravated by what the Chinese refer to as unequal treaties between Imperial Russia and Imperial China prior to the twentieth century. As a result of these treaties Russia gained a number of territories from the Chinese—a gain which present-day communist Chinese feel to have been unfair, unwarranted, and thereby illegal. In larger scope, the inequality of treatment on the part of the Western nations of weak and defenseless China in the nineteenth century has contributed to the strong anti-Western feelings of communist China in the 1960's. One effect of Chinese history, then, has been to prejudice many educated Chinese against Western nations and the USSR, and thus make it easier for the communist regime to carry out anti-Western and anti-Soviet foreign policies—even though, in Marxism-Leninism, the regime adopted a Western ideology.

These brief and sketchy examples attempt to suggest some of the impact which the political history of these nations exerts on modern communist internationalism. It is an impact which is pervasive—perhaps in the long run crippling—for the international communist movement.

GEOGRAPHICAL DETERMINANTS

Additional determinants of a nation's foreign policy include—apart from location—size and natural wealth. The large territory and important geographical position of the USSR and of China measurably contribute to the importance of these two states in world affairs, communism notwithstanding. The USSR, sitting astride parts of two continents, the largest territorial state in the world, quite naturally was destined for great power status both within and outside of the group of communist states. Geography also has influenced, if not dictated, certain foreign policies for both tsarist Russia and the Soviet Union, for example, in efforts to influence Europe—particularly Eastern Europe—the Far East, and especially China and Japan.

On the other end of the scale are the small, remote, and undeveloped states of Albania and Mongolia. These states seem relegated to insignificance within the international world, and communism has not compensated for their geographical limitations.

The vulnerable location of Poland and Czechoslovakia within central Europe has doomed them in recent centuries to being dominated, and at times occupied, by the great European powers. In the case of Poland, its dismemberment at the hands of Hitler and Stalin in 1939 led to a postwar grant of former German lands as a western extension of Poland: a gift of Stalin. As a result, and also because of the Soviet guarantee of protection for Poland's newer western borders, Poland has been politically tied to the USSR in no small degree. In the case of Czechoslovakia, the Munich disaster of 1938—in which the Western powers forced the Czechoslovaks to look eastward toward the USSR for help—was very important in shaping Czechoslovakia's foreign policy in international affairs as pro-Soviet. In 1968, the strategic geographical location of Czechoslovakia within central Europe was one of the motivating causes for the Soviet invasion of that country. Soviet leaders were particularly worried over the possible defection of Czechoslovakia to the West. The case of the GDR, with its perennial involvement in East-West relations, is also due chiefly to its strategic and vulnerable location in Europe. As close proximity of the Eastern European states makes them susceptible to Soviet concern because they fall within the Soviet "sphere of influence," so Cuba is similarly related to the United States. The abortive American invasion of Cuba in 1962, for example, was intended to cancel out an alien (communist) "threat" to the United States in an area in which many Americans feel to be within their sphere of influence.

There are other direct geographical influences on communist international relations. The political independence of Cuba and Yugoslavia from Moscow, for example, is in no small part a result of their physical distance, hence independence, from the USSR. Similarly, the relative remoteness of North Korea and North Vietnam from Moscow contributes to their occasional sympathy for Peking's leadership within the international communist movement. The geographical position of these two smaller communist states, like that of Cuba, requires their foreign policies to be more directly concerned (at times, confronted) with the United States than is the case with the Eastern European communist states.

Numerous examples could be used, of course, to illustrate the influence of geography on any nation's foreign policy. In the case of the communist states, the point is that the desire for an international communist organization must reckon with the given geographical determinants with which these states have to deal.

IDEOLOGY

Marxist-Leninist ideology teaches several concepts about the world of international relations and about foreign policies of nations having to do business in the international scene. For Marx, communism in international and socialist-communist parties should not be motivated by narrow nationalistic desires. Instead, all communists should seek the rapid spread of revolution so that the old order will be overcome and replaced by communism. Accordingly, Marxists support, at least morally, revolutionary movements and civil wars which seek to put communists, or at the least, noncapitalists in power.

Lenin wrote of capitalism in the age of imperialism, meaning that advanced capitalist nations gain control over and exploit underdeveloped colonies for economic advantage. Thus, following Lenin, communists support revolutionary struggle in the nonindustrialized areas—even supporting bourgeois nationalists if they oppose the parent capitalist-imperialist regime. According to Lenin, then, the world of international relations is one in which there is constant strife and turmoil, one of wars between nations (caused by capitalists fighting among themselves over markets in the under-developed world). It is a world, too, in which the exploited people on occasion rise up against their capitalist oppressors.

For communists there are several lessons to be learned from this Marxist-Leninist approach and some specific tasks to undertake. Capitalist-imperialist nations are always bitterly opposed to socialist-communist states and, accordingly, they seek to defeat "progressive" political movements wherever they might occur in the world. The capitalist nations are weakened, however, as a result of their own wars and by occasional revolts from the subjected colonial peoples. This makes these nations at times vulnerable. To successfully defeat a worldwide group of imperialistic states, however, requires a unified and dedicated organization of communists who will work with all exploited people to throw off the capitalistic yoke. Defeat of capitalism-imperialism is not only called for in the name of establishing progressive, humanitarian peace throughout the world, but is the only assurance that communist states will themselves be able to live in peace, safe from attack by the enemy. Accordingly, communist-party states cannot trust capitalistic governments, and the era of permanent world peace requires the eventual elimination of capitalism throughout the world.

Hypothesis 5, to be examined in this chapter, specifies that communist political systems support a bloc of fellow communist states; oppose capitalist governments; support anticapitalist, anti-imperialist revolutionary movements; and orient their foreign policies toward achieving these ends.

COMMUNIST SYSTEM BUILDING

Comintern. Following shortly on the Bolshevik Revolution, in 1919, Lenin and his colleagues created the Third, or Communist, International (Comintern).[2] This organization was considered by Lenin to be the general staff for the worldwide spread of communism. At the Second Congress of the Comintern in 1920 twenty-one rules or "conditions," chiefly drawn up by Lenin, were decided upon, which set requirements for membership of parties in the Comintern. Among these rules were the following: any aspiring party group must be bound by the decisions of Comintern head-quarters; moreover, these groups should actively promote the growth of communism in their respective nations and they should support the new Soviet regime; communists, in whichever country they operate, must be placed in responsible positions, for example, in controlling the press; illegal organizations, including communist cells, must be set up by communists where the communist move-ment is held to be illegal, and communists should at all times propagandize to spread communist ideas, especially in the army, in the countryside, and in trade unions; finally, all such groups wishing to join the Comintern must rename themselves the "Communist Party of (a given nation), Section of the Third Communist Inter-national."[3]

Comintern headquarters were set up in Moscow; and by that action its founders laid the foundation stones for what they hoped would be, at long last, a viable, international, and Russian-led socialist organization, with the goal of guiding the world's masses toward communism. With the establishment of the Comintern, the international communist movement was born.

The Comintern attempted to organize foreign revolutionaries against their respective governments and against the various groups of moderate, more accommodating socialists within the particular nations. The Comintern's objective appeared radical enough. Its task, in the words of its first manifesto as written by Trotsky, was to mobilize the forces of all genuinely revolutionary parties among the world proletariat, thereby hastening the victory of communist revo-lution throughout the world. Under the banner of revolutionary struggle for power and for the "dictatorship of the proletariat," Trotsky urged workers of all countries to unite.[4] These early calls for communist revolution, following the Russian pattern, anticipated great upheavals within society which then would usher in the new order.

Organizationally, the Comintern, unlike the rather loose structure of the First and Second Internationals, possessed a central executive committee with authority, between the larger policy-setting con-gresses, to issue binding instructions to member communist parties.

Even political communication between member parties was to pass, normally, only through the executive committee of the Comintern.

The May, 1919, manifesto of the Comintern described that organization as an international fellowship of proletarians of all countries having, as its primary task, the overthrow of the bourgeoisie and the establishment of an "international Soviet republic." At the Second Congress of the Comintern in 1920, the statutes read: "It is the aim of the Communist International to fight by all available means, including armed struggle, for the overthrow of the international bourgeoisie and for the creation of an international Soviet republic as a transitional stage to the complete abolition of the State. . . . The Communist International undertakes to support every Soviet republic, wherever it may be found."[5] Other Comintern statements referred to a "United States of Socialist Europe" (1926), a "World communist system" (1928), and a "World Union of Socialist Soviet Republics" (1928). The Comintern had already announced its intention to oppose capitalist governments (with force if necessary) and to organize some kind of vague world system of communism. Just how this would be done, what form the new system would take, or when it could be realized, was not yet clear.

The Sixth Congress of the Comintern in 1928 contained in its program several pertinent points. It called for a voluntary union of all peoples liberated from capitalism and for a centralization of their military and economic forces. The resultant organization of the world proletariat would come about by way of the victory of "socialism" in individual countries or groups of countries which, little by little, apparently would join together to form the world union of socialist republics.[6] But what of the role of the new Soviet state in the international world in relation to the Comintern? Would there not arise a conflict of interests between the Soviet Union as a single, sovereign nation-state, and the Soviet Union as headquarters for an international communist movement?

In 1919 Lenin argued that the new Soviet Republic which he headed could not exist in a world with imperialist states; one or the other must triumph in the end. In another statement, Lenin observed that future Soviet republics in countries more cultured than Russia—in countries where the workers had greater weight and influence—would have every chance of overtaking Russia.[7] For Lenin, in other words, this was both a period of optimism for the spread of communist revolutions in other countries, and of concern that the new "Bolshevik" state might have to fight alone to protect itself in a hostile world. For Trotsky, the proletariat could come to power only at a time of national upheaval, of sweeping national enthusiasm. As a revolutionary representative of the people, the proletariat fights against absolutism and barbaric feudalism, and for positive legislation and revolutionary politics.[8] Thus, Lenin opposed the existence of imperialist states and anticipated additional, non-Russian "Soviet" republics; while Trotsky anticipated proletarian government ushered in by great national upheaval.

Stalin reiterated Lenin's idea of the inevitable clash between the two centers: the "socialist" center and the "capitalist" center. In elaborating the socialism-in-one-country doctrine for which he became famous, Stalin in 1924 noted that one country (the USSR) could be used as a base for the coming world revolution, for the overthrow of imperialism in all countries.[9] In 1936, however, Stalin was interviewed by a foreign newsman (Roy Howard), and he pointed out that the Soviet Union never had harbored world revolutionary plans. In response to a query as to Soviet intentions to force its political system on other nations, Stalin replied that the Soviet people would welcome change in other nations, but the question of change really was a question for those other nations to decide.[10] Furthermore, in the late 1940's Stalin argued, privately, that "socialism" was possible even under the English monarchy. "Revolution is no longer necessary everywhere," he said.[11]

The confusion resulting from vague theoretical pronouncements like these points to the role within communism that is played by ideology—which is to justify, but not determine, the nature of action. Communist analyses of history and predictions for the future society often are misinterpreted in the West to be statements of positive intent. Where the communist outlines an area of philosophical belief, Westerners often understood this to signal a plan for direct action. The two, of course, are not the same at all. Statements by Soviet leaders to the effect that a "world communism" is their eventual goal, in Kautsky's view, are of the magnitude of goals relating to world liberty and world justice made by other leaders.[12] The communist ideological statements are symbolic professions of faith, not blueprints for positive action. Thus, the picture clears if a sharp distinction can be made between intent and declaration, between ideology and practice.

Even considered merely as statements of intent, however, the program of the Comintern was not viable enough to warrant its continuation indefinitely. Djilas quotes Stalin on the Comintern's abolition.

> The situation with the Comintern was becoming more and more abnormal. Here Vyacheslav Mikhailovich [Molotov] and I were racking our brains [trying to work out Soviet foreign policy], while the Comintern was pulling in its own direction—and the discord grew worse. . . . Most important of all, there was something abnormal, something unnatural about the very existence of a general Communist forum at a time when the Communist parties should have been searching for a national language and fighting under the conditions prevailing in their own countries.[13]

Stalin's comment that communist parties should search for a "national language" perceptively reveals what in later years, following Stalin's death, became a truism. Nationalism proved to be a worthy contender for international communism in almost every one of the communist-party states by the mid-1960's. No international organization or scheme in which communist-party states have been involved—and this is especially true for the USSR—from the Comintern days on has been attractive enough to replace nationalism in these states. The rather undistinguished Comintern history, in the analysis of one of its former supporters, was a history of intrigues and schisms and of such unmitigated arrogance on the part of Russian communists that a number of the Comintern's member parties left it.[14] As Nollau has said, when the Comintern no longer served the interests of Soviet foreign policy, it was readily abandoned by Stalin.[15] As far as directing revolutions, the impact of Comintern operations on European communism in actuality was to dry up spontaneous revolutionary response.[16] The Comintern was abolished in 1943 following almost two and a half decades of modest success as a supporting arm of Soviet foreign policy. Its success as an international clearinghouse for revolutions, however, was lacking.

Cominform. In 1947 the Communist Information Bureau (Cominform) was organized "to tighten discipline within the new Soviet empire and consolidate Stalin's control there."[17] It was composed of

Soviet and Eastern European communist states (except Albania and the GDR), in addition to the communist parties of France and Italy. The Cominform, as a Comintern of a new type, was headquartered in Belgrade, later moving to Bucharest following Yugoslavia's expulsion from the Soviet Bloc. In comparison to the Comintern, the Cominform was considerably weaker in its mechanisms for controlling member parties, in part because it lacked the highly organized and dedicated central headquarters which characterized the Comintern. Failing to achieve any worthwhile successes, the Cominform was abolished by Khrushchev in 1956 as a conciliatory gesture to Tito in hopes of Yugoslavia rejoining the Soviet Bloc.

Although the Comintern and Cominform failed to internationalize communism completely, the leaders of the CPSU were able nevertheless by means of these organizations to join together for a period of time a group of fellow-communist states into a common front against the anticommunist nations. At the end of World War II, furthermore, Soviet troops in a number of countries in Eastern Europe and in part of Korea helped put into power native communist governments which were pro-Soviet. This development, coupled with the coming to power of friendly communist governments in other places (Czechoslovakia, Yugoslavia, Albania, China), enabled the Soviet Union to forge an impressive alliance of communist party-states—popularly referred to in the west as the Soviet Bloc, or among communists as the camp of brotherly socialist nations. The Bloc included, for a short time at least, the Soviet Union plus the Eastern European communist states of Albania, Bulgaria, Czechoslovakia, the GDR, Hungary, Poland, Rumania and Yugoslavia. In Asia it included China, North Korea, and Mongolia. This was an imposing group of twelve nations in the late 1940's, covering a great land area and including a combined population of approximately one billion people. Certainly this group of communist states, if it were unified and persistent, could exert a very forceful impact on world politics.

CMEA. In 1949 the Council for Mutual Assistance (CMEA), or as it sometimes is referred to, the Comecon, was established as a Soviet-inspired communist alternative to Western Europe's Marshall Plan. Membership in the CMEA included the Soviet Union and the communist states of Eastern Europe (except Yugoslavia) and Mongolia. Acting as an international communist organ which has attempted to strengthen economically the member states, the CMEA has made efforts to set up an autarkic bloc of nations in which each produces a number of specialty items for the entire bloc. After Stalin's death, CMEA, in the view of Triska and Finley, has been steadily rising in stature to the point of becoming the major organizational instrument in the Soviet effort to retain control of the Eastern European communist states.[18]

The linchpin of CMEA's success from the beginning was to have been a very strong sense of dedication, sacrifice, and cooperation among the member nations. Virulent nationalism, however, eventually eroded these necessary ingredients. The Soviet Union itself has been the most notable offender in using CMEA for her own selfish interest, for example, in buying Polish coal prior to 1957 at a price less than that offered on the world market, or in forcing unwise investments in other states in the interest not of those particular states, but of the Soviet Union, and perhaps even of the Soviet Bloc as an entity. Rumanian semi-independence from Soviet control in the 1960's was caused in part by economic restrictions forced on Rumania via the CMEA. Moreover, in the 1970's we still cannot anticipate any significant decline in political nationalism among these communist states sufficient to ensure closer economic cooperation among them.

Warsaw Pact. In 1955 the Warsaw Pact was organized, again by the USSR, in part as a belated military counterpart to NATO. The Pact was to provide a powerful military force of communist states for their own mutual protection. Membership in the Pact, at its origin, included in addition to the USSR all of the Eastern European communist states except, again, Yugoslavia. Top command of the Pact forces has always remained in Russian hands. The intention of the Soviet leaders, no doubt, was to discourage NATO from any potential aggressive moves; if successful, that alone was to justify the organization for the communist states. In 1956, however, the revolutionary Hungarian government pulled out of the Pact, but was quickly pulled back in again by the Russians as an aftermath of their invasion of Hungary. Other limitations have stemmed from Rumania's threats partially to disengage from the Pact and from the widespread liberalizations which Czechoslovakia attempted prior to the Soviet invasion of that country in 1968—liberalizations which threatened increased independence from the USSR by

Czechoslovakia. Of course, the Pact always has been considered by the Russians as a defensive protection for the USSR. At the same time, the Pact has not prevented the Russians from signing bilateral military alliances with other communist states.

System building and system maintenance. The 1950 Sino-Soviet mutual defense treaty was an attempted link-up between the two groups of communist states—European and Asian—competition between the two having been involved even in Soviet and Chinese aid of, and support for, the governments and their war efforts in North Korea and in North Vietnam. In 1957 and again in 1960, world summit meetings of communist parties were held in Moscow with the hope of patching up the weakening international communist movement. At the 1957 meeting of communist-party states, the following statement was issued regarding the growth of communism: "The Communist Parties stand for the establishment of cooperation with socialist parties both in the struggle for improving the working people's living conditions, for extending and preserving their democratic rights, for winning and defending national independence and for peace among peoples and in the struggle for winning power and building socialism."[19] Significantly, "democratic rights" and "national independence" appear more prominent than "cooperation" in this passage.

At the 1960 summit meeting in Moscow, the problem of a Chinese challenge to Soviet leadership was dealt with and the following statement was issued from the meeting: "The Communist and Workers' Parties unanimously declare that the Communist Party of the Soviet Union has been, and remains, the universally recognized vanguard of the world Communist movement, being the most experienced and steeled contingent of the international Communist movement."[20] Even though the Chinese communists joined in this statement, they soon set it aside when the Sino-Soviet controversy heated up in the early 1960's. They apparently had little intention of honoring the superior position of the Soviet Communist party except superficially. In the spring of 1969 still another world communist meeting was held in Moscow, but the large number of absences from the meeting and the disagreements (chiefly between the Rumanians and the Russians) signaled another failure at building anything like a world communist system.

The hope and expectation of communist leaders from Lenin on has been to create a dynamic bloc of communist states which would offer mutual advantage to all member nations. Soviet involvement in—if not domination of—defense policy, foreign policy, even economic planning in the other communist states, attests to the great energy on the part of the Soviet Union which has been devoted to communist system building, albeit of Soviet-centered systems. Lowenthal argues, indeed, that Khrushchev's rise to leadership of the Soviet empire was linked with an effort to replace the obsolete model of a totalitarian world party by a more flexible, yet still single-centered system of international cooperation under which communist states, ostensibly independent, would submit voluntarily to the ideological leadership of the "leading party."[21] Successes in these endeavors have included economic rehabilitation of some communist states, establishment of a strong and collective defense posture, various programs of joint mutual assistance, and launching of several of the states on the road to modernity. Failures to develop a more successful international system, though, focus on a post-Stalin recrudescence of nationalism within the various communist-party states.

DISINTEGRATION OF COMMUNIST INTERNATIONALISM

The world communist movement, from the establishment of the Comintern in 1919 to the early 1960's, has recorded more setbacks than advances. After 1919 communism came to power chiefly on its own in several states (Albania, Czechoslovakia, North Vietnam, Yugoslavia, and China) and was helped to power by the Soviet Army in several others (Bulgaria, GDR, Hungary, Mongolia, North Korea, Poland, Rumania). In most other nations of the world communism either was vigorously opposed or it was hardly an issue at all. Even among the communist states, by the late 1950's and early 1960's, international solidarity rapidly was splitting apart over matters of ideology, policy, and tactics. The growing problems faced within the Soviet Bloc were not caused solely by latter-day events, however.

As we have already suggested, Lenin had never succeeded in setting up a truly viable, coordinated international movement. The Comintern was mildly successful only as an instrument of Soviet foreign policy, and not for too many years at that. The very Soviet-ization and nationalization of international communism at the hands of the Russians, in fact, measurably detracted from the effectiveness of the Comintern as a viable international movement. These Russian actions, plus the stresses brought about by World War II, caused the eventual demise of the Comintern. The Comintern's successor after World War II, the Cominform, was even less influential than its predecessor and died at the age of nine years. Its demise, like that of the Comintern, resulted from the requirements of Soviet foreign policy.

The origins of Tito's quarrels with Stalin arose out of World War II and culminated in Stalin's expulsion of Yugoslavia from the Soviet Bloc in 1948. (Among the more important Stalin-Tito disagreements —which also included, of course, Tito's "nationalist" tendencies— Stalin had failed to give Tito requested military assistance in World War II and, following the war's end, upset Tito and his colleagues by trying to recruit Yugoslavs in Yugoslavia to work for Soviet intelligence.) This momentous event, a brother communist state thrown out of the communist family by the family's patriarch, was caused mainly, however, by Stalin's refusal to concede Yugoslavia's feelings and desires for nationalism. Titoism, or national communism, in essense is communism independent of Soviet control. It also reflects an innovating type of practical experimentation in forms of governmental, economic, and social controls. Repercussions from Yugoslavia's expulsion from the Bloc included imprisonment, even execution, of certain other nationalist-minded communist leaders in Albania, Bulgaria, Czechoslovakia, Hungary, and Poland.

Although sporadic workers' riots occurred in Czechoslovakia and the GDR in 1953, open revolt nearly took place in Poland in 1956— revealing latent anti-Stalinism, anti-Russianism, and a growing dis-enchantment over communism in general in that country. The Hungarian Revolution of 1956, finally, resulted in a popular movement to take Hungary out of the Soviet Bloc, both diplomatically and militarily.

According to the plans of the temporary leader, Imre Nagy, Hungary was to withdraw from the Warsaw Pact and become an independent nation, which would improve its trade and diplomatic ties with selected Western nations. From the standpoint of the Soviet leaders, these actions endangered the Eastern European buffer zone which the USSR had so carefully constructed after World War II. To the Soviet leaders, the loss of Hungary to the Bloc was unacceptable. On October 30, 1956, the Soviet government issued a declaration titled Principles of Development and Further Strengthening of Friendship and Cooperation Between the Soviet Union and Other Socialist States. ". . . the dark forces of reaction and counterrevolution attached themselves to this just and progressive movement of the working people and are attempting to utilize the discontent of part of the working population to undermine the foundations of the people's democratic system in Hungary and re-establish landlord and capitalist rule."[22] The subsequent Soviet invasion of Hungary put down the revolution and the "dark forces of reaction" and restored the Hungarian communist (pro-Moscow group) fully to power. Apparently the invasion was successful, from the viewpoint of the Soviet leadership, because Hungary was kept in the Bloc. Hungary's foreign policy, too, by the late 1960's appeared to be sufficiently pro-Soviet, including such goals as the following:

1. Defense of the national independence and sovereignty of the Hungarian People's Republic against all imperialist intrigues.
2. Consolidation of the unity and solidarity of the socialist countries, enhancement of their political, economic, and military prestige.
3. Solidarity with our brothers, the workers in the capitalist countries . . . support for the national liberation movements against colonialism and neo-colonialism, against imperialist oppression and aggression.
4. Promotion of cooperation with the independent countries of Asia, Africa, and Latin America.
5. Promotion of the peaceful coexistence among countries of differing social systems.
6. The task of eliminating the threat of a world war by rallying the peace forces of the world.[23]

In yet another disagreement within the Soviet Bloc, Albania, previously a loyal supporter of Moscow, in 1961 opposed Soviet efforts directed toward a rapprochement with Yugoslavia. Albania had for some time been fearful of a Yugoslav take-over, a proposal once suggested to the Yugoslavian communist leaders by Stalin and Molotov. The Albanian regime also objected to de-Stalinization efforts in the USSR, which indirectly criticized all arbitrary, Stalin-like communist leaders, including Hoxha of Albania. The final break saw Albania leave the Soviet Bloc and seek moral support from the outspoken opponent of both Yugoslavia and the USSR—China. Thus was born the rather odd alliance between these two communist states.

By the mid-1960's the leadership of Rumania and the USSR disagreed on (1) the role which China should play within the international communist movement (Rumania remained uncommitted in the Sino-Soviet conflict); (2) the continued vitality if not actual existence of the Warsaw Pact; and (3) the position within the bloc-wide economic coordinating agency (CMEA) to be carried out by Rumania. More significantly, Rumania began reviewing her ties with Western nations. In 1967 Rumania officially recognized one of the Soviet Union's historic enemies, West Germany. In a Moscow conference on Nazi war criminals, Rumania refused to sign a resolution which attacked West Germany, Israel, and the United States. In 1969, Rumania's leaders embarrassed the Russians by inviting the new American President to visit Rumania, a popular event, as it turned out. What the Rumanian leadership had been doing was different from internal liberalization (like that of Yugoslavia and Czechoslovakia): it did not include weakening the dictatorship, nor were there moves toward greater democratizations for the citizens. What was happening was that Rumania was declaring her independence from the Soviet Union. Included in this development was growing military and economic independence, as well as political independence. Between the years 1964–67 the Soviet share of Rumanian foreign trade declined from 42 percent of the total to 27 percent. With all of the CMEA nations, including the USSR, Rumanian foreign trade declined from 72 percent in 1960 to less than 50 percent in 1967.[24] Thus, the Rumanian party leaders had decided that it would be in Rumania's interest to carry out a selfishly Rumanian policy in dealing with other nations, rather than a communist-bloc policy or a Soviet-dictated policy. By the early 1970's, Rumanian independence, if anything, had increased.

The aftermath of the Cuban missile crisis of 1962 also resulted in a deterioration in the previously close alliance between Cuba and the USSR. The Soviet neglect of sensitive Cuban feelings which arose from fear of creating a danger to the Soviet Union, while logical from the Soviet point of view, nevertheless affronted Castro. Following the event, Castro became perceptibly more neutral toward the Soviet Bloc, while at the same time broadening his contacts with the Chinese communists. Other Cuban-Soviet differences have centered on how to proceed with revolutions in Latin America, with the Russians supporting old-line communist parties in the area and Castro pursuing his own independent line in disregard of these Latin American communists. Since 1968, however, there has occurred a slight Cuban-Soviet rapprochement, as Cuba has sided with the Soviet Union toward Czechoslovakia and toward the Middle East.

In 1961 the Italian communist leader Togliatti pointed out that there could be no single guiding communist state. There must be, this author of the term "polycentrism" argued, a multiplicity of directing centers within the communist movement.[25] Indeed, by the early 1960's there had emerged within the international communist movement several contravening centers of power. In addition to Moscow, the capitals of Belgrade, Peking, and Tirana had become independent sources of ideological pronouncements.

In 1968, however, a serious blow weakened the voluntary unity of the Eastern European communist states while strengthening Soviet forced unity: the USSR—along with troops from the GDR, Poland, Hungary, and Bulgaria—invaded and occupied Czechoslovakia to force cancellation of the political liberalizations which had been developing in Czechoslovakia since 1967.

Following the invasion, which later became known in the West as the "Brezhnev doctrine," Soviet leaders justified their action by arguing that changes and developments in Czechoslovakia constituted a danger to communism throughout the "socialist camp." There had arisen in Czechoslovakia, according to the Russians, a right-wing, antisocialist, counterrevolutionary force such as to endanger socialism in that country. "It was precisely this that was the chief cause for the concern shown by the CPSU and the other fraternal parties. . . ." Defending socialism in Czechoslovakia was not only the problem of that country, but also a problem of defending world socialism. Thus, history has evolved "in such a way that the Soviet Union bears enormous responsibility for the security of the socialist camp."[26] Later, *Pravda* noted that Czechoslovakian self-determination—that is, its separation from the Bloc—would not be in Czechoslovakia's fundamental interest and would, as a result, inevitably harm the other socialist nations. This self-determination, for instance, might result in NATO troops approaching the Soviet border, to dismember the several Eastern European communist nations.[27]

In a 1970 speech to the United Nations General Assembly, expressing forcefully the desire for independence of the Eastern European communist states, the Rumanian communist-party leader Ceausescu called for the abolition of all military blocs and the withdrawal of all armed forces abroad to their own national borders. However, if the Soviet Union could without much difficulty physically discipline Hungary in 1956 and Czechoslovakia in 1968, the problem raised by open Chinese opposition to the Soviet Union constituted a larger and more serious challenge to Soviet leadership of the communist world.

Disagreement between the Soviet and Chinese communist parties is an old story which reaches back into the late 1920's, when Stalin forced poor advice on the Chinese communists relative to building a proletariat instead of a peasant revolutionary base in that nation. By the mid-1930's Mao Tse-tung had, without so declaring, begun to lead the Chinese Communist party independently of Moscow. By this time Mao also had been setting up himself as an original contributor to Marxist-Leninist theory. Particularly, Mao and his colleagues opposed Stalin's unrealistic directions to organize the Chinese proletariat in the 1920's, objected to Stalin's support for Chiang Kai-shek and the Kuomintang even after World War II, and differed with the Russians over which nation (China or the Soviet Union) should dominate Mongolia. Other disagreements arose over Eastern Europe (to what degree these communist states should be independent from Moscow), over the Chinese clash with India in the border dispute of 1962, and over prosecution of the war in Southeast Asia. Most importantly, though, China and the Soviet Union fell out in the 1960's over the question of relations with the United States.

China has viewed the United States prior to 1971 as its number-one enemy, both ideologically and strategically since it became communist in 1949. The largest capitalist nation also happens to have been the one to seemingly frustrate China at every turn in Asia. United States forces stationed on Formosa denied China full title to Chinese territory. Close United States-Japanese relations, including the long

United States occupation of Okinawa, plus American troops in South Korea, all totaled up to a belligerency which arose to the level of a direct threat to China herself. Moreover, American military activities in Southeast Asia, in addition to its past anticommunist alliances with other nations, have suggested to the Chinese leaders that the United States was laying the groundwork for an eventual attack on China. Consequently, all Soviet efforts directed toward a Soviet-American detente have been seen in Peking as a Soviet sell-out to the capitalist West, especially to the United States. In addition, the Chinese communists have rated the Soviet leadership as inept because of the failures of Soviet policies in Berlin, Cuba, and in Eastern Europe. Another result of this Chinese assessment has been active competition between China and the Soviet Union in attempting to win the support of developing nations. In the case of the small Middle Eastern nation of Southern Yemen, for example, each of the two big communist nations had sent delegations which were expected to include several hundred instructors, advisers, and technicians.[28] These and yet other causes of the Sino-Soviet rift do not signal any foreseeable change in this situation. Moreover, American-Chinese discussions since 1971 have eased strained relations between the two countries; and at the same time they might encourage continued Chinese independence from, if not opposition to, the Soviet Union. These discussions raise old Russian fears of an American Chinese rapproachement in East Asia.

By the late 1960's firm unity of the communist states no longer existed and there were indications that this unity, along with effective Soviet control over the communist states, was a phenomenon of the past—perhaps it constituted a stage in development through which communist political systems have passed. The list of national defections from Soviet control, some piecemeal and not always successful, includes Yugoslavia (1948); Hungary, and to a lesser extent Poland (1956); China (late 1950's); Albania and Rumania (early 1960's); and Czechoslovakia (1968). In addition to disagreements regarding independence from the Soviet Union, other disagreements have occurred among the communist states to further destroy communist unity.

Aspaturian sums up the period from World War II as one in which the Soviet leaders attempted to mesh their own policies with the requirements of international communism. According to his analysis the communist interstate system followed the Hegemonic Model of Soviet dominance from 1945–56, the Consensus Model from 1956–68, and the Polarization Model (mainly China vs. USSR) since 1968.[29]

COMMUNIST-BLOC UNITY AND DISUNITY

The communist states in the 1970's might be divided into several groupings with respect to the international world. In the first one (Table 10), the states are rated in their attitude and posture, as of the early 1970's, toward retaining and renewing Communist-bloc unity under the overall influence and guidance of the Soviet Union. In the low category are those states least desirous of such unity and in the high category are those most desirous of it.

In the second grouping (Table 11) the states are rated in their attitude and posture toward Western, noncommunist nations in the early 1970's. Those states in the low category favor a more hard-nosed policy toward the West, and are cool toward more coopera-

TABLE 10
Support for Soviet-Sponsored Bloc Unity

Low	Medium	High
Albania	Cuba	Bulgaria
China	Hungary	Czechoslovakia
North Korea	North Vietnam	GDR
Rumania		Mongolia
Yugoslavia		Poland
		USSR

TABLE 11
Support for Increased Contacts with the West, 1950–1970

Low	Medium	High
Albania	Bulgaria	Hungary
China	Czechoslovakia	Rumania
Cuba	North Vietnam	Yugoslavia
Mongolia	Poland	
North Korea	USSR	
GDR		

tive international contacts with the noncommunist nations. Those in the high category favor freer trade and increased economic relations with the West, more international cooperation and peaceful co-existence with other nations.[30]

In both of these tables, the ratings are judgments of the author rather than empirically based. Nevertheless, they do bear a logical connection to the foreign policies of these states. Where to place Czechoslovakia in Table 11, for example, is complicated by the Soviet invasion of 1968. From 1967 to 1969 Czechoslovakia seems to deserve a high rating, but the postinvasion regime in that country suggests a lower rating. China's low rating might well change in the future if she continues to expand and develop her contacts with Western nations as begun in 1971.

In the third grouping (Table 12) the communist states are categorized by national alliance.

TABLE 12
Communist States by National Alliance

USSR Group	China Group	Semi-independent Alliance	Unaligned Nations
Bulgaria	Albania	Cuba	North Vietnam
Czechoslovakia	China	North Korea	Yugoslavia
GDR		Rumania	
Hungary			
Poland			
Mongolia			
USSR			

Cuba and Rumania are closer to the USSR than they are to China, but in both cases the alliance is weak. North Korea also appears a bit more inclined toward Soviet leadership, although in the past she has lined herself closer to China.

SUPPORT FOR REVOLUTIONARY ACTIVITY

Communist-party states have, from time to time, supported anti-capitalist, anti-imperialist revolutionary movements, as called for in *hypothesis 5*. Lenin considered the Comintern at one time to be the general staff for world revolution, and that organization did over a number of years help foreign revolutionaries to carry out anti-governmental activities. Post-Lenin Soviet experience in this regard, however, appears minimal. Stalin, for example, was reluctant to see the Chinese Communist party oppose the Nationalist Government prior to and immediately following World War II. In Greece and Turkey after the war, Stalin contributed a small amount of help to the revolutionaries, whose efforts proved fruitless. Soviet experience since World War II has probably convinced the Russian leaders that revolutionary civil wars utilizing Soviet assistance might be successful only in very limited circumstances, such as in Vietnam.[31]

In 1965 China's then Defense Minister, Lin Piao, elaborated the Chinese communist theory of world revolution.

Taking the entire globe, if North America and Western Europe can be called "the cities of the world," then Asia, Africa, and Latin America constitute "the rural areas of the world." . . . In a sense, the contemporary world revolution also presents a picture of the encirclement of cities by the rural areas. In the final analysis, the whole cause of world revolution hinges on the revolutionary struggles of the Asian, African, and Latin American peoples who make up the overwhelming majority of the world's population. The socialist countries should regard it as their internationalist duty to support the people's revolutionary struggles in Asia, Africa, and Latin America. As for revolutionary wars waged by the oppressed nations and peoples, so far from opposing them, we invariably give them firm support and active aid. It has been so in the past, it remains so in the present and, when we grow in strength as time goes on, we will give them still more support and aid in the future. . . . Of course, every revolution in a country stems from the demands of its own people. Only when the people in a country are awakened, mobilized, organized, and armed can they overthrow the reactionary rule of imperialism and its lackeys through struggle; their role cannot be replaced or taken over by any people from outside. In this sense, revolution cannot be imported.[32]

In this passage there are several important themes, including, first, mention of the anticipated success of "rural areas" (Asia, Africa, and Latin America) in their struggles with the "cities" (North America, Europe); and, second, mention of the point that successful revolutions come about from internal causes—hence revolution, even Chinese communist type of revolution, cannot be imported from abroad. This latter assessment, of course, grows out of the particular revolutionary experience of the Chinese communists. Chinese support for the National Liberation Front in Vietnam in the form of military supplies, as with Soviet aid in that area, appears to be an exception rather than the rule.

Cuba, on the other hand, has supported revolutionary movements in Latin America for virtually a decade. Cuban volunteers have contributed both moral and material support for these movements, and Cuban volunteers have even died in battles.[33]

The long-run trend, it seems, is for communist states to de-emphasize their support for actual revolutionary movements. Stalin could have given considerably more help to the several revolutionary movements in Greece, Turkey, and China following World War II. He revealed, however, only slight interest in such revolutions. Lin Piao's 1965 statement, as we have just seen, refers to a cardinal theme of Chinese communist ideology, the nonexportability of revolution. More recently, Cuba too has cooled toward support for revolutionary activity in Latin America, becoming much more concerned with Cuba's internal economic problems.[34]

In support of developing, ex-colonial nations, communist-party states seem to prefer trade, and financial and technical assistance, over sheer revolutionary activity. In 1966 General Secretary Brezhnev of the Soviet Communist party noted that some 600 industrial, agricultural, and other projects were being built in African and Asian nations with Soviet help. In addition, Soviet assistance contributed to building more than 100 educational, medical, and scientific centers in these nations.[35] Table 13 lists communist offers of aid to developing countries for a fourteen-year period from 1954–68.

In recent years China has measurably increased its aid to African countries, including building and staffing hospitals, supervising the digging of wells, constructing dockyards, advising on agricultural problems, building railways, advising the military and providing it with some arms. In a revealing statement from a Tanzanian government official, referring to the above assistance, Chinese aid officials in Tanzania were quoted as saying this time the Chinese have come simply as friends to help, "not to subvert as they used to do."[36]

To sum up: The hypothesis for this chapter states that communist political systems support a block of fellow communist nations; that they oppose capitalist governments; and that they give support to anticapitalist and anti-imperialist revolutionary movements. Examination of the foreign policies of the communist-party states reveals fairly wide agreement with the first part of the hypothesis: support

TABLE 13
Communist Offers of Aid to Developing Countries, 1954–68
(in millions of dollars)

1954–67	USSR	Eastern Europe[3]	China	Total	Percent
Africa	925	435	340	1,700	18.5
Asia	2,775	710	390	3,875	42.0
Latin America[1]	200	315	—	515	5.6
Middle East[2]	2,060	925	145	3,130	33.9
Total 1954–67	5,960	2,385	875	9,220	100.0
Percent	64.6	25.9	9.5	100.0	
1968					
Africa	—	60	—	60	7.9
Asia	135	15	—	150	19.7
Latin America[1]	—	60	—	60	7.9
Middle East[2]	205	275	12	492	64.5
Total 1968	340	410	12	762	100.0
Percent	44.6	53.8	1.6	100.0	

Total 1954–68	USSR	Eastern Europe[3]	China	Total	Percent
Africa	925	495	340	1,760	17.6
Asia	2,910	725	390	4,025	40.3
Latin America[1]	200	375	—	575	5.8
Middle East[2]	2,265	1,200	157	3,622	36.3
Grand Total 1954–68	6,300	2,795	887	9,982	100.0
Percent	63.1	28.0	8.9	100.0	

[1] Excluding Cuba　　[2] Including UAR　　[3] Excluding Yugoslavia
Source: Communist Economic Aid in 1968 (Radio Liberty Committee, New York: April 8, 1969), p. 8.

for fellow communist states. The problem here stems from which communist state, or group of states, to support. Certainly the communist states do not all cooperate with one another. Albania, China, and Yugoslavia, particularly, have withdrawn their earlier support for the Soviet Union. The failures of the CMEA, also, testify to national reluctance for a common bloc-wide economic planning organization.

The experience of communist political systems displays the eventual, long-run impracticality of holding a socialist bloc together voluntarily. For a number of reasons bloc unity is artificial because it fails to allow for the unique requirements of any given state. Thus, while cooperation from time to time is possible in some circumstances, unification is not only impractical, but even might be considered to be undesirable. Foreign policy by its very nature is selfish, as Stalin well understood, and to consider it otherwise only points to an unnatural assignment—selfless dedication to the interests of another state. When a state neglects its own needs—say, in foreign trade, defensive posture, or helpful contacts with certain other states—even though it may be in the name of ideological internationalism, it eventually weakens its own position within the competitive world of nation-states. The record of the communist political systems seems to prove this point.

Above all, the object of Soviet control over the foreign policies of other communist states has never been anything other than service to the wishes and demands of Soviet leaders for the sole national interest of the Soviet Union. Thus, the Soviet Union, as the first communist state calling for sacrifices for international communism, was in practice the worst example of such unselfish internationalism. It has not yet set any example for such cooperation.

Other communist leaders, of course, have realized the selfish basis of Soviet internationalism; and some of them have tried hard to gain for their own countries more independence from Soviet control. In all, the traditional and nationalistic political cultures of the communist-party states have not really been weakened simply because of the Russian call for communist internationalism.

The second part of *hypothesis 5* is only partially verified because by the 1970's a number of the communist states did not appear actively to be opposing capitalist governments. Vigorous opposition to capitalist governments, when it appears in the communist states, appears at an early stage in their development after coming to power. Regarding this point one should recall expanding trade between communist and capitalist states, continuing attempts by states such as Rumania and Yugoslavia to seek more friendly relations with Western capitalist nations, and China's new look since 1971.

The last part of *hypothesis 5*—that communist states support anti-capitalist revolutionary movements—is only slightly verified. While such support no doubt remains secret, at least for awhile, the apparent lack of success of communist-supported revolutionary efforts in Asia, the Middle East, Africa, and Latin America argues for a minimal commitment on the part of leaders of the communist-party states. In the long run, financial and technical aid appear considerably more fruitful than subversion.

NOTES

1. All communist states, in Aspaturian's portrayal, function in three distinct spheres: (1) the communist interstate subsystem; (2) the general international system; and (3) the international communist movement. Vernon Aspaturian, "Patterns of Variation in the Foreign Policies of Communist States." Paper (mimeographed, unpublished) delivered at the Sixty-sixth Annual Meeting of the American Political Science Association, Los Angeles, September, 1970, p. 6.

2. The First International Working Men's Association (1864–74) was formed under Marx's guidance in London as a guiding force for socialist parties and movements. The Second International (1889–1914) was not much more successful than its predecessor as a worldwide organization of socialists. The Second International fell before the overpowering nationalism which arose out of World War I.

3. Jane Degras, ed., *The Communist International, 1919–1943: Documents* (London: Oxford University Press, 1958), vol. 1, pp. 167 ff.

4. *Ibid.*. pp. 38, 47.

5. *Ibid.*, pp. 163–64.

6. *Ibid.*, vol. 2, pp. 492, 497, 508.

7. V. I. Lenin, *Selected Works* (International Publishers, 1943), vol. 8, p. 33; vol. 1, p. 35. Lenin wrote this in April, 1919.

8. Robert V. Daniels, *A Documentary History of Communism* (New York: Random House, 1960), p. 44.

9. J. Stalin, *The October Revolution and the Tactics of the Russian Communists* (Moscow: Foreign Languages Publishing House, 1950), pp. 58, 63.

10. *New York Times*, March 5, 1936.

11. Milovan Djilas, *Conversations With Stalin* (New York: Harcourt, Brace and World, 1962), p. 113.

12. John Kautsky, in *Contemporary Communism: Theory and Practice*, Howard R. Swearer and Richard P. Longaker, eds. (Belmont: Wadsworth, 1963), p. 50.

13. Djilas, *op. cit.*, pp. 80–81.

14. Ignazio Silone, in *The God That Failed*, Richard Crossman, ed. (New York: Harper, 1950), pp. 105–06.

15. Gunther Nollau, *International Communism and World Revolution* (New York: Praeger, 1961), p. 209.

16. Adam Ulam, *Unfinished Revolution* (New York: Random House, 1960), p. 240.

17. Jan F. Triska and David D. Finley, *Soviet Foreign Policy* (New York: Macmillan Company, 1968), p. 13.

18. *Ibid.*, p. 205.

19. *Current Digest of the Soviet Press*, vol. IX, no. 47 (January 1, 1958), p. 6.

20. *Current Digest of the Soviet Press*, vol. XII, no. 49 (January 4, 1961), p. 7.

21. Richard Lowenthal, *World Communism* (New York: Oxford University Press, 1966), p. 232.

22. Quoted in *International Relations Among Communists*, Robert H. McNeal, ed. (Englewood Cliffs, N.J.: Prentice-Hall, 1967), p. 93.

23. From the 9th Congress of the Hungarian Socialist Workers' Party. *World Marxist Review*, January, 1967, p. 63.

24. Paul Lendvai, *Eagles in Cobwebs: Nationalism and Communism in the Balkans* (Garden City: Doubleday, 1969), pp. 338–39.

25. Quoted in Alexander Dallin, ed., *Diversity in International Communism* (New York: Columbia University Press, 1963), p. 419.

26. *Pravda*, August 22, 1968.

27. *Ibid.*, September 26, 1968.

28. *New York Times*, January 10, 1971.

29. Aspaturian, *op. cit.* (above, n. 1), pp. 15, 30, 45.

30. Triska and Finley rate the communist states on a level of "internationalization," with the higher figures associated with more internationalization. Thus, Czechoslovakia, Yugoslavia, and the USSR rate high; North Vietnam, North Korea, and China rate quite low; with the remainder of the states in between these two groups. The states were rated on the basis of participation in the United Nations, membership in other international organizations, per capita imports of foreign goods, and communications with foreign nations. See Triska and Finley, *op. cit.* (above, n. 17), p. 185.

31. See the discussion in J. M. Mackintosh, *Strategy and Tactics of Soviet Foreign Policy* (New York: Oxford University Press, 1963), p. 288.

32. Lin Piao, "Long Live the Victory of People's War," *Peking Review*, September 3, 1965. Note also in this connection Stalin's description of the world being divided into two camps: the handful of civilized nations possessing finance capital who exploit others, and the camp of oppressed and exploited peoples in colonies and dependent countries, who comprise the majority. Joseph Stalin, *Foundations of Leninism* (New York: International Publishers, 1939), p. 82.

33. See James F. Petras, "Socialism in One Island: A Decade of Cuban Revolutionary Government," *Politics and Society*, February, 1971, p. 218.

34. *Ibid.*, pp. 220 ff.

35. *Pravda*, March 30, 1966.

36. *New York Times*, April 9, 1971.

7

Success of Communist
Political Systems

Preceding chapters of this book outlined and discussed certain
basic elements of communist political systems in both descriptive
and analytical terms, though with greater emphasis on the former.
Hopefully by now the reader has an understanding of some of the
more important structures, functions, and behavior of communist
political systems. What remains to be carried out at this point is a
little deeper analysis: to suggest several conclusions as to the degree
of success of these systems and to indicate probable directions in
which they appear to be moving.

THE MARXIST-LENINIST MODEL

One might ask just how "communist" are the communist-party
states? The record of these states might now be matched against the

model set forth in the first chapter. In addition, the record of communist achievements might be examined with respect to such communist goals as economic equality, economic abundance, and worker rule. Still another guideline for measurement, to be referred to later, involves a checklist of economic and political development for the communist states.

From the Marxist-Leninist Model we derived several controlling hypotheses for examining certain data. The five hypotheses might now be reiterated and summary comments provided regarding their verification in this study.

Hypothesis 1. To be communist, a new political system is placed in power which is clearly labeled as "Marxist-Leninist," and which has as its main objective the bringing into full operation of a Marxist-Leninist, or communist, society.

All of the fourteen communist-party states fit this hypothesis with the partial exception of Cuba, whose Castro-led regime did not initially come to power in order to bring into being a Marxist-Leninist society. Rather, this objective was added at a later time.

Inaugurating a Marxist-Leninist system, as far as ideology goes, might be accomplished simply by official announcement. In coming to power, however, communists use a number of techniques, such as forming temporary alliances with various groups of people, heavy reliance on propaganda, infiltration and physical take-over of key governmental offices, and unremitting pressure to eliminate their opponents. In a number of communist states, the assistance of the Soviet Army was of great importance in the party's coming to power. Moreover, what might loosely be termed "preconditions" to communism reveal that all of the states that became communist had earlier suffered from political feebleness, contrasted with periods of authoritarian rule; widespread popular alienation from the old system; underdeveloped industry; and, often, postwar economic and political chaos. The question now posed is whether these new Marxist-Leninist systems would enjoy political legitimacy.

Hypothesis 2. In a communist political system, the communist party (a) assumes political control over society; (b) serves as the spokesman for and represents the interests of the working class.

All communist states except Cuba have successfully carried out the first part of this hypothesis. This internal supremacy of communist-party rule is, no doubt, the single most salient feature of communist political systems. Nonetheless, in some of the states absolute party rule from time to time has been questioned: the USSR during the Great Purge (1936–38), China during and immediately following the Cultural Revolution (1966–69), Hungary in 1956, Czechoslovakia in 1968, and Yugoslavia since 1960. Prior to the Polish workers' riots in 1970—in yet another case—both Soviet and GDR communist leaders feared that the Polish Communist party was acting too arbitrarily and precipitously to ensure political stability.[1]

Cuba is an exception to this pattern because rule by the communist party in that state is questionable. Although it is the only visible party at present, it assists in actual political rule only at Castro's pleasure. The Cuban Communist party, unlike those in the other communist party-states, does not appear to have any extensive and elaborate network of well-disciplined organizations and officials distributed throughout the nation for purposes of control and supervision of regional and local levels of government, or of such activities as industry and agriculture.[2]

At least part of the communist party's problem with respect to winning legitimacy stems from another item of the hypothesis: that the party represents the interests of the working class. Although all communist regimes make this claim of truly representing workers, temporary lapses of firm party control—added to workers' strikes and riots in the GDR, Hungary, Poland, Yugoslavia, and even the USSR—throw doubt on the legitimacy of this claim. In any event, ruling communist parties do not allow other political parties or movements to challenge their supremacy, so that a free and unrestricted expression of worker support for the communist regime is not allowed to be registered. Are communist political systems and their regimes, then, truly legitimate? The communists in power have not presented any substantial evidence that they represent the interests of the working class, so this part of the hypothesis remains unverified.

Hypothesis 3. A communist political system transforms an economy from private ownership to public-socialist ownership and governmental control.

This hypothesis is fairly well verified in the communist-party states, with the limited exceptions of some light and service industries in a few of the states, and of agriculture in Poland and Yugoslavia.

Communists also claim that their economic system will lead to rapid industrialization, to a form of egalitarianism as all citizens share in the wealth of the society, and to an eventual economy of abundance. Socialization of the economy, including nationalization of industry and collectivization of agriculture, has proceeded a long way in the communist states. Almost all of them have nationalized their industry and trade, and collectivized their agriculture, at least ostensibly so.

The record of the communist states, however, fails to bear out their claim that communism brings rapid industrialization. Although the Soviet Union industrialized itself within a few decades, some of the other states are not even close to an industrialized status. Even more clearly to be seen is that collectivization of agriculture exists in only some of the states. It was abandoned in Poland and Yugoslavia, markedly altered in China in the early 1960's, and enjoys some notable exceptions in the GDR and in the USSR.

Economic egalitarianism has been seriously attempted, although never fully achieved, under communism. Extensive private wealth has been eliminated, however, and efforts continue to provide every deserving citizen with a minimum income. In the Soviet Union, for example, official salaries range from a low of less than 100 rubles a month to a high of some 2,000 rubles, although there are exceptions to this—for example, a very successful writer may earn considerably more than this in royalties. And yet, something of a rough equality of income is claimed by providing both a salaried income and a "social wage" for each reputable citizen (with such as vagrants and criminals excepted). Although balance and a measure of equality in the distribution of society's wealth continues as a main theme for communist leaders, their achievements are still debatable.

As for economic abundance, communist states are still reaching for this goal, but with none even close to achieving it in the early 1970's in the sense of adequate goods, including a variety of desirable types for all citizens. This may not be the important question, though, since no nation, communist or noncommunist, has yet reached this level of economic output. More appropriately, the question should be, can a communist system reach the level of economic abundance more rapidly and more surely than a non-communist system? As is the case with rapid industrialization, there is no evidence that communist states can achieve economic abundance more rapidly or more surely than noncommunist ones.

Hypothesis 4. A communist political system (a) organizes structures for popular participation; (b) achieves viable worker rule through these structures.

Communist-party states do organize structures for popular worker rule, including elective legislatures, trade unions, a court system, and mass organizations of citizens. Through the structures communist leaders seek both to administer their political rule and to legitimate their entire political system. In the eyes of these leaders, their system definitely is of and for the people, and wide-scale popular participation hopefully will prove the point both to citizens at home and to the world at large. This is not an insignificant point; for the single most important claim of communists is that their system, above all others, more fully permits the worker (including all honestly employed citizens and pensioners) to rule himself. This has been, of course, the main promise of Marxism. Workers' self-rule continues as the ultimate justification for the dominance of the communist party.

All communist states have provided appropriate structures for popular participation, such as an elected legislature, trade unions, and mass organizations. Some of the states have added elective governing bodies at the regional and local levels, workers' councils to supplement trade unions, quasi-official tribunals run by average citizens to mete out popular justice, and numerous volunteer committees of citizens to assist in the practical administering of the communist society. The various communist leaderships have done much to popularize their systems, including improving the rights of women; protecting the rights of children; and raising levels of literacy, education, and health. Various forms of social insurance and official responsibility for job placement as well as job training are also features of modern communism.

In several of these institutions—such as legislatures—influence on party policy-making has been on the increase. This has been the case most notably in the legislatures of Poland, Czechoslovakia, Yugoslavia, and the Soviet Union. Communist leaders have per-

mitted, even encouraged, broad popular participation in such significant activities as constitution-making; draft legislation dealing with
family law and pensions; and, indeed, in China, the entire panorama
of the Cultural Revolution. There is, then, large-scale popular
participation of citizens in communist systems. Moreover, these
systems are so structured as to require massive citizen activity. The
significance of these popular inputs into the system should not be
underestimated. Many economic decisions of the governments, for
example, reflect consumer desires and the list of such decisions
grows continuously. The ultimate importance of popular inputs,
though, relates to their indirection.

Citizens in communist-party states influence their political leaderships in a number of low-keyed, indirect ways. In all this, what
these citizens cannot do is to directly challenge the political supremacy of the communist party. There are struggles for power within
communist systems, of course, but these are usually confined to the
members of the party hierarchy. Popular participation is seen more
in the execution of policy than in the determination of that policy.
Communist systems remain authoritarian, ruled by one-party elite
dictatorships. Consequently, a number of demands by specific
groups of people (minority peoples for independence, writers for
more literary freedoms) may often be ignored by the regime with
impunity. Where the citizens can influence their leaders is by subtle
indirection rather than by confrontational politics in the open arenas
of public life.

Popular participation in communist systems does not extend so
far as to include direct democratic processes. Citizen influence on
communist systems, although growing, continues to be indirect,
modest, and subject to the waxing and waning of autocratic power
at any given time. With respect to *hypothesis 4,* communist societies
do not permit popular worker rule, even though they display an
elaborate facade for such rule. There is considerable worker influence and many worker inputs, but no worker rule. This fact reveals
the widest single gap between communist ideological myth and
communist political practice. The first part of *hypothesis 4,* then, is
verified in all of the communist-party states, but the second part by
and large remains unverified.

*Hypothesis 5. A communist political system (a) supports a bloc
of fellow communist states; (b) opposes capitalist governments;*

(c) *supports anticapitalist, anti-imperialist revolutionary move-ments.*

Toward reaching the goal of organizing a socialist bloc of states, a number of attempts have been made and a few successes scored. The Comintern, for example, functioned from 1919–43; the Cominform, from 1947–56. To these early internationalizing efforts of communist states was added the CMEA in 1949, for joint economic cooperation; and the military Warsaw Pact in 1955. Prior to the Warsaw Pact, in 1950, the Sino-Soviet Treaty had been signed for the purpose of mutual military defense. World summit conferences of communist parties—following on the demise of the Comintern and Cominform—met in Moscow in 1957, 1960, and in 1969. Despite these numerous organizational efforts to promote a coordinated international communist movement and cooperatively to protect the communist-party states, the failures of the communists in this regard have clearly outnumbered their successes.

The Comintern failed to weld together an international workers' movement and its short-term successor, the Cominform, was no more successful because both were corrupted and thereby tainted by their subordination to Soviet foreign policy. The CMEA has throughout its existence received only minimal support from its member nations in their individual reluctance to sacrifice national economic advantage for an elusive intra-bloc cooperative effort which they have apparently believed, in any event, was advantageous only to the Soviet Union. The Warsaw Pact has been more successful than these other organizations. But even so, Yugoslavia was never a member; Albania left the organization; Hungary tried to leave in 1956; and the Rumanians in 1970 called for the end to all military blocs, of both East and West. A considerable loss in prestige, if not credibility, for the Pact resulted from the mid-1968 invasion by Pact members, led by the Soviet Union, on the capital of a fellow member, Czechoslovakia.

The world summit conferences of communist parties elaborated cooperative foreign policy stands in 1957 and 1960, but these were soon abandoned as the Sino-Soviet split began in the late 1950's. By the 1969 meeting a number of communist parties simply failed to attend.

Part (a) of *hypothesis 5,* then, is partially verified; but China and

Yugoslavia are two of the notable exceptions. Part (b) occurs from time to time, but the exceptions appear numerous enough to leave this part only partially verified at best. Part (c) is only slightly verified, and as with (b), seems more viable in the early stages of development in some of the states (USSR, China).

As the communist-party states try to make their ideology operational, do they closely fit the Marxist-Leninist Model? The foregoing discussion, centering on the five hypotheses derived from this model, indicates that they do not. Of the five hypotheses, numbers 1 and 3 are largely verified by the record of the communist-party states; while numbers 2 and 4 are only half verified, and number 5 is only slightly verified. The most obvious exceptions to the model are in the areas of worker rule, direct popular influence on political decision-making, and selfless communist internationalism. Consequently, it seems in order to conclude that the ideological goals of Marxist-Leninism either cannot be realized in entirety by the leaders of the communist-party states, or else they refuse to do so.

It should be noted, again, that the communism of Cuba might be questioned because Cuba differs from all of the other thirteen communist states in two respects. First, the regime did not come to power in order to inaugurate Marxism-Leninism. Second, the Cuban Communist party cannot be said to rule Cuba as do the communist parties of the other thirteen communist states. Is Cuba, then, communist? The answer probably should be a qualified yes. It appears to be communist because it is moving in that direction, along with the other communist-party states, but it is doing so in a more unorthodox manner.

Apart from use of the Marxist-Leninist Model, there are other ways of evaluating the accomplishments and successes of communist political systems. One of these is found in the developmental approach.

POLITICAL-ECONOMIC DEVELOPMENT

Marxism provides a foundation for looking at communism developmentally because it interprets history as a progression from feudalism, through industrial capitalism, into transitional socialism, finally entering the millennium of communism. Politically, the development proceeds from capitalist political rule, through a transitional period of communist rule, then into the final phase of worker rule. Communism might therefore be viewed as the end result of a long history of developmental steps.

In attempting to define "development," perhaps the key concept is that of process rather than structure, or even function. The process involves modernization. In the view of Pye, modernization can be thought of as a diffusion of a world culture based on an advanced technology, the spirit of science, nationalism, a secular approach to society, a feeling for justice in public affairs, and a belief in the primacy of the nation-state. As a consequence of these attitudes and approaches, modernization implies greater ability and increased governmental power, as expressed in modern administrative or bureaucratic structures, to deal with a larger range of problems.[3] Cutright notes, in this connection, that developed nations enjoy complex and specialized institutions.[4] This latter concept is similar to Almond's in portraying a modern political system as possessing differentiated political structures, such as a legislature that legislates and interest groups which articulate popular demands.[5]

One might suggest other attributes of a developed society, including industrialization; a broad spectrum of educational facilities; an expanded, efficient, and widespread network of transportation and communications; an efficient political system which accommodates popular demands. To these a Marxist would add the ingredients of economic planning, nationalized industry, nationalized and/or collectivized agriculture, and centralized governmental controls—all of these being supervised by a proficient communist party.

In these several ingredients of modernization, one looks for the dominant feature. Is it nationalism, industrialization? Is it the drive for modernity, the quality of economic capability and flexibility, or parliamentary democracy? The questions come easier than the answers. As for the communists themselves, they have tended to equate Soviet experiences (such as economic planning, industrialization) with development. Even in China, the Soviet model of developmental-modernization was followed in the early years after 1949, although by the 1960's the Chinese regime has strongly criticized Soviet foreign and domestic policy and the Soviet model.

We might raise the question of the inevitability of political development. In this, communist ideology and the mystique of Western political systems appear to converge. Both act on the assumption of the inevitability of political development, which in this sense is tied almost inextricably to economic development.[6] Here, the concepts of political mobilization and mass participation may be considered a part of political development. Sharlet believes that accompanying political development in communist political systems is a progressive increase in the breadth and generality of both mass and individual involvement in the implementation of public policy.[7]

For purposes of this analysis, development in communist political systems accents both economic and political features as these pass through suggested evolutionary stages, or levels.[8] This is, of course, a restricted use of the concept of development. Thus in the area of economics, as set forth in the checklist below, development appears to be more of a process than an accomplishment, an adoption of certain administrative techniques on the part of communist states rather than the attainment of certain levels of production or investment.

The items which make up this checklist have been selected for the first level because they represent actions taken early in the development of communist systems. The leaders of all communist states, for example, have nationalized industry and established a dictatorship. For the second level, most of the communist states have attempted some of these items, such as reforms in economic planning and downgrading the role of the political police. For the third level, the items are largely projections of actions logical to earlier ones already attempted and they also seem to be requirements of a modern, technologically oriented society—for example, a wider articulation of popular demands and the use of market indicators in the economy.[9]

Taking the communist-party states individually, the author has attempted a judgmental evaluation of them to see to what extent they do or do not seem to match the ten items of economic management and the ten items of political development as set forth in the above checklist. The assigned values in Table 14 are based on the data contained in the preceding chapters and the author's interpretations of that data. The numerical ratings used in the evaluation carry the following weight:

0 – no identification with the items.
1 – low, or slight identification with the item.
2 – moderate, or average identification.
3 – high, or considerable identification.
—no data available.

DEVELOPMENTAL CHECKLIST FOR COMMUNIST POLITICAL SYSTEMS

	Economic Management	*Political Development*
First Level	1. Nationalization of industry	Taking power by communist party
	2. Collectivization/socialization of agriculture	Setting up the apparatus of a dictatorship
	3. Inauguration of economic planning	Elimination of political opposition
Second Level	4. Decentralization of economic organization and management	De-emphasis of extremes of the dictatorship; elimination of much of the terror; downgrading of political police; easing of legal punishments
	5. Reform of economic planning: decentralization and simplification	Decentralization of some governmental functions
	6. Managerial rationalization: increase in autonomy and flexibility for lower-level managers	Increase in responsibility and autonomy of legislature
	7. Striving for industrialization	Increase in electoral vitality: multi-candidacies, contested elections
Third Level	8. Introduction of small-scale private enterprise	De-emphasis in monopoly power of communist party
	9. Decollectivization/socialization of agriculture	Wider articulation of popular demands through mass organizations, interest groups
	10. Use of market indicators: profits, consumer demands, price reform	Increase in internal political diversity

Certainly, development in communist systems cannot be reduced to simple quantification. The value which these ratings may have would be to note some differences among the several systems and to suggest possible trends for their future development.

The judgmental evaluation or ratings in Table 14, if they are at all valid, suggest several interpretations. A few of the states appear to have developed very little in economic management (Albania, for example), while others seem clearly to be passing through the several levels of economic development (especially apparent for Yugoslavia). Similar disparities appear in the political side of the checklist. Albania, on the low side, is contrasted with Czechoslovakia and Yugoslavia, on the high side.[10] For the remainder of the states, the development of economic management appears to correlate fairly well with political development. Reasons for such correlation might include the measurement, in both cases, of related phenomena.[11] Development, one might suggest, is development whether it be economic or political. At least in this checklist, development appears as a process of transforming elementary methods into more sophisticated ones, accompanied by an increase in popular participation. Decentralization in economic management finds its natural counterpart in greater independence for regional and local governments. Thus, the logic of decentralization resists compartmentalization into economic or political categories. A record of liberalization in one argues the desirability for liberalization in the other.

The results of the ratings in Table 14 are presented as percentages of fulfillment in Table 15 and graphically in Figure 1 to illustrate the degree of linear progression. Three states were dropped from Table 15 and Figure 1 because of a lack of pertinent data. The premise of the Developmental Checklist is that each communist party state will proceed through the first, second, and third levels in that order. If the states have not completed all three levels, then they should demonstrate relatively greater accomplishment in the earlier ones. As Figure 1 shows, eight of the eleven states on the economic side, and seven of the eleven on the political side follow this pattern. Another way to portray this is to note that of the sixty-six ratings in Table 15, only nine of them deviate from the projected pattern. Thus, in 87 per cent of the cases these communist states followed the patterned development set forth in the checklist.

There are, as the tables and the figure reveal, slight deviations from this pattern: Hungary and Poland on the economic side, and

TABLE 14
Ratings for Developmental Checklist, 1970

	Economic			Political		
level	1	2	3	1	2	3
Checklist item	1 2 3	4 5 6 7	8 9 10	1 2 3	4 5 6 7	8 9 10
Albania	3 3 3	1 1 1 0	0 0 0	3 3 3	1 0 0 0	0 0 0
Bulgaria	3 3 3	2 2 2 1	0 0 2	3 3 3	1 2 1 0	0 0 1
China	3 3 3	1 1 1 0	1 1 0	3 3 3	0 0 0 0	0 2 0
Cuba	1 3 3	1 0 0 1	0 0 0	1 3 3	1 0 0 0	2 0 0
Czechoslovakia	3 3 3	3 2 2 3	3 0 2	3 3 3	3 2 2 2	2 3 3
GDR	3 2 3	2 2 2 3	3 0 2	3 3 3	1 2 1 1	0 2 0
Hungary	3 3 3	2 2 2 2	3 2 3	3 3 3	2 2 2 0	1 2 2
Mongolia	3 3 3	– – – 0	– – –	3 3 3	– – – 0	0 – 0
North Korea	3 3 3	1 1 – 1	– – –	3 3 3	– – – 0	0 – –
North Vietnam	3 3 3	– – – 0	– – –	3 3 3	– – – 0	0 – –
Poland	3 1 3	1 1 2 2	3 3 1	3 3 3	2 2 2 0	0 2 2
Rumania	3 3 3	1 1 2 2	1 0 1	3 3 3	2 1 0 0	0 1 0
USSR	3 3 3	2 2 2 3	0 0 1	3 3 3	2 2 1 0	0 2 1
Yugoslavia	3 1 3	3 3 3 1	3 3 3	3 3 3	3 3 2 2	2 3 2

China, Cuba, Czechoslovakia, Hungary, and Poland on the political side. Only Yugoslavia, on the economic side, reverses this patterned development. No doubt this reflects her unusual experimentation under Titoism.

What conclusions, finally, might be drawn from the checklist for development that might be useful to our analysis? The checklist clearly suggests certain directions which communist political systems are taking as they evolve their economic and political patterns. Spe-

TABLE 15
Percentage Completion by Level of Development

	Economic			Political		
level	1	2	3	1	2	3
Albania	100	25	0	100	8	0
Bulgaria	100	58	22	100	33	11
China	100	33	22	100	0	22
Cuba	77	16	0	77	8	22
Czechoslovakia	100	83	55	100	75	88
GDR	88	75	55	100	41	22
Hungary	100	66	88	100	50	55
Poland	77	50	77	100	50	44
Rumania	100	50	22	100	25	11
USSR	100	75	11	100	41	33
Yugoslavia	77	83	100	100	83	77

These figures are the percentage of completion of the three levels of development based on the ratings from Table 14. Mongolia, North Korea and North Vietnam have not been included in this table nor in Figure 1 because of a lack of pertinent data.

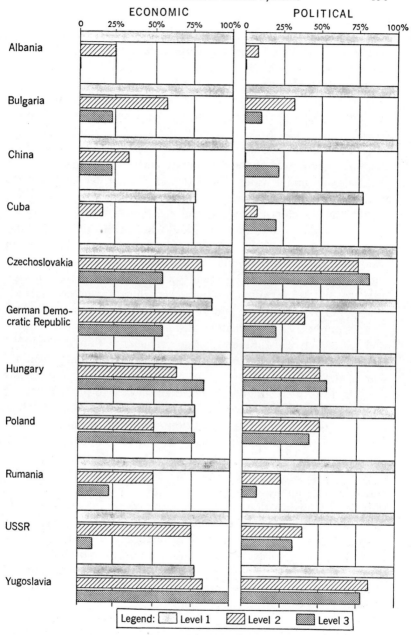

Figure 1
Percentage Development by Level

cifically, these states follow trends set forth in the checklist such as adopting more sophisticated managerial techniques, decentralizing economic administrative and governmental functions, and scaling down the harshness of the dictatorship. Although we are less confident of whether communist party states will proceed through level three, nevertheless, following the logic of the checklist as well as the accomplishments of these states so far, we would predict more decollectivization of agriculture, additions to the amounts of private enterprise, heavier reliance on market indicators, a de-emphasis in the monopoly power of the communist party with respect to other organizations, and a wider articulation of popular demands into the political system.

In the introductory chapter several questions were raised as to the nature of communist political rule, and whether this rule constitutes a distinct type of political system. Communist political rule, in a way, must be somewhat similar to noncommunist rule, as functionalists would remind us. Organized society must be watched over, guarded, and led by an authoritative government, whatever label is attached to the political system. In modern societies, moreover, complex requirements of demand satisfaction argue for even closer similarities between different states: problems within the political system of the USSR, in some respects (scientific management research, defense technology) bear more resemblance to problems faced by the American government than they do to problems faced by a fellow communist state which is undeveloped (Albania, Mongolia). Nonetheless, in a number of other respects communist states appear distinctive enough to qualify as a special or unique type of political system.

There exists among communist states a commonality of structures and ruling techniques (commitment to Marxism-Leninism, a functioning dictatorship dominated by the apparatus of a communist party, a centrally planned economy, a nationalized industry, a collectivized agriculture, a mass-participant society, and some alliance with other communist states). Communist leaders of the various states also share similar objectives (continuance of party rule, industrialization, economic egalitarianism) and these states tend to develop along similar lines. We should know reasonably well, then, what a communist political system will look like while, or even before it is established. To the extent that Cuba under Castro, or perhaps Chile under Allende, for example, match elements of the ideological framework and developmental checklist, perhaps to that extent we may be able to label them "communist" or "noncommunist" political systems.

Communist systems appear mildly progressive economically as they establish national planning and carry out programs of social welfare. They also appear somewhat politically progressive, although less so than in the economic realm. This political progressiveness, however, is different from that found in Western parliamentary democracies. Where the communist society stresses broad popular participation in administering the nation within a frame of dictatorship, in democracies such participation includes open opposition to the political rulers. Thus, while communist societies may well represent the beliefs, wishes, and demands of a majority of their citizenry, the self-selected ruling elites do not permit popular mandates to be expressed on their rule; political participation yes, but political decision-making by the citizens, no.

Are communist political systems successful? Effective? Is communist rule instrumental to communist goals? The answer to these questions must be a qualified yes. The communist party remains politically dominant and elite rule continues; but citizen self-government, even the "dictatorship of the proletariat," has not been achieved. Although capitalistic structures have ended, by and large, and the economies have been fairly well nationalized, it seems doubtful that these economies enjoy any advantage over capitalistic ones. While some of the communist states have seen solid accomplishments in industrialization, collectivization of agriculture has been a noted failure in increasing agricultural production. What communist political systems have achieved is a working format of dictatorship, which has sought widely to be granted legitimacy by its citizens.

NOTES

1. Djilas has written that communist parties of the future are destined to become socio-political movements, more democratic and possessing less of a bureaucratic monopoly over society. Milovan Djilas, *The Unperfect Society: Beyond the New Class* (New York: Harcourt, Brace and World, 1969), pp. 40, 48, 52.

2. Control of the nation, in the observation of Thomas, is in the hands of several institutions: the communist party, the neighborhood Committees for the Defense of the Revolution (CDR's), and the armed forces. "Castro has created," he continues, "a strong, ruthless but original and popular despotism, with many remarkable social reforms to its credit. . . ." Hugh Thomas, *Cuba: The Pursuit of Freedom* (New York: Harper & Row, 1971), pp. 1457–58, 1492.

3. Lucian W. Pye, *Aspects of Political Development* (Boston: Little, Brown and Company, 1966), pp. 8, 16. Anderson argues that scarcity of resources may be the distinguishing characteristic of underdevelopment. Charles W. Anderson, *et al., Issues of Political Development* (Englewood Cliffs: Prentice-Hall, 1967), p. 66.

4. Philip Cutright, "National Political Development: Measurement and Analysis," *American Sociological Review*, April, 1963, p. 255. For Black, the communist party's policy of modernization places a high priority on industrialization, scientific and technical education, and public health, and a low priority on legality, standard of living, and consumer goods. Cyril E. Black and Thomas P. Thornton, eds., *Communism and Revolution: The Strategic Uses of Violence* (Princeton: Princeton University Press, 1964), p. 16. Once a nation has set a course toward modernization, in Black's view, the most disputed issues of domestic politics then center on how leaders are to be selected, allocation of governmental powers, distribution of the tax burden, and the proper relationship between the individual and the state. *Ibid.*, p. 12.

5. On the relationship between the two, consult Norman H. Nie, *et al.*, "Social Structure and Political Participation: Developmental Relationships, II," *American Political Science Review*, September, 1969, pp. 808, 816, 825.

6. Jerzy J. Wiatr, "Political Parties, Interest Representation and Economic Development in Poland," *American Political Science Review*, December, 1970, p. 1245.

7. Robert S. Sharlet, in *Communist Studies and the Social Sciences*, Frederic J. Fleron, Jr., ed. (Chicago: Rand-McNally, 1969), pp. 248–50. One study found no positive correlation between the most economically developed party-state elites and efforts to make their respective political systems more responsive and less coercive. Dennis C. Pirages, "Socio-economic Development and Political Access in the Communist Party-States," in *Communist Party States*, Jan F. Triska, ed. (New York: Bobbs-Merrill Co., 1969), p. 271.

8. There are, in the view of Almond and Powell, three interrelated variables in political development (role differentiation, subsystem autonomy, and secularization) which tend to vary together during processes of change. Gabriel Almond and G. Bingham Powell, *Comparative Politics: A Developmental Approach* (Boston: Little, Brown and Company, 1966), p. 306.

9. One writer argues that development of communist systems away from the Stalinist model toward a more liberal system expands the func-

tions of public opinion. Zvi Gitelman, "Public Opinion and the Political System in Eastern Europe." Paper (unpublished, mimeographed) delivered at the Annual Meeting of the American Political Science Association, Los Angeles, September, 1970, p. 6.

10. Mongolia, North Korea and North Vietnam were not rated on a number of the items because of a lack of available information.

11. Lenski has suggested that a limited advance in technology causes, or makes possible, a major advance in political organization; thus, at certain levels of technological development, a considerable degree of variation in political development becomes possible. Gerhard Lenski, *Power and Privilege: A Theory of Social Stratification* (New York: McGraw-Hill, 1966), pp. 435–36.

Selected Bibliography

Of the great number of books in English on communism, only a few deal with the subject on a cross-national and comparative basis. The following books and articles attempt to discuss, comparatively, both theoretical and empirical aspects of communism as an ongoing political system.

BOOKS

Barnett, A. Doak, ed. *Communist Strategies in Asia: A Comparative Analysis of Governments and Parties.* New York: Frederick A. Praeger, 1963. Considers Russian and Chinese models of communism prior to taking up other Asian communist parties and systems.

Brown, J. F. *The New Eastern Europe: The Khrushchev Era and After.* New York: Frederick A. Praeger, 1966. Treats such subjects as political development, reforms in industry and agriculture, and international relations.

Brzezinski, Zbigniew K. *The Soviet Bloc, Unity and Conflict,* 2nd edition. Cambridge: Harvard University Press, 1967. Discusses and analyzes internal structures and policies as well as international relations among member states of the Bloc.

Burks, R. V. *The Dynamics of Communism in Eastern Europe.* Princeton: Princeton University Press, 1961. Takes up the political culture within which communism has developed and includes an analysis of ethnic groups and the role they have played in communist movements.

Dallin, Alexander and George W. Breslauer. *Political Terror in Communist Systems.* Stanford: Stanford University Press, 1970. A specialized comparative study set within an analytic framework of progressive stages in the implementation of terror within communist systems. Concludes with a summary chapter.

Farrell, R. Barry, ed. *Political Leadership in Eastern Europe and the Soviet Union.* Chicago: Aldine Publishing Co., 1970. Discusses the theory of leadership under communism, the top leaders themselves, and certain features of political leadership in practice.

Fleron, Frederick J. Jr., ed. *Communist Studies and the Social Sciences.* Chicago: Rand-McNally and Co., 1969. A compilation of many articles which range over wide areas, while focusing on the theoretical problems involved in comparative communist studies.

Gamarnikow, Michael. *Economic Reforms in Eastern Europe.* Detroit: Wayne State University Press, 1968. Describes economic reforms both theoretically and practically, with emphasis on specific managerial problems involved.

Hazard, John N. *Communists and Their Law: A Search for the Common Core of the Legal Systems of the Marxian Socialist States.* Chicago: University of Chicago Press, 1969. Treats all communist states, but emphasizes USSR, Poland, Czechoslovakia, Yugoslavia, and China. Highlights the economic and political distinctiveness of the communist law.

Ionescu, Ghita. *The Politics of the European Communist States.* New York: Frederick A. Praeger, 1967. Within a framework of pluralism, the various communist organizations (*apparats*) are treated as interest groups exerting checks on, occasionally even expressing dissents from, the policies of the party leaders.

Jacobs, Dan N. *The New Communisms.* New York: Harper & Row, 1969. Covers internal and external relations of communist party states as well as communism in other areas of the world.

Johnson, Chalmers, ed. *Change in Communist Systems.* Stanford: Stanford University Press, 1970. Cross-national comparative analyses beginning with a general introductory essay; includes comparisons of economic, party, pluralistic, and power features of communist systems.

Kanet, Roger E., ed. *The Behavioral Revolution and Communist Studies, Applications of Behaviorally Oriented Political Research on the Soviet Union and Eastern Europe.* New York: The Free Press, 1971. Concentrating chiefly on the Soviet Union, this collection of articles and essays takes up selected topics utilizing current research methodologies.

Kautsky, John H. *Communism and the Politics of Development: Persistent Myths and Changing Behavior.* New York: John Wiley, 1968. Compares theories of Marxism, Leninism, and Maoism; uses models of communism; and includes an essay on the relation of communist-party strength to economic development.

Rubinstein, Alvin Z., ed. *Communist Political Systems.* Englewood Cliffs: Prentice-Hall, 1966. Takes up communist systems in their historical setting; considers their coming into power, their ideologies, governmental structures, and policies; includes an extensive selection of articles on economics and on political culture.

Scalapino, Robert A., ed. *The Communist Revolution in Asia: Tactics, Goals and Achievements.* Englewood Cliffs: Prentice-Hall, 1969. Includes chapters on China, Mongolia, North Korea, and North Vietnam, as well as on other Asian communist parties. An introductory chapter places Asian communism within a comparative framework.

Seton-Watson, Hugh. *Nationalism and Communism: Essays 1946–1963.* New York: Frederick A. Praeger, 1964. Accents historical developments with comparative discussions on the policies of the communist parties and evaluations on the impact of communism on the Eastern European states.

Skilling, H. Gordon. *Communism National and International.* Toronto: University of Toronto Press, 1964. Describes orthodox, unorthodox, and "ex" satellites, with an opening general statement on communism and nationalism.

————. *The Governments of Communist East Europe:* New York: Thomas V. Crowell Co., 1966. Treats both structures and functions of government; covers a wide range of subjects; discusses future prospects of these states.

Spulber, Nicolas. *The Economics of Communist Eastern Europe.* New York: John Wiley, 1957. Although quite dated, includes a great deal of information on all aspects of the economics of these states.

Swearer, Howard R. and Richard P. Longaker, eds. *Contemporary Communism: Theory and Practice.* Belmont: Wadsworth, 1963. A large and varied selection of a number of subject-matter articles presenting a worldwide coverage of communist parties and communist systems.

Toma, Peter A., ed. *The Changing Face of Communism in Eastern Europe.* Tucson: University of Arizona Press, 1970. Includes general comparisons and analysis in addition to country studies.

Triska, Jan, ed. *Communist Party States: Comparative and International Studies.* Indianapolis: Bobbs-Merrill, 1969. Both theoretical concepts and empirical studies are brought to bear on the internal and foreign policies of the communist states.

Wellisz, Stanislaw. *The Economies of the Soviet Bloc: A Study of Decision-Making and Resource Allocation.* New York: McGraw-Hill, 1964. Includes a treatment of planning in its various forms, a discussion on decision-making, and a discussion on the efficacy of the Soviet model.

ARTICLES

Armstrong, John A. "Comparative Politics and Communist Systems." *Slavic Review,* March, 1967.

Benjamin, Roger W. and John H. Kautsky. "Communism and Political Development." *American Political Science Review,* March, 1968.

Brzezinski, Zbigniew K. "The Communist Middle Class in the USSR and Poland." *Survey,* Autumn, 1969.

Cattell, David T. "A Non-Marxist Theory of Comparative Analysis." *Slavic Review,* December, 1967.

Cornell, Richard. "A Comparative Analysis of Communist Movements." *Journal of Politics,* February, 1968.

Fleron, Frederic J., Jr. "Soviet Area Studies and the Social Sciences; Some Methodological Problems in Communist Studies." *Soviet Studies,* January, 1968.

Gamarnikow, Michael. "Political Patterns and Economic Reforms." *Problems of Communism,* March–April, 1969.

Hollander, Paul. "Observations on Bureaucracy, Totalitarianism, and the Comparative Study of Communism." *Slavic Review,* June, 1967.

Jacobs, Dan N. "Area Studies and Communist Systems." *Slavic Review,* March, 1967.

Korbonski, Andrzej. "Comparing Liberalization Processes in Eastern Europe: A Comparative Analysis." *Comparative Politics,* January, 1972.

Lowenthal, Richard. "Development vs. Utopia in Communist Policy." *Survey,* Winter–Spring, 1970.

Luck, David. "Soviet and Chinese Political Development." *Survey,* Winter–Spring, 1970.

Meyer, Alfred G. "The Comparative Study of Communist Political Systems." *Slavic Review,* March, 1967.

Pryor, Frederic L., "Barriers to Market Socialism in Eastern Europe in the Mid-1960's." *Studies in Comparative Communism,* April, 1970.

Sharlet, Robert S. "Concept Formation in Political Science and Communist Studies: Conceptualizing Political Participation." *Canadian Slavic Studies,* Winter, 1967.

―――. "Systematic Political Science and Communist Systems." *Slavic Review,* March, 1967.

Shoup, Paul. "Comparing Communist Nations: Prospects for an Empirical Approach." *American Political Science Review,* March, 1968. This article includes an extensive bibliographic essay.

Skilling, H. Gordon. "Interest Groups and Communist Politics." *World Politics,* January, 1966.

―――. "Soviet and Communist Politics: A Comparative Approach." *Journal of Politics,* May, 1960.

Tucker, Robert. "On the Comparative Study of Communism." *World Politics,* January, 1967.

Index